My
Windows® 10
Tablet

Jim Cheshire

800 East 96th Street,
Indianapolis, Indiana 46240 USA

My Windows® 10 Tablet

Copyright © 2016 by Pearson Education, Inc.

ISBN-13: 978-0-7897-5545-2
ISBN-10: 0-7897-5545-9

Library of Congress Control Number: 2015944471

Printed in the United States of America

First Printing: September 2015

Trademarks

All terms mentioned in this book that are known to be trademarks or service marks have been appropriately capitalized. Que Publishing cannot attest to the accuracy of this information. Use of a term in this book should not be regarded as affecting the validity of any trademark or service mark.

Windows is a registered trademark of Microsoft Corporation.

Warning and Disclaimer

Every effort has been made to make this book as complete and as accurate as possible, but no warranty or fitness is implied. The information provided is on an "as is" basis. The author and the publisher shall have neither liability nor responsibility to any person or entity with respect to any loss or damages arising from the information contained in this book.

Special Sales

For information about buying this title in bulk quantities, or for special sales opportunities (which may include electronic versions; custom cover designs; and content particular to your business, training goals, marketing focus, or branding interests), please contact our corporate sales department at corpsales@pearsoned.com or (800) 382-3419.

For government sales inquiries, please contact governmentsales@pearsoned.com.

For questions about sales outside the U.S., please contact international@pearsoned.com.

Editor-in-Chief
Greg Wiegand

Acquisitions Editor
Michelle Newcomb

Development Editor
Brandon Cackowski-Schnell

Managing Editor
Sandra Schroeder

Senior Project Editor
Tonya Simpson

Copy Editor
Bart Reed

Indexer
WordWise Publishing Services, LLC

Proofreader
Kathy Ruiz

Technical Editor
Vince Averello

Editorial Assistant
Cindy Teeters

Cover Designer
Mark Shirar

Compositor
Bumpy Design

Contents at a Glance

Table of Contents

11 **Using Calendar** **241**

15   Watching Video   315

16   Using Photos   329

About the Author

Jim Cheshire has been using Microsoft software for decades. He has worked for Microsoft for almost 20 years and currently works in the cloud computing world of Azure. He has written more than a dozen books on technology. When not working, you'll usually find Jim spending time with his wife and two children or bass fishing with his son.

You can contact Jim at cheshire@outlook.com.

Dedication

This book is dedicated to my mom, who died shortly before I began work on it. She'll always be remembered as a faithful and loving wife and a devoted mother. She spent her life helping others, and I hope that spirit lives on within these pages. I love you, Mom.

Acknowledgments

This book would not have been possible if not for the tireless work of so many people at Que Publishing. I owe much thanks to Michelle Newcomb for coordinating things behind the scenes and for keeping everything on track with the crazy schedules mandated by unpredictable beta releases of Windows 10. This book would not have been possible without Todd Brakke, Brandon Cackowski-Schnell, and Bart Reed, the three of whom worked to make sure that what came out of my head would make sense going into yours. The end result of this project is due to the excellent work by Tonya Simpson, who coordinated the myriad changes that seemed to be never-ending. I owe a great deal to all of those who worked to lay out all the beautiful pages in this book. Getting each step's callout just right is tedious and time-consuming, and they did a great job! Finally, thanks are in order for my family for their patience and tolerance while I worked on another book. I know they'll be happy to have a respite from hearing, "Sorry, I can't. I have to write."

We Want to Hear from You!

As the reader of this book, *you* are our most important critic and commentator. We value your opinion and want to know what we're doing right, what we could do better, what areas you'd like to see us publish in, and any other words of wisdom you're willing to pass our way.

We welcome your comments. You can email or write to let us know what you did or didn't like about this book—as well as what we can do to make our books better.

Please note that we cannot help you with technical problems related to the topic of this book.

When you write, please be sure to include this book's title and author as well as your name and email address. We will carefully review your comments and share them with the author and editors who worked on the book.

Email: feedback@quepublishing.com

Mail: Que Publishing
ATTN: Reader Feedback
800 East 96th Street
Indianapolis, IN 46240 USA

Reader Services

Visit our website and register this book at quepublishing.com/register for convenient access to any updates, downloads, or errata that might be available for this book.

Introduction

Windows 10 is Microsoft's latest iteration of the Windows operating system, and it represents a pretty dramatic departure from the Windows of the past. Although it might look familiar to many, its underlying design is quite fresh and new. Windows 10 is designed from the ground up for touch on a tablet computer. Windows 8 was Microsoft's first attempt at making Windows a touch-enabled operating system. Windows 10 is not just an iteration of that first attempt. It's a dramatic evolution.

As you use Windows 10 on your tablet, you might be surprised to find that the evolution is just beginning. Microsoft is no longer updating Windows with major updates every year or two. They are going to be updating Windows regularly and frequently, and you'll benefit from new features and new functionality along the way.

What You'll Find Inside

Windows 10 is made for work and play. You'll find Office apps such as Word, Excel, PowerPoint, and OneNote in the Windows Store, but Windows 10 includes many other apps for information, entertainment, and productivity.

Here are just some of the things you can do with your Windows 10 tablet:

- Read news from major news outlets, from sources for all your favorite topics, and even based on your own web searches.

- Get the latest weather, sports scores, travel ideas, stock quotes, and more.

- Listen to your music, discover new music, stream music, and buy music.

- Rent and purchase movies and TV shows from the Windows Store.

- Access all your social networks.

- Browse and edit pictures that are stored on your device or on OneDrive.

- Watch video using Netflix, Hulu Plus, and more.

- Enhance your tablet with apps from the Windows Store.

Why You'll Love *My Windows 10 Tablet*

Windows 10 is accessible to all kinds of users, and so is *My Windows 10 Tablet*. If you're a nontechnical person, you'll find the step-by-step approach in *My Windows 10 Tablet* to be refreshing and helpful. If you're a technical person new to Windows 10, you'll find plenty of tips and tricks to help you get the most out of your new tablet.

The book covers all the capabilities of your Windows 10 tablet. I show you how to get the most out of each feature using a step-by-step approach, complete with figures that correspond to each step. You never have to wonder what or where to tap. Each task shows you how to interact with your tablet using simple symbols that illustrate what you should do.

This icon means that you should tap and hold an object on the screen:

This icon means that you should drag an item on the screen:

This icon indicates that you should pinch on the screen:

This icon means that you should "reverse pinch":

This icon indicates that you need to swipe on the screen:

Along the way, I add plenty of tips that help you better understand a feature or task. I also warn you with It's Not All Good sidebars when you need to be careful with a particular task or when there are pitfalls you need to know about.

Finally, for those of you with the paperback version of this book, you might notice that it isn't a big and bulky book. It's a handy size for taking with you when you go places with your tablet. That way, you can always find the steps necessary to do what you want to do. Of course, if you prefer not to carry the book with you, you can always purchase the e-book version and read it on your tablet.

What You'll Find in the Book

Your tablet is full of surprises. The major functions are easy to discover, but some of the neater features are hidden away. As you read through this book, you'll find yourself saying, "Wow, I didn't know I could do that!" This book is designed to invoke just that kind of reaction.

Here are the things covered in this book:

- Chapter 1, "An Introduction to Windows 10," provides an introduction to Windows 10 and how to interact with it on your tablet.

- Chapter 2, "Connecting to Networks," shows you how to connect to wireless networks, how you can access shared resources on your network, and how you can remote in to other computers on your network using your tablet.

- Chapter 3, "Using and Customizing the Start Menu and Taskbar," walks you through using the new Windows Start menu and the Taskbar, including details on how you can customize both and make them uniquely yours.

- Chapter 4, "Security and Windows 10," shows you how to use user accounts and secure your tablet.

- Chapter 5, "Using Microsoft Family," provides a thorough view of Microsoft Family, a feature that makes it easy to control what family members can do on your Windows 10 devices, which apps they can use, and when they are able to use your devices. You also learn how you can get reports on activity that kids and other family members are engaging in.

- Chapter 6, "Backing Up Your Data with File History," shows you how to use the unique features in Windows 10 to back up your data and keep it safe from data loss.

- Chapter 7, "Finding Information on the Internet," covers Microsoft Edge, the new browser introduced in Windows 10.

- Chapter 8, "Using Cortana," shows you how to use Cortana, the digital personal assistant built in to Windows 10.

- Chapter 9, "Connecting with People," demonstrates how you can interact with friends and family on Windows 10.

- Chapter 10, "Using Mail," covers the Mail app in Windows 10 and explains how to send and receive email.

- Chapter 11, "Using Calendar," walks you through using the Calendar app to keep track of your appointments.

- Chapter 12, "Keeping Up to Date with News," shows you how to read news and other information from sources all over the Web from within the News app.

- Chapter 13, "HomeGroups and OneDrive," explains how you can share data with others on your network with HomeGroups and how to use Microsoft OneDrive to store and share files in the cloud.

- Chapter 14, "Discovering and Playing Music," provides information on using the Groove Music app to play your own music, how to buy music from the Windows Store, and how to use a Groove Music Pass to stream and download music.

- Chapter 15, "Watching Video," covers the Movies & TV app as well as renting and buying movies and TV shows from the Windows Store.

- Chapter 16, "Using Photos," shows you how to use the Photos app to view and edit pictures from your tablet and from OneDrive.

- Chapter 17, "Using Maps," walks you through using Maps, an app that provides detailed maps as well as directions.

- Chapter 18, "Creating Documents with Microsoft Word Mobile," covers using Microsoft Word Mobile to create and edit documents.

- Chapter 19, "Crunching Numbers with Microsoft Excel Mobile," walks you through using Microsoft Excel Mobile to create workbooks, including how you can use formulas and functions to create complex sheets.

- Chapter 20, "Presenting with Microsoft PowerPoint Mobile," walks you through using Microsoft PowerPoint Mobile to create compelling presentations.

- Chapter 21, "Organizing Notes with Microsoft OneNote," shows you how to use Microsoft OneNote to organize notes, synchronize them across your devices, and access them from anywhere.

- Chapter 22, "Enhancing Windows with Apps," shows you how to enhance the operation of your tablet using apps from the Windows Store.

- Chapter 23, "Updating and Troubleshooting Windows 10," shows you how to update Windows 10 and how to troubleshoot and repair problems that you might encounter.

Go Deeper

Now that you know what's in store, it's time to start having fun digging deeper into Windows 10 on your tablet. You're sure to learn new things and experience the thrill of what your tablet can do—and you'll have fun doing it. Let's get started!

Use the Touch Keyboard to type and
a stylus to interact with Windows
using your own handwriting.

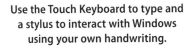

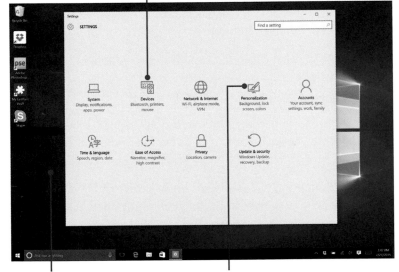

Learn the basics of
using and customizing
Windows 10.

Make Windows your own by
personalizing settings that can even
follow you from PC to PC.

In this chapter, you learn the basics of how to use Windows 10 and how to customize how Windows looks and how it works. You learn about

→ Windows 10 Basics

→ Additional Settings

→ Moving On

An Introduction to Windows 10

Windows 10 represents Microsoft's latest move at making the Windows operating system optimized for touch devices such as your Windows 10 tablet. Windows 8 and Windows 8.1 were solid moves in that direction, but Microsoft got plenty of feedback from people who felt like these versions were too focused on touch. Windows 10 addresses a lot of that feedback, and I think Microsoft has done a great job of making an operating system that makes you feel just at home using touch as you do using a mouse or trackpad and a keyboard.

Windows 10 in More Detail

I don't cover everything about Windows 10 in this overview. If you need an in-depth guide to Windows 10, I recommend that you read *My Windows 10* from Que Publishing.

Windows 10 Basics

You need to know some basic things to get around in the new Windows 10 interface. This chapter gives you an introduction to these features, and I'll point you to places in the book where you can read more about them where applicable.

The Start Menu

The Start menu is the primary way you will start apps and access settings and other features of Windows. Using the Start menu, you can start your apps, access Windows settings, personalize Windows, and much more.

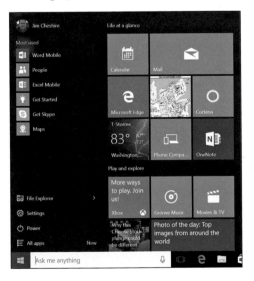

You can personalize the Start menu by arranging and resizing the tiles that appear on the right side. You can also create tile groups and rearrange those groups so that the apps you use most often are easy to access.

More Info on the Start Menu

For more information about using and customizing the Start menu, see Chapter 3, "Using and Customizing the Start Menu and Taskbar."

Task View

If you've been a Windows user for any period of time, you're probably already familiar with switching between running apps and maybe even with displaying multiple apps on the screen at the same time. Windows 10 takes that a huge step forward with Task View.

Using Task View, you can actually create multiple virtual desktops so that you can further separate your apps. For example, you can have one desktop running apps that you use for work, such as Microsoft Excel, an email application, and Microsoft Word, while another desktop is running fun apps such as a web browser, the Netflix app, and so on. This allows you to use your tablet with a less cluttered interface.

Even if you don't want to create multiple desktops, Task View makes it easier to switch between running apps on your tablet.

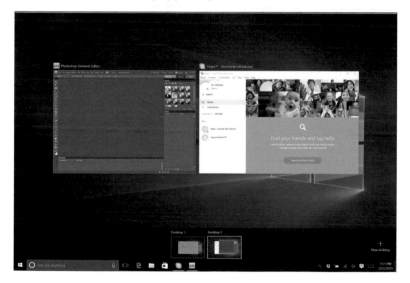

More Info on Task View

For more information on using Task View, see the section "Using Task View" in Chapter 3.

Typing in Windows 10

One of the great things about a tablet is the touch interface, which you can easily use without having a keyboard attached to the tablet. There are certainly times when you will want to use a physical keyboard (such as I'm doing while writing this book), but at other times, you likely will want the convenience of a pure tablet.

When you don't have a physical keyboard attached to your tablet, you can use the Touch Keyboard provided by Windows 10 to type.

1. Tap inside a text field.

2. Tap Touch Keyboard.

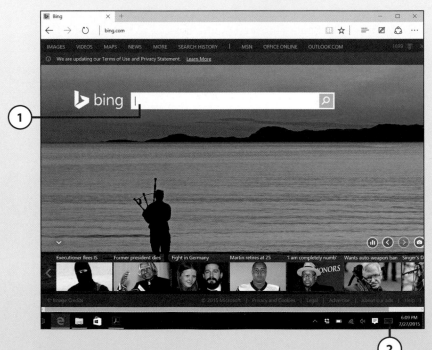

3. Tap the keyboard to input text.

4. Tap a recommended word to complete it.

5. Tap and drag Move to move the keyboard to another location on the screen.

6. Tap Dock to dock the keyboard to the bottom of the screen.

7. Tap &123 to switch to a keyboard where you can enter symbols and numbers.

8. Tap the Smiley to access emojis.

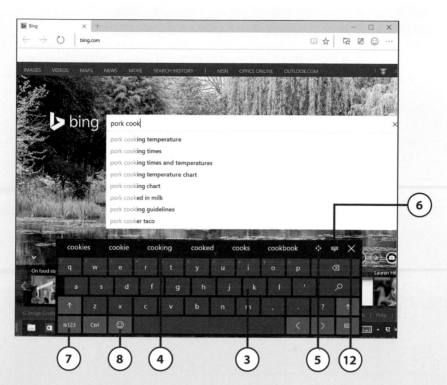

9. Tap an emoji type to see other emojis.

10. Tap an emoji to insert it.

11. Tap the Smiley to exit the emoji keyboard.

12. Tap Close or leave the text field to close the touch keyboard.

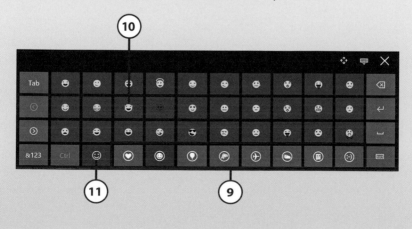

Handwriting in Windows 10

Not all tablets come with a stylus. Even if your tablet didn't come with one, you can buy one to use with it. Make sure you don't buy one of the cheap styluses with a large rubber tip. Instead, buy a quality writing stylus such as the DotPen. It will cost you quite a bit more money than a rubber-tipped stylus, but it's well worth it.

If you'd prefer, you can use a stylus to write text in your own handwriting.

1. Tap inside a text input area with a stylus.

2. Write the text you want to enter.

3. Tap a recommended word to complete it.

Writing Hand

To make handwriting in Windows 10 as reliable as possible, it's a good idea to tell Windows which hand you write with. From the Settings app, tap Devices and then tap Pen. From there, you can set the hand that you write with.

Tablet Mode

It's a little bit of a misnomer to call a Windows 10 tablet a true "tablet." Although your tablet can certainly be used as such in the true sense of the word, you can also use it like a traditional notebook computer by attaching a keyboard to it. Some tablets (such as Microsoft's Surface and Surface Pro tablets) even have a keyboard attachment that makes them operate very much like a traditional notebook PC.

Microsoft understands the versatile nature of these devices, and Windows 10 can switch into Tablet Mode when it senses you are using your tablet without a keyboard and mouse. Tablet Mode causes all apps to open full screen so that they're easier to work with using touch.

You can enable Tablet Mode manually, but you can also configure Windows 10 so that it will detect when Tablet Mode might be needed.

Tablet Mode for Small Tablets

If your tablet's screen is 10 inches or smaller, Windows will boot into Tablet Mode automatically to make your tablet easier to use.

1. From the Start menu, tap or click Settings.

2. From the Settings screen, tap or click System.

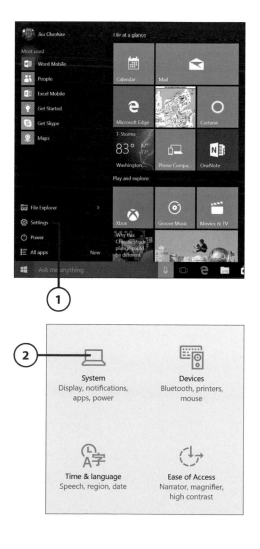

3. Tap or click Tablet Mode.

4. Tap or click Make Windows More Touch-Friendly when Using Your Device as a Tablet to turn Tablet Mode on manually.

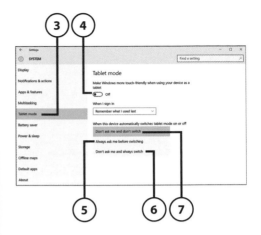

5. Tap or click When This Device Automatically Switches Tablet Mode On or Off and choose Always Ask Me Before Switching if you want Windows 10 to prompt you when it believes Tablet Mode should be enabled.

6. Tap or click Don't Ask Me and Always Switch if you want Windows 10 to switch to Tablet Mode automatically without prompting when it detects Tablet Mode should be enabled.

7. Tap Don't Ask Me and Don't Switch if you want to prevent Windows 10 from detecting when Tablet Mode should be used or not.

Detecting Tablet Mode

Windows 10 will detect that Tablet Mode should be enabled when you, for example, detach a removable keyboard or turn your tablet display sideways so that it's in portrait mode.

It's Not All Good

Detection Not Always Supported

Windows 10 cannot detect when it should change to Tablet Mode for all tablets. Some of the detection relies on the tablet itself. Microsoft is continuing to work with PC makers to add Tablet Mode detection to more PCs.

Storage Settings

One of the drawbacks to a tablet is that you can't install additional hard drives in them. The only way to get a bigger hard drive is to buy a new tablet with a bigger drive in it, and that's not financially reasonable. Most tablets enable you to add a memory card to them for storing additional data, but Windows has traditionally not made it easy to use drive space on a memory card.

Windows 10 changes all of that with new Storage settings. Windows 10 sees all the drives connected to your tablet (including memory cards you've inserted) and enables you to easily use that extra drive space for documents, music, pictures, and video that you store on your device.

It's Not All Good

No Apps

You will see a storage setting for choosing a location to which new apps should be saved, but it's grayed out and cannot be changed. Microsoft has decided not to allow apps to be installed on a microSD card for now. It plans to enable that feature in a future release of Windows 10.

1. From the System page in Settings, tap or click Storage.

⚙	**SYSTEM**
Display	
Notifications & actions	
Apps & features	
Multitasking	
Tablet mode	
Battery saver	
Power & sleep	
① Storage	

2. Tap or click a storage location to see what items are taking up space in that location.

3. Tap or click a drop-down under Save Locations to choose where items are saved by default.

This PC (C:)
29.4 GB used out of 119 GB

SDXC (D:)
1.12 MB used out of 59.4 GB

②

Save locations

Change where your apps, documents, music, pictures and videos are saved by default.

New apps will save to:

This PC (C:) ⌄

③

New documents will save to:

This PC (C:) ⌄

New music will save to:

SDXC (D:) ⌄

New pictures will save to:

This PC (C:) ⌄

New videos will save to:

SDXC (D:) ⌄

Battery Saver

Because your Windows 10 tablet is a full-fledged PC and not just a tablet, it uses a lot of power. How much power depends on what you do with it. If you're only browsing the Internet and checking email, you won't use a lot of power. However, if you run other apps, you might find that your battery level drops faster than you might expect.

To maximize battery life, Windows 10 users a feature called Battery Saver to reduce the amount of work happening in the background to save battery life.

Battery Saver turns on automatically when battery life is 20% or below. You can adjust when Battery Saver turns on, or you can turn it off completely.

1. From the System page in Settings, tap or click Battery Saver.

2. Tap or click Battery Use to see which applications are using the most battery power.

3. Tap or click Battery Saver Settings.

4. Tap or click the slider and drag it to a new percentage setting to control when Battery Saver is automatically enabled.

5. Tap or click Turn Battery Saver On Automatically If My Battery Falls Below to uncheck the box and disable Battery Saver.

6. Tap or click Allow Push Notifications from Any App While in Battery Saver to check the box and enable apps to send push notifications when Battery Saver is enabled.

7. Tap or click Lower Screen Brightness While in Battery Saver to uncheck the box and prevent Battery Saver from reducing screen brightness when it's enabled.

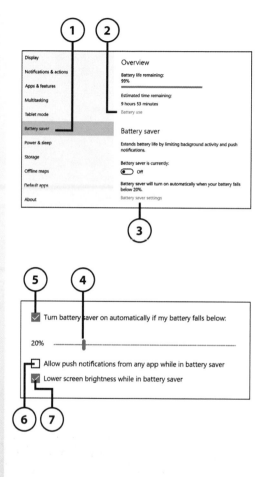

Battery Usage and Screen Brightness

If you feel that your battery's charge is going down faster than it should, check Battery Usage in step 2. It will help you to isolate what's using most of your battery.

Here's a hint: The display uses more power than just about anything else, so reducing the brightness of your display can really save a lot of battery life. I show you how you can change the display brightness in the "Screen Brightness and Rotation Lock" section later in this chapter.

Viewing Notifications

Many Windows applications will display notifications when certain things happen. For example, a mail app might display a notification when new mail arrives, Facebook's app displays a notification when someone interacts with you on Facebook, and Windows displays notifications when apps are installed and so forth. You can view a list of past notifications in case you missed one.

1. Tap or click the Notifications icon in the system tray to display the Action Center.

2. Tap or click a notification to see more information on it if available.

3. Tap a notification or an app to mark it as viewed and remove it. (You can also hover over it with a mouse and click the X to remove it.)

4. Tap or click Clear All to remove all notifications.

Controlling Notifications

You can turn on and off notifications for individual apps in the Notifications & Actions settings screen in System settings.

Changing Quick Actions

Along the bottom of the Action Center, you'll see four buttons and an Expand link. These four buttons are called Quick Action buttons and they allow you quick access to settings on your tablet.

The first four Quick Action buttons always appear at the bottom of the Action Center. You can customize which four buttons appear so that you can quickly access the settings you use most often.

1. From the System settings page, tap or click Notifications & Actions.

2. Tap or click one of the four Quick Action buttons to change it.

⚙ **SYSTEM**	
Display	**Quick actions**
① ─ Notifications & actions	Choose your quick actions
Apps & features	
Multitasking	Select which icons appear on the taskbar
Tablet mode	Turn system icons on or off
Battery saver	
Power & sleep	**Notifications**
Storage	Show me tips about Windows
Offline maps	⬤ On
Default apps	Show app notifications
	⬤ On

3. Tap a Quick Action option to set the selected button to that option.

Expand for All Quick Actions
If you tap or click Expand in the Action Center, you'll see all of the Quick Action buttons available.

Additional Settings

You might find yourself wanting to adjust several other settings in Windows 10 as you use your tablet. This section goes over a few of them, but I encourage you to examine all the settings available to you to customize your tablet just the way you want it.

Screen Brightness and Rotation Lock

As I mentioned earlier, the brightness of your screen is one of the primary factors in battery usage. Adjusting the brightness of your screen is a good way to save on battery life. You can also configure Windows to automatically adjust the brightness of your display based on ambient lighting.

1. From System settings, tap or click Display.

2. Tap or click Brightness Level, and then drag the slider to adjust the brightness of the display.

3. Tap or click Adjust My Screen Brightness Automatically to enable or disable automatic brightness.

Shutting Down, Sleeping, and Restarting

Your Windows 10 tablet is designed to stay turned on practically all the time. If you press the power button, it will go into a low-power state so that it uses less battery power, but it can still jump on the Internet quickly to check for mail and other data.

If you aren't going to use your tablet for a while, you might want to allow it to sleep so that it uses almost no power at all. You can also shut it down completely so that it doesn't use any power.

1. Tap or click the Start button.

2. Tap or click Power.

3. Tap or click Sleep to put your tablet into a low-power sleep state.

4. Tap or click Shut Down to shut down your tablet completely. (This is the safe way to turn off your tablet completely.)

5. Tap Restart to restart Windows on your tablet.

Sync Settings

One of the advantages of logging in with a Microsoft account is that your settings can be synchronized across multiple PCs. For example, if you use a favorite picture for your desktop wallpaper on one PC, you can have that same picture automatically appear as your wallpaper on your other PCs.

You can control whether your settings are synced and which settings follow you from PC to PC.

1. From the Settings screen, tap or click Accounts.

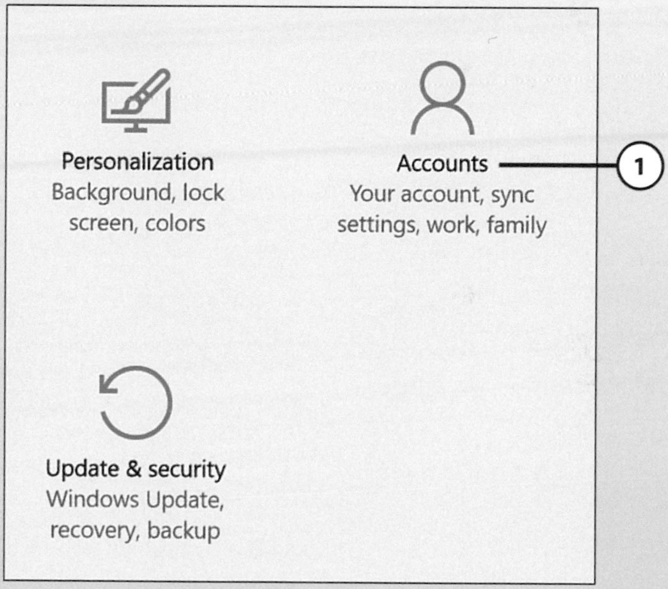

Personalization
Background, lock
screen, colors

Accounts ——①
Your account, sync
settings, work, family

Update & security
Windows Update,
recovery, backup

2. Tap or click Sync Your Settings.

3. Tap or click Sync Settings to turn syncing on or off.

4. Tap or click Theme to enable or disable syncing of the Windows theme. (This impacts desktop wallpaper, colors, and so forth.)

5. Tap or click Web Browser Settings to enable or disable syncing of settings in your web browser, such as Favorites and so forth.

6. Tap or click Passwords to enable or disable syncing of passwords that you've saved in Windows.

7. Tap or click Language Preferences to enable or disable syncing of language settings.

8. Tap or click Ease of Access to enable or disable syncing of Ease of Access settings such as Narrator, Magnifier, and so forth.

9. Tap or click Other Windows Settings to enable or disable syncing of Windows Explorer and mouse settings.

Moving On

I started this chapter by telling you that I was only going to scratch the surface of using Windows. You learned how to change some of the more common settings and the basics of how to interact with your tablet, but you didn't learn how to efficiently work with the file system in Windows, how to create and manage users, and other more advanced topics. That doesn't mean those things aren't important! We just don't have enough pages in this book to cover them all. If those are topics you aren't comfortable with, I highly encourage you to read a book on using Windows itself so that you can make the most of your tablet.

In the chapters that follow, you're going to learn a lot about how you can use your tablet to do more than you might imagine. You'll be entertained, you'll get some work done, you'll interact with friends and family in a rich and satisfying way, and you'll do it all using one of the most advanced and user-friendly operating systems ever created.

Let's get started!

Connect to Wi-Fi networks.

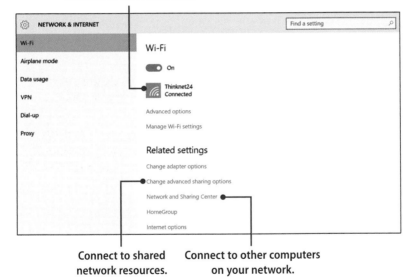

Connect to shared network resources.

Connect to other computers on your network.

In this chapter, you learn how to connect to wireless networks, how you can share content on your tablet with other computers, and even how you can log in to your tablet or other computers on your network remotely. You learn about

→ Wireless Networking

→ Network Sharing and Discovery

→ Remoting In to Other Computers

Connecting to Networks

When you turn on your tablet for the first time, you're walked through a series of steps to get the device ready for use. One of those steps is to connect to a wireless network, and for good reason—Internet access is an absolute necessity when you're using Windows 10.

Always Connected

You don't have to always be connected to the Internet to use your tablet. You'll find plenty of applications you can use without being connected, but many of your apps require the Internet, and being able to synchronize your settings and files does as well.

Wireless Networking

Wireless networks (also called Wi-Fi networks) are everywhere these days. They're in fast-food restaurants, quick oil change service centers, doctor's offices, and just about everywhere else. Of course, you also likely have a wireless network in your home. You can connect to any of those wireless networks with your Windows 10 tablet.

Connecting to a Wireless Network

Your tablet can display a list of all wireless networks that are within range. You can connect to one of those networks easily.

1. From the Settings app, tap or click Network & Internet.

2. Tap or click Wi-Fi.

3. Tap or click the network to which you want to connect.

4. Tap or click Connect Automatically if you want Windows to remember this network and reconnect you automatically from now on.

5. Tap or click Connect.

6. Enter the network's security key.

7. Tap or click Next.

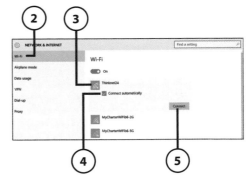

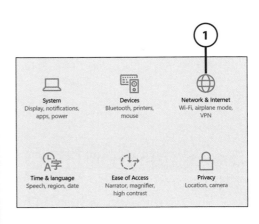

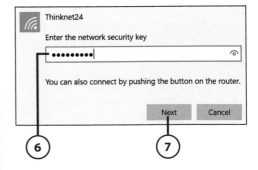

8. Tap or click Yes if you want your tablet to be discoverable by other devices on the network automatically. (If you're on a public Wi-Fi access point, tap or click No.)

Thinknet24

Do you want to allow your PC to be discoverable by other PCs and devices on this network?

We recommend allowing this on your home and work networks, but not public ones.

| Yes | No |

8

Connecting Automatically

If you choose to connect to multiple networks automatically, Windows 10 selects the network to connect to based on signal strength.

Disconnecting from a Network

If you no longer want to connect to a particular network, you can disconnect from it. If you decide to connect to the network later, you'll have to reconnect manually, but Windows will still remember the network's security key so that you don't have to enter it again.

1. Tap Wi-Fi in the system tray.

2. Tap the wireless network from which you want to disconnect.

3. Tap Disconnect.

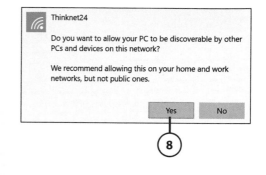

2   **3**

Thinknet24
Connected

Disconnect

MyCharterWiFib6-2G

PSCGG

TB Proprietary Channel. D2

Lukas

MyCharterWiFib6-5G

Network settings

Thinknet24   Airplane mode

8:06 AM
7/28/2015

1

Forgetting a Wireless Network

You can choose to "forget" a wireless network, which causes Windows to not only stop automatically connecting to the network, but also to forget the network key and other information about the network.

If you want to make sure no one is able to easily reconnect to a particular wireless network in the future, you can go through these steps to forget that network:

1. From Wi-Fi settings in Network & Internet, tap or click Manage Wi-Fi Settings.

2. Tap or click the network you want to forget.

3. Tap or click Forget to forget the network.

Rejoining a Forgotten Network

If you forget a network, you'll have to go through the steps in "Connecting to a Wireless Network" if you want to reconnect to it.

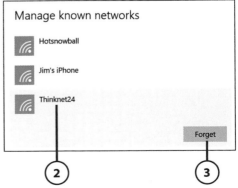

Using Airplane Mode

In some cases (such as when you are on an airplane), you might need to turn off all the radios on your tablet. When this need arises, you can enable Airplane mode.

1. From Network & Internet settings, tap Airplane Mode.

2. Tap Airplane Mode to change the setting to On. When Airplane mode is turned on, the Wi-Fi and Bluetooth radios on your tablet are turned off.

3. Tap Airplane Mode again to turn off Airplane mode and turn on the radios again.

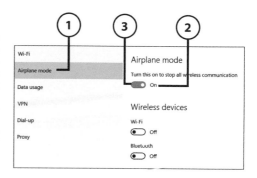

Quick Access to Airplane Mode

For fast access to Airplane mode, you can set one of your Quick Action buttons to activate it. For information on doing that, see the "Changing Quick Actions" section of Chapter 1, "An Introduction to Windows 10."

Network Sharing and Discovery

Windows 10 includes a network sharing feature that makes it easy for you to share files and devices (such as networked printers) with other computers on your network. Windows will automatically discover shared network resources and configure them for you. You can turn these sharing and discovery features on or off.

Sharing and Public Networks

If you are connected to a public network, you should not enable sharing because it can allow others on the network to see your files and devices.

Turning Sharing and Discovery On or Off

You can easily turn sharing and discovery on or off as necessary.

1. From the Wi-Fi settings screen, swipe up or scroll down and tap or click Change Advanced Sharing Options.

Related settings

Change adapter options

Change advanced sharing options ──────①

Network and Sharing Center

HomeGroup

Internet options

Windows Firewall

2. Tap or click Turn on Automatic Setup of Network Connected Devices to enable or disable automatic configuration of devices such as shared network printers and so forth.

3. Tap or click Turn Off Network Discovery to disable the discovery of networked devices when connected to networks.

4. Tap or click Turn Off File and Printer Sharing to disable sharing of files or printers on your tablet with others on the network.

5. Tap Save Changes.

Public and Private

In the Advanced Sharing Settings dialog, you might notice that the settings shown are in a section called Private. Windows maintains different sets of settings—one called Private, one called Public, and a third called All Networks that applies to both Public and Private. Private settings are for private networks and Public settings are for public networks. This enables you to use different sharing and discovery settings for public wireless networks. In fact, Windows automatically disables sharing and discovery on such public networks, but using the steps in "Turning Sharing and Discovery On or Off," you can override those settings if you want to.

Keep in mind that it's highly recommended that you not share network resources on public networks because you never know who else is on those networks.

Accessing Network Resources

If sharing is turned on, you can use File Explorer to view resources on your network.

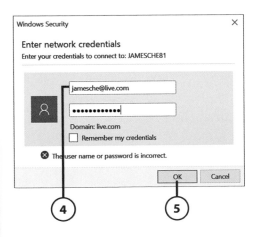

1. Tap or click File Explorer on the Taskbar. (If you've unpinned File Explorer, you can find it on the Start menu.)

2. In File Explorer, tap or click Network to see network resources.

3. Double-tap or double-click a resource to connect to it.

4. Enter a username and password if prompted.

5. Tap OK to continue.

Incorrect Username and Password

If you are prompted for a username and password, you might notice that Windows displays an error in the initial username/password dialog that tells you that the username and password were incorrect. That's because Windows attempted to log you in to the network resource using the username and password you used to log in to Windows on your tablet, and it failed. If you attempt to access a network resource that uses the same username and password that you use on your tablet, the automatic login will succeed and you won't even be prompted for a username and password.

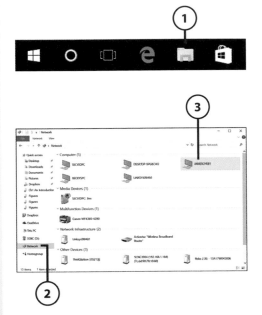

6. Browse to the network resource in which you're interested.

Accessing Unlisted Computers

If you want to access a folder on a computer that isn't listed under Network, you can use a different method. Tap and hold or right-click the Start button, and then tap or click Run. In the dialog, enter **\\computer\folder** to access the computer. For example, to access a "videos" folder on a computer called MomsComputer, you would enter **\\momscomputer\videos**. You might be prompted for a username and password just as you were in the "Accessing Network Resources" step-by-step.

Remoting In to Other Computers

Windows 10 enables you to remotely connect to other Windows computers or to connect from other computers to your tablet. When you remote in to a computer, what you see on your screen is exactly what appears on the remote PC, and you can interact with that PC just as though you were using it directly.

Remote connections to other computers are established using a Remote Desktop Connection. By default, Windows does not allow remote connections, so to remote in to a computer, you must first enable remote connections.

Enabling Connections on the Remote Computer

These steps should be carried out on the remote computer to which you want to connect. The computer can be running any version of Windows from Windows XP onward. I show you steps for Windows 10, but the steps are almost identical on other versions of Windows.

Because you might be doing this on a PC that doesn't have a touch screen, I provide instructions using a trackpad or a mouse and keyboard. (If you want to remotely connect to your Windows 10 tablet, you should complete these steps on your tablet.)

1. Right-click the Start button and click System.

2. Click Remote Settings.

Computer Name

Toward the bottom of the System dialog, you'll see the computer name. Make note of it because you'll use it to connect to this computer later.

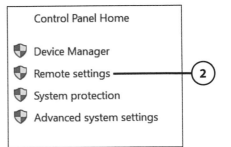

3. Click Allow Remote Connections to This Computer.

4. If the PC is a tablet or a notebook computer, you will be notified that you might want to change the computer settings so that it doesn't sleep or hibernate. Do that if you want to, and then click OK.

5. Click OK.

System Properties

Computer Name | Hardware | Advanced | System Protection | Remote

Remote Assistance

☑ Allow Remote Assistance connections to this computer

What happens when I enable Remote Assistance?

Advanced...

Remote Desktop

Choose an option, and then specify who can connect.

○ Don't allow remote connections to this computer

● Allow remote connections to this computer

☑ Allow connections only from computers running Remote Desktop with Network Level Authentication (recommended)

Help me choose

Select Users...

OK   Cancel   Apply

3

Remote Desktop

⚠ This computer is set up to go to sleep or hibernation when not in use. While the computer sleeps or hibernates, people cannot connect to it remotely. To change this setting, go to Power Options in Control Panel.

OK

4

Remote Desktop

Choose an option, and then specify who can connect.

○ Don't allow remote connections to this computer

● Allow remote connections to this computer

☑ Allow connections only from computers running Remote Desktop with Network Level Authentication (recommended)

Help me choose

Select Users...

OK   Cancel   Apply

5

Connecting to Remote Computers

After you've enabled remote connections on your remote computer, you can connect to it from another PC. I provide instructions for using a trackpad or mouse and keyboard in these steps in case you don't have a touch screen.

1. Click the Start button.

2. On your keyboard, enter **remote desktop**.

3. Click Remote Desktop Connection.

4. Enter the computer name of the remote computer.

5. Click Connect.

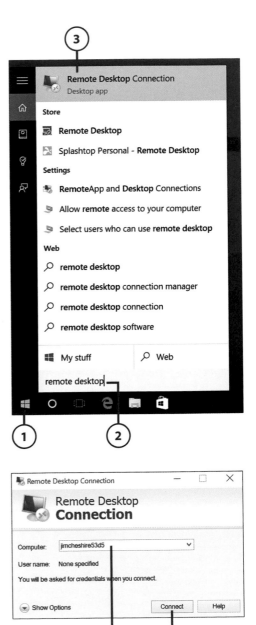

6. Enter your password. If necessary, click Use Another Account and enter a username and password.

7. Click to check Remember My Credentials if you want Windows 10 to remember your username and password.

8. Click OK.

Use Microsoft Accounts

If you are connecting to a Windows 8 or later PC, you can make this process much easier by using the same Microsoft account on the remote PC that you are using on your local PC.

9. Click Yes in the Remote Desktop Connection dialog that appears to alert you of any certificate errors. (You can safely ignore the certificate problem in this specific case.)

10. To disconnect from the computer, click the X in the Remote Desktop title bar.

Windows Security   ✕

Enter your credentials
These credentials will be used to connect to jimcheshire53d5.

Jim Cheshire
MicrosoftAccount\cheshire@outloo...

••••••••

Use another account

☐ Remember my credentials

OK   Cancel

⑦   ⑥   ⑧

Remote Desktop Connection   ✕

The identity of the remote computer cannot be verified. Do you want to connect anyway?

The remote computer could not be authenticated due to problems with its security certificate. It may be unsafe to proceed.

Certificate name

Name in the certificate from the remote computer:
JIMCHESHIRE53D5

Certificate errors

The following errors were encountered while validating the remote computer's certificate:

⚠ The certificate is not from a trusted certifying authority.

Do you want to connect despite these certificate errors?

☐ Don't ask me again for connections to this computer

View certificate...   Yes   No

⑨

⑩

H ..ll   jimcheshire53d5

Launch your apps.

Customize your Start menu.

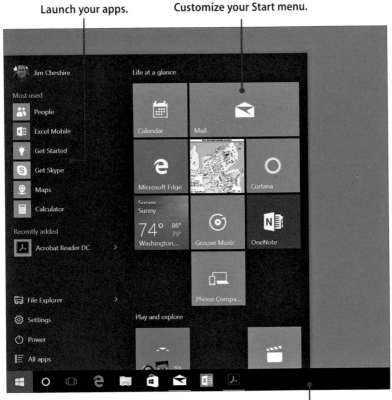

Control apps with the Taskbar.

In this chapter, you learn how to use and customize the Windows 10 Start menu and Taskbar. You learn about

→ Locating and Launching Apps

→ Switching Between Apps

→ Using Task View

→ Organizing the Start Menu and Taskbar

→ Customizing the Start Menu and Taskbar

Using and Customizing the Start Menu and Taskbar

Windows 8 introduced a new Start screen to Windows that threw many Windows users for a loop. It was unlike any user-interface Microsoft had ever used, but the hope was that users would eventually grow accustomed to it and would learn to love it. That didn't happen, and the new Start menu in Windows 10 is evidence of that. The Windows 10 Start menu has all the interactivity and visual appeal of the Windows 8 Start screen, but it brings back the familiar elements of earlier versions of Windows.

Locating and Launching Apps

The Start menu in Windows 10 shows you both Windows Desktop apps and what Microsoft calls Windows Store Apps, which are apps that either come preinstalled in Windows or are purchased from the Windows Store.

By default, the Start menu shows you only some of the apps installed on your tablet. However, you can easily view all apps with the click of a button, and you can also search for hard-to-find apps.

Launching Apps from the Start Menu

You can easily locate an app from the Start menu and launch it.

1. Tap or click the Start button to show the Start menu.

2. To locate apps not currently visible on the Start menu, tap or click All Apps.

3. Slide or scroll up and down to locate the app you want to launch.

4. Tap or click the app's icon to launch the app.

Launching Apps from the Taskbar

The Taskbar provides a fast and convenient way to launch often-used apps.

1. If the Taskbar is hidden, tap the edge of the screen or move your mouse corner to the edge where the Taskbar is located.

2. Tap or click the Taskbar button for the app that you want to launch.

3. After the app launches, a line appears at the bottom of the app's button on the Taskbar.

Active Apps
If an app is active, the line under the app's taskbar button will be slightly wider than otherwise.

Searching for Apps

If you have a lot of apps installed, you might have a hard time locating an app on your Start menu. You can quickly find the app you want by searching for it.

1. Tap or click the Start button.

2. On your keyboard, enter one or more letters included in your app's name.

3. Locate the app from the list of apps.

4. Tap or click the app to launch it.

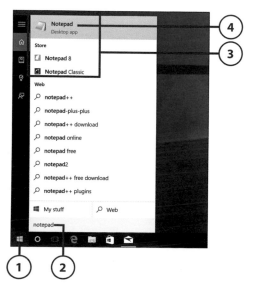

Switching Between Apps

Windows 10 is designed to run multiple apps at the same time. You can run a single app full screen, but you can also display multiple apps at the same time so that you can copy and paste between apps or so that you can reference one app while using another.

Switching Between Running Apps

Each app that is running will have a button displayed on the Taskbar. You can easily switch between apps using the Taskbar buttons.

One App with Multiple Windows

Some apps enable you to have multiple windows open. For example, your web browser enables you to have multiple websites open at one time. By default, the Taskbar will display multiple overlapping Taskbar buttons when an app has multiple windows open.

1. Tap or click the Taskbar button of the app you want to switch to.

2. If the app has multiple windows, tap or click the preview of the window you want to activate.

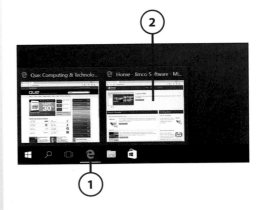

Displaying a List of Running Apps

If you have a lot of apps running, it can be convenient to see a list of running apps. Windows Task Manager can display a list of them.

1. Tap and hold or right-click an empty area of the Taskbar.

2. If tapping, release your finger to display the context menu.

3. Tap or click Task Manager.

4. Tap or click an app to switch to that app.

Quick App Switching

Pressing Ctrl+Tab will display thumbnails of currently running apps. Each subsequent press of Ctrl+Tab will highlight the next app in the list. Release the Ctrl key to switch to the highlighted app.

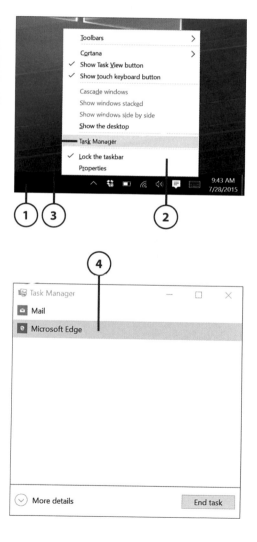

Displaying Two Apps Simultaneously

You might encounter situations in which you want to use two different apps simultaneously. For example, you might be copying information from your email that you want to add to a Microsoft Word document. In such situations, being able to display two apps onscreen at the same time can be quite helpful.

1. Open the first app you want to display.

Activating an App That's Already Open

If an app is already running but you can't see the app's window, use the steps in "Switching Between Running Apps" earlier in this chapter to activate the app's window.

2. Tap or click and hold on the app's title bar and drag it to the right or left edge of the screen.

3. Release your finger or the mouse button when you see a shaded app window on the screen. The app will snap to that size and position.

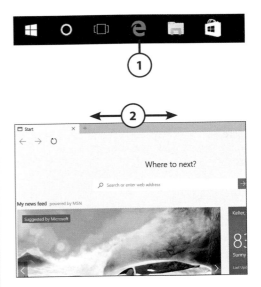

4. From the Task View previews, tap or click the app you want to show in the remaining portion of your screen.

Using the Keyboard

You can snap an app to the side of the screen quickly using the keyboard. After you activate the app, press Winkey+left arrow to snap the app to the left side of the screen or Winkey+right arrow to snap the app to the right side of the screen.

It's Not All Good

App Won't Snap to Side of Screen

You may notice that an app might not snap to the side of the screen when you drag the title bar to the left or right edge. If that happens, you can fix it by changing your position on the title bar. If you are dragging the app to the right edge of the screen, tap or click the app's title bar to the left of center when dragging the app's window. If you are dragging the app to the left edge of the screen, tap or click the app's title bar to the right of center when dragging the app's window.

Using Task View

Tablets are convenient and portable computers, but they don't come with the giant screen you might have for a desktop computer. Because of that, running a lot of apps simultaneously can really clutter your Taskbar and make for a less-than-optimal computing experience. Windows 10's Task View can rescue you from that kind of frustrating experience.

Task View makes it easy to create one or more virtual desktops. Each virtual desktop can have completely different apps running; by default, each desktop's Taskbar will show only the apps running on that desktop.

Creating a Virtual Desktop

You can easily and quickly create new virtual desktops to better organize your tablet experience.

1. Tap or click the Task View button on the Taskbar to launch Task View.

2. Tap or click New Desktop to create a new desktop.
3. Tap or click the desktop you'd like to make active.

Desktop Names

Your original desktop (the one you see when you first log in to Windows) will always be called "Desktop 1." The first virtual desktop you create will be called "Desktop 2," and each subsequent desktop will use a name with an incremented number. Unfortunately, you cannot rename desktops.

Deleting a Virtual Desktop

You can delete a virtual desktop if you no longer want to use it.

1. Tap or click Task View.

2. If you're not using touch, hover your mouse pointer over the desktop you want to delete.

3. Tap or click the Close button at the top of the desktop.

Deleting a Desktop with Open Apps

If there are any open apps on a desktop you delete, they will be moved to the desktop that appears immediately to the left of the deleted desktop in Task View. For example, open apps on Desktop 2 will be automatically moved to Desktop 1 if you delete Desktop 2.

Switching Desktops

You can switch between desktops you create so that you can use apps on any desktop.

1. Tap or click Task View.

2. Tap or click a desktop to switch to that desktop.

Switching Desktops with the Keyboard

You can switch between desktops quickly with your keyboard. Press Winkey+Ctrl+right arrow to move to the next desktop or Winkey+Ctrl+left arrow to move to the previous desktop.

Moving Apps Between Desktops

By default, an app will appear on the desktop that was active when the app was launched. However, you can move an app to another desktop easily.

1. Switch to the desktop running the app you want to move to another desktop.

2. Tap and hold or right-click the app you want to move to show the context menu.

3. Tap on or hover over Move To.

4. Tap or click the desktop to which you want the app to be moved.

5. Tap a desktop to make it the active desktop.

Dragging Apps Between Desktops

You can also drag an app to a new desktop. Instead of using the context menu in step 2, tap or click and then hold and drag the app to the desired desktop. Make sure you tap or click somewhere on the app other than on the title bar. If you tap or click the title bar, you won't be able to drag the app.

Organizing the Start Menu and Taskbar

The right side of the Start menu is reserved for displaying tiles for apps. After you've installed some of your own apps, the tiles on your Start menu might begin to get a little unwieldy. You can bring order back to your Start menu by organizing tiles into groups.

Rearranging Apps on the Start Menu

You can move a tile to a new location by dragging it.

1. Tap or click and then drag the tile to release it from its current location.

2. Drag the tile to a new location. Other tiles will move to accommodate the tile you are moving.

3. Release the tile when it is in the desired location.

4. To create a new tile group, drag the tile to a blank area at the top edge of the Start menu and release it when a highlighted group separator appears.

Adding New Tiles

You can drag an app from the list on the left side of the Start menu to a group on the right side, and a new tile will be added for that app. You'll learn how to do that step-by-step in the "Pinning Apps to the Start Menu" section later in this chapter.

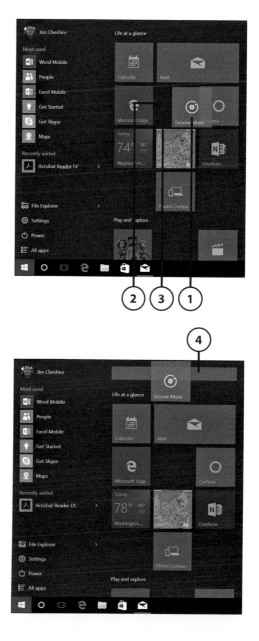

Naming Start Menu Groups

Naming groups of tiles is another way of providing additional organization to your Start menu.

1. Tap just above a tile in the group you want to rename or hover your mouse above the tile until the group separator appears, and then click.

2. Type a name for the group and press Enter to add the group name.

Groups with No Name

Tile groups aren't required to have a name. If a tile group has no name assigned to it, you will see a space between those tiles and other tiles, but no name will appear in the group separator.

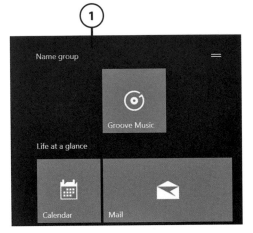

Changing or Removing a Start Menu Group Name

You can change the name of a group that you named previously or remove the group name.

1. Tap or click the existing group name.

2. Enter the new name and press Enter.

3. To remove a group name, tap or click the X.

Rearranging Start Menu Groups

You can change the order of groups on the Start menu by dragging a group to a new location.

1. Tap or click and then hold on the handle on the right edge of the group separator.

2. While holding your finger or the mouse button, drag the group separator to the desired location.

3. Release your finger or mouse button to move the group.

Tiles Move with Groups

When you move a group, any tiles in that group move along with it. However, as you are moving the group separator, you won't see the tiles. The tiles reappear when you finish moving the group.

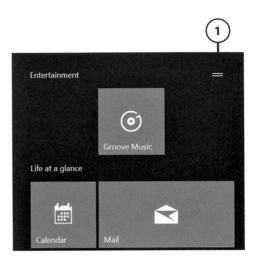

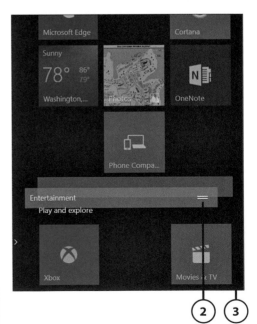

Rearranging Taskbar Buttons

You can move Taskbar buttons so that they are organized the way you want them. You can move buttons for open apps and for apps that are pinned to the Taskbar but not currently open.

Pinning Apps to the Taskbar
You learn how to pin apps to the Taskbar in the "Pinning Apps to the Taskbar" section later in this chapter.

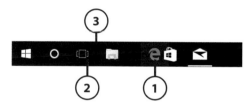

1. Tap or click and then hold on the Taskbar button you want to move.

2. Drag the button to the desired location on the Taskbar.

3. Release your finger or mouse button to move the Taskbar button.

Customizing the Start Menu and Taskbar

You can customize the Start menu by adding and removing apps and changing tile sizes. You can customize the Taskbar by adding and removing Taskbar buttons and by changing on which edge of the screen the Taskbar is located.

Pinning Apps to the Start Menu

You can pin an app to the Start menu so that a tile is displayed for the app. Doing so makes it easier to find your most often used apps.

1. From the list of apps on the left side of the Start menu, tap and hold or right-click the app you want to pin to the Start menu.

2. Tap Pin to Start to pin the app to the Start menu.

Cannot Find Pinned App

When you pin an app to the Start menu, it gets added to a new group at the bottom of the Start menu. You can move the app to a new group if you want.

Pinning Apps to the Taskbar

If you want to add a button to the Taskbar for an app that you use a lot, you can pin the app to the Taskbar. After you pin an app to the Taskbar, the Taskbar will show a button for the app even when it's not running so that you can launch the app quickly.

1. From the Start menu, tap and hold or right-click an app that you want to pin to the Taskbar.

2. Tap Pin to Taskbar to pin the app to the Taskbar.

Pinning Running Apps to the Taskbar

If an app is running, you can tap and hold or right-click the app's Taskbar button and tap Pin to Taskbar on the menu to pin the app to the Taskbar more easily.

Removing Apps from the Start Menu

You can remove a tile from the Start screen by unpinning it. You can unpin any tile that you no longer want displayed on your Start menu, including those that are included on the Start menu by default.

1. Tap and hold or right-click the tile you want to remove to display the context menu.

2. Tap or click Unpin from Start to remove the tile.

Removing Buttons from the Taskbar

You can remove a button from the Taskbar for an app that has been pinned to the Taskbar.

1. Tap and hold or right-click the Taskbar button you want to remove to display the context menu.

2. Tap Unpin from Taskbar to remove the button.

Removing the Button for a Running App

If you remove a button for an app that is currently running, the button will remain until you close the app.

Removing Apps from the Most Used List

Windows 10 displays the seven most-often-used apps in the Most Used list on the Start menu. If you would like to remove an app from the Most Used list, you can.

1. Tap and hold or right-click the app you want to remove from the list.

2. Tap Don't Show in This List to remove the app from the list.

Always Seven Apps

The Most Used list will always contain seven apps. If you remove an app from the list, Windows will add the eighth most-used app to the bottom of the list.

Changing the Start Menu Tile Size

Tiles can appear in up to four different sizes that are labeled Small, Medium, Wide, and Large. Because Windows 10 uses Live Tiles (tiles that display useful information directly), making a tile larger can allow more information to be displayed on the tile.

1. Tap and hold or right-click the tile you want to resize.

2. Tap or point to Resize.

3. Tap or click the desired tile size.

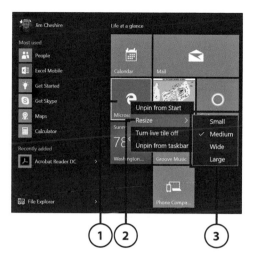

Changing the Taskbar Location

By default, the Taskbar is at the bottom of the screen. You might find it more convenient to have the Taskbar on the left or right edge or possibly even the top of the screen. Moving the Taskbar might be especially helpful if you use touch a lot and you want to move the Taskbar so that it's closer to where your fingers rest when you are holding your tablet.

1. Tap and hold or right-click a blank area of the Taskbar.

2. If Lock the Taskbar is checked, tap or click this option to unlock the Taskbar.

3. Tap or click and hold on a blank area of the Taskbar.

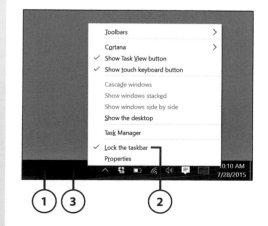

4. Drag the Taskbar to the desired edge of the screen until it snaps into place.

Locking the Taskbar

If you want to prevent the Taskbar from being accidentally removed, you can tap and hold or right-click a blank area of the Taskbar after moving it and then check the Lock the Taskbar option again.

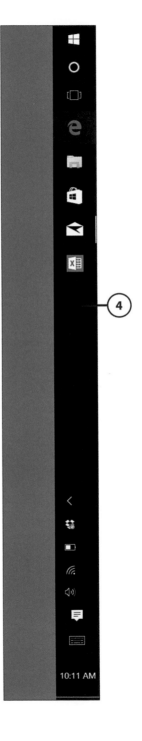

Sign in with a PIN or a
picture password.

Secure your tablet with
your Microsoft account.

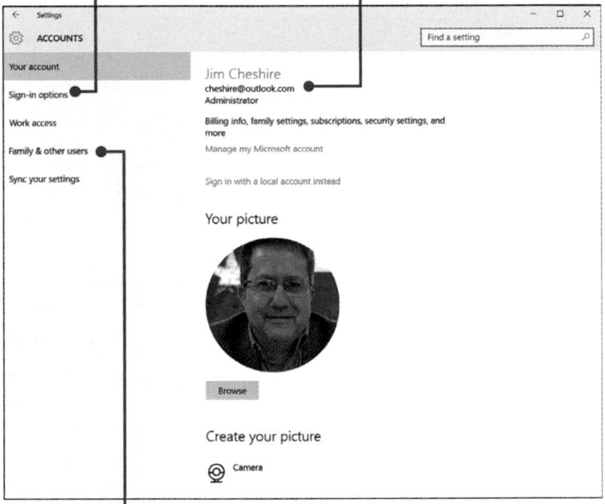

Create other
user accounts.

In this chapter, you learn how you can keep your Windows 10 tablet secure with a password and how you can give other people access to your tablet. You learn about

→ Securing Your Tablet

→ Using Picture Passwords

→ Using PINs

→ Using a Fingerprint Reader

→ Managing User Accounts

Security and Windows 10

Your Windows 10 tablet is quite secure by design. You can encrypt all files on your hard drive, and apps you run are isolated to their own environment and aren't allowed to access sensitive information stored on the PC. Windows 10 also contains many features deep under the hood that are designed to prevent infections from viruses and other malware. It's not at all hyperbolic to say that Windows 10 is the most secure version of Windows ever made.

With that said, you will still want to take steps to secure your tablet. Today's connected devices offer access to more information than ever before, and it's more important than ever to ensure that access to your tablet is controlled. You also might want to let your kids play a game on your tablet without worrying that they are going to delete your emails or get access to information that should be kept private.

Securing Your Tablet

You secure your tablet using a password. If I were to ask you what your password is, you obviously wouldn't tell me (I hope). Even so, if your password is a weak one, you might as well give it to everyone. What do I mean by a "weak" password? I mean a password that consists of a word that appears in the dictionary or is the name of your pet, spouse, or some other word that someone might easily guess. You should protect your password vigilantly, and that means choosing one that's impossible to guess.

Creating a Strong Password

A good password would be something like this: h028w5y358j3. Believe it or not, remembering this password is pretty easy. It's simply "now is the time" on my keyboard with the spaces removed and with my fingers shifted up one row when I typed it. I use that trick often to create strong passwords.

Changing Your Password on a Microsoft Account

If reading this chapter's introduction made you realize that your password needs to be stronger, you can easily change it. It's not a bad idea to change your password periodically as a security precaution.

It's recommended that you sign in to your tablet using a Microsoft account. If you are using a local account instead, see the steps in the "Changing Your Password on a Local Account" section that follows these steps.

1. From the Start menu, tap or click Settings.

2. Tap or click Accounts.

3. Tap or click Manage My Microsoft Account. This will launch your web browser so that you can change your password.

4. In the Basics section, tap or click Change Password.

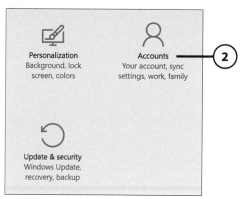

5. Enter your current password and tap or click Sign In.

6. Enter your current password again.

7. Enter a new password.

8. Enter your new password again.

9. Tap or click Save.

Sign in

Because you're accessing sensitive info, you need to verify your password.

cheshire@outlook.com

•••••••••• ✳

Sign in

Can't access your account?
Sign in with a different Microsoft account

5

6 **7**

Change your password

A strong password helps prevent unauthorized access to your email account.

Microsoft account
cheshire@outlook.com

Current password
•••••••••• ✳
Forgot your password?

New password
•••••••••
8-character minimum; case sensitive

Reenter password
•••••••••

☐ Make me change my password every 72 days

Save   Cancel

9 **8**

Changing Your Password on a Local Account

If you are using a local account instead of a Microsoft account, you can change your password within Windows rather than using your web browser.

1. From the Settings screen, tap or click Accounts.

2. Tap or click Sign-In Options.

3. In the Password section, tap or click Change.

4. Enter your current password.

5. Tap or click Next.

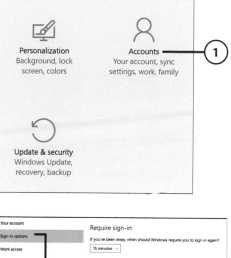

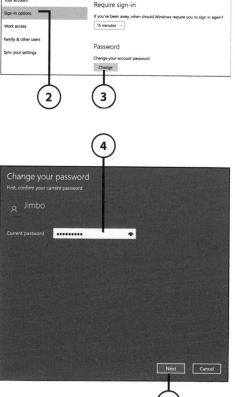

6. Enter a new password.

7. Reenter your new password.

8. Enter a password hint.

9. Tap or click Next.

10. Tap or click Finish.

Faster Password Change

You can also change your local password by pressing Ctrl+Alt+Delete and tapping or clicking Change Password. To get to the Ctrl+Alt+Delete screen without a keyboard, press and hold the Windows button on your tablet, and then press and release the power button quickly.

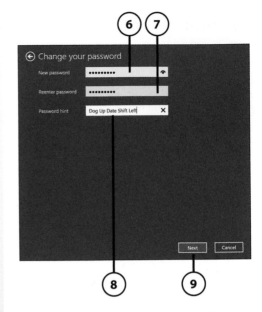

Locking Your Tablet

When you're not using your tablet, it's a good idea to lock it. When your tablet is locked, your password must be entered to access the apps and information on it.

Your tablet sleeps automatically when it has been idle for 15 minutes, but you can also explicitly lock it immediately. (You can change the time interval for the automatic locking feature, and I'll show you how later in this chapter.)

1. From the Start menu, tap or click your username in the top-left corner.

2. Tap Lock on the menu to lock your tablet.

Locking Faster

You can quickly lock your tablet by pressing Winkey+L on your keyboard.

Signing Out of Your Tablet

You can also sign out (log off) of your tablet. Signing out is similar to locking the tablet, except that it closes all apps you are using and completely signs you out of the tablet.

1. From the Start menu, tap your username in the top-left corner.

2. Tap Sign Out.

Configuring Auto-Lock

By default, Windows 10 will ask you to enter your password when you wake up your tablet from sleep. You can configure how soon your tablet sleeps when inactive so that it automatically locks after a certain amount of time.

1. From the Settings app, tap or click System.

2. Tap or click Power & Sleep.

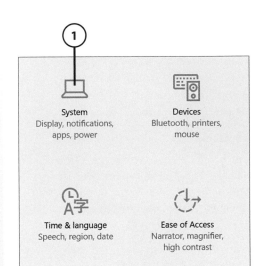

System
Display, notifications, apps, power

Devices
Bluetooth, printers, mouse

Time & language
Speech, region, date

Ease of Access
Narrator, magnifier, high contrast

⚙ **SYSTEM**

Display

Notifications & actions

Apps & features

Multitasking

Tablet mode

Battery saver

Power & sleep

Storage

3. Tap or click On Battery Power, PC Goes to Sleep After and select a desired time period.

Change Power Settings

If you regularly use your tablet while it's plugged in, you might want to configure it to go to sleep after being inactive when it's plugged in. The setting is available on the Power & Sleep page directly under the setting you changed in step 3.

Turning Off the Screen

You can also configure a time period after which your screen turns off. Windows 10 also will lock your tablet when the screen turns off.

③

Sleep

On battery power, PC goes to sleep after

| 15 minutes | ∨ |

3 minutes

5 minutes   to sleep after

10 minutes

15 minutes

20 minutes   connected to Wi-Fi while asleep

25 minutes
                              connected to Wi-Fi while asleep
30 minutes

45 minutes

1 hour

Using Picture Passwords

A picture password enables you to use a series of gestures (taps, circles, and lines) on a picture instead of entering a password. The location, size, and direction of your gestures are all part of your picture password. A picture password is a fast and convenient way to log in to your tablet.

Creating a Picture Password

You can create a picture password using a picture that is included with Windows or you can use one of your own pictures.

1. From the Picture Password section of Sign-in Options, tap or click Add.

2. Enter your current password.

3. Tap or click OK.

4. Tap or click Choose Picture.

PIN

You can use this PIN to sign in to Windows, apps, and services.

Change   I forgot my PIN

Picture password

Sign in to Windows using a favorite photo

Add

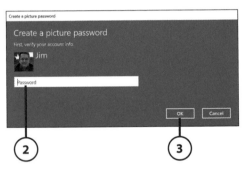

Create a picture password

Create a picture password

First, verify your account info.

Jim

Password

OK   Cancel

Welcome to picture password

Picture password is a new way to help you protect your touchscreen PC. You choose the picture — and the gestures you use with it — to create a password that's uniquely yours.

When you've chosen a picture, you "draw" directly on the touchscreen to create a combination of circles, straight lines, and taps. The size, position, and direction of your gestures become part of your picture password.

Choose picture

5. To change to a new folder, tap or click This PC and select a new folder.

6. Tap or click the picture you'd like to use for your picture password.

7. Tap or click Open.

8. Drag to position the picture the way you want it.

9. Tap or click Use This Picture.

10. Draw three gestures on your picture using the guidelines provided.

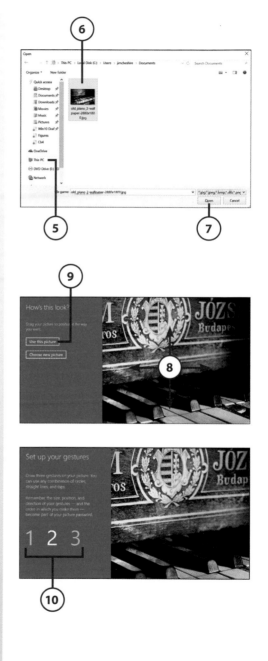

11. Repeat your gestures to confirm them.

12. Tap or click Finish to complete your picture password.

Picture Password with a Mouse

If you plan on using a picture password with your mouse instead of with touch, you'll only be able to create gestures that consist of straight lines and dots. The picture password feature is more secure if you use touch and use multiple types of shapes.

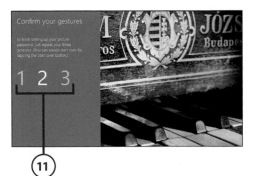

Confirm your gestures

To finish setting up your picture password, just repeat your three gestures. (You can always start over by tapping the Start over button.)

1 2 3

(11)

Congratulations!

You've successfully created your picture password. Use it the next time you sign in to Windows.

Finish (12)

Changing Your Picture Password

If you want to change the picture used for your picture password, you can do so. You might also want to change the gestures used while keeping the same picture.

1. From the Sign-in Options screen in Accounts, tap or click Change.

2. Enter your password to confirm it.

3. Tap or click OK.

4. Tap or click Use This Picture to keep using the existing picture or Choose New Picture to select a new picture.

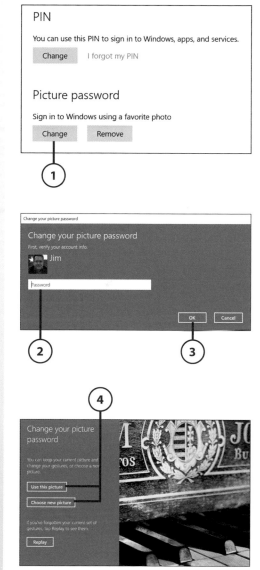

5. Enter the desired gestures for your picture password.

6. Reenter your gestures.

7. Tap or click Finish.

⑤ ⑥

Change your picture password

Congratulations, you have successfully changed your picture password.

Finish —⑦

Replaying Your Picture Password

If you've forgotten the gestures you used for your picture password, Windows can play them back for you.

1. From the Sign-in Options in Accounts, tap or click Change.

2. Enter your password and tap or click OK.

3. Tap or click Replay.

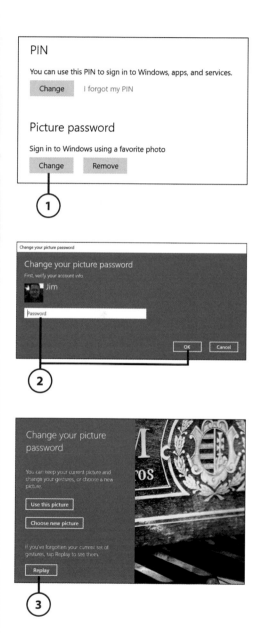

4. Trace the gestures displayed on the screen.

5. Repeat your three gestures.

6. Tap or click Finish.

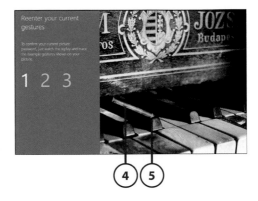

Reenter your current gestures

To confirm your current picture password, just watch the replay and trace the example gestures shown on your picture.

1 2 3

Relearn your picture password

Congratulations, you have successfully relearned your picture password.

Finish

Removing Your Picture Password

You can remove your picture password, after which you must enter your textual password when signing in.

1. From the Accounts screen, tap or click Sign-in Options.

2. Tap or click Remove to remove your picture password.

Using PINs

If you want, you can use a four-digit PIN to sign in to your tablet instead of using a password.

Creating a PIN

You create a PIN by entering a series of four numbers you want to use when signing in or when unlocking your tablet.

1. From the Sign-in Options screen, tap or click Add under PIN.

2. Enter your password to confirm it before creating your PIN.

3. Tap or click OK.

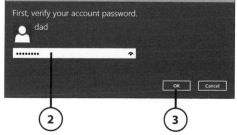

4. Enter your PIN.

5. Confirm your PIN.

6. Tap or click OK.

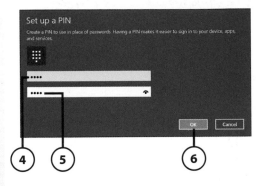

Changing a PIN

You can change your PIN easily.

1. From the PIN section on the Sign-in Options screen, tap or click Change.

2. Enter your current PIN.

3. Enter a new PIN.

4. Confirm your new PIN.

5. Tap or click OK.

Removing a PIN

You can remove a PIN by tapping or clicking I Forgot My PIN. When you get to the point where you are asked to enter a new PIN, tap or click Cancel and your PIN will be removed.

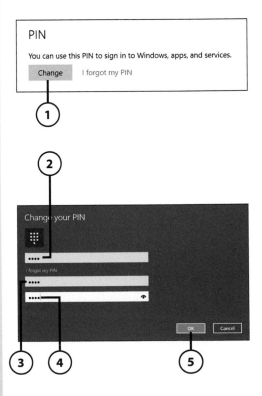

Signing In with a PIN

When a PIN is set for your account, signing in will prompt you for your PIN instead of a password.

1. Swipe up from the lock screen.
2. Enter your PIN to sign in.

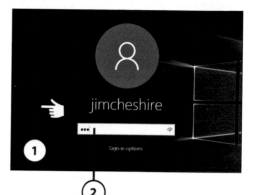

Using a PIN When a Picture Password Is Set

If you have a picture password set, you'll need to use these steps to use your PIN for the first time.

1. Swipe up from the lock screen.
2. Tap or click Sign-in Options.
3. Tap or click the PIN keypad button and enter your PIN to sign in.

Changing Sign-in Options

When you tap Sign-in Options, you'll see various buttons depending on whether you've configured a picture password or a PIN. Tap the appropriate button to choose your sign-in option.

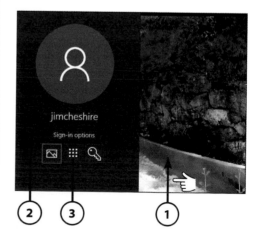

Using a Fingerprint Reader

Not all tablets have a fingerprint reader, but if your tablet does, you can use a swipe of your finger to log in to Windows. Modern fingerprint readers don't suffer from the problems that early readers had; today's fingerprint readers are reliable and extremely secure.

Logging In with a Fingerprint

After you've added one or more fingerprints, you can log in to Windows with a fingerprint using the Sign-in Options link you used earlier. After tapping or clicking it, tap the fingerprint to log in using a fingerprint reader.

Windows Hello

Fingerprint login is part of Windows Hello and requires your tablet to support the biometric features in Windows. Not all tablets support Windows Hello.

Adding a Fingerprint

Before you can use a fingerprint to log in to Windows, you need to add the fingerprint from at least one finger to Windows. You should add the fingerprint from multiple fingers so that you won't be prevented from using your fingerprint reader if you cut a finger or otherwise injure yourself and change your fingerprint.

1. From the Sign-in Options screen, tap or click Set Up in the Windows Hello section.

2. Tap or click Get Started.

Windows Hello

Sign in to Windows, apps and services using

Fingerprint

① ─ Set up

Picture password

Sign in to Windows using a favorite photo

Add

Windows Hello setup   ✕

Welcome to Windows Hello

Your device just got more personal. Say goodbye to entering complex passwords and start using Windows Hello to unlock your device, verify your identity, and buy things in the Store using your fingerprint.

Learn more

② ─ Get started   Cancel

3. Enter your PIN. (If you don't have a PIN, enter your password.)

4. Swipe your finger on your fingerprint reader. Windows will have you repeat this several times. Make sure you swipe the same finger each time.

5. When Windows has enough swipes of your fingerprint and it tells you that you're done, tap or click Add Another to add another fingerprint or Close to finish the process.

Adding Another Finger

You can add fingerprints from additional fingers later. Tap or click Add Another in Sign-in Options and repeat the process of adding a fingerprint.

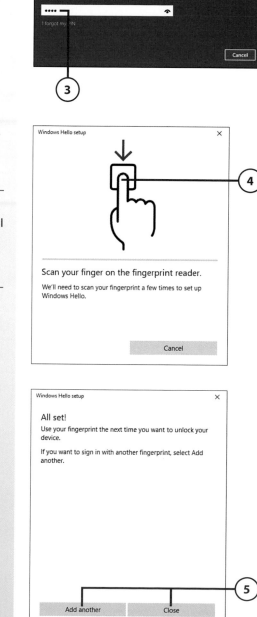

Making sure it's you

I forgot my PIN

Cancel

③

Windows Hello setup

Scan your finger on the fingerprint reader.

We'll need to scan your fingerprint a few times to set up Windows Hello.

Cancel

④

Windows Hello setup

All set!

Use your fingerprint the next time you want to unlock your device.

If you want to sign in with another fingerprint, select Add another.

Add another   Close

⑤

Removing Fingerprints

You can remove fingerprints if you no longer want to sign in using your fingerprints.

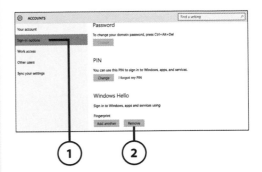

1. From the Account screen, tap Sign-in Options.

2. In the Windows Hello section, tap or click Remove. (If you have more than one fingerprint added, tap or click Remove All.)

It's Not All Good

Cannot Remove Single Fingerprints

You cannot remove a single fingerprint. When you remove fingerprints, all the fingerprints you've added are removed in one step.

Managing User Accounts

User accounts are used to identify particular people using a PC. Windows not only gives each user a unique sign-in ID, but also separates each user's data into folders that are accessible only by that user or by an administrator.

Administrators

Administrators have the ability to access any folder on the system, change any system setting, and so forth. By default, users you add are not administrators. If you want to make a user an administrator, see "Changing an Account Type" later in this chapter.

You can add two types of accounts: local accounts and Microsoft accounts. A local account is tied to the particular PC where it was created. A Microsoft account is tied to a particular Microsoft ID and automatically synchronizes settings and other information via the Internet.

Microsoft Accounts

If you don't already have a Microsoft account, you can get one by browsing to https://signup.live.com.

Adding a Local Account

You can add a new local account that isn't associated with a Microsoft account. This is a convenient way of adding an account for a child or someone else who doesn't have a Microsoft account.

1. From the Accounts screen, tap or click Family & Other Users.

2. Tap or click Add Someone Else to This PC.

Why a Local Account Is Not Recommended

Microsoft doesn't recommend a local account because that account will not be able to synchronize settings across PCs.

3. Tap or click The Person I Want to Add Doesn't Have an Email Address.

4. Tap or click Add a User Without a Microsoft Account.

5. Enter a username for the new user.

6. Enter a password for the new user.

7. Reenter the password to confirm it.

8. Enter a password hint. (A user can display this when signing in if he or she forgets the password.)

9. Tap or click Next to add the new account.

Create an account for this PC

If you want to use a password, choose something that will be easy for you to remember but hard for others to guess.

Who's going to use this PC?

Jimbo

Make it secure.

•••••••••

•••••••••

Secret Password   ✕

Back   Next

Your Family
You might notice an option to add family members. I cover how to do that in Chapter 5, "Using Microsoft Family."

Adding a Microsoft Account

A Microsoft account enables the user to have a more consistent experience across multiple PCs. Settings made on one PC are synchronized to other PCs.

1. From the Family & Other Users screen, tap or click the Add Someone Else to This PC button to add a user account.

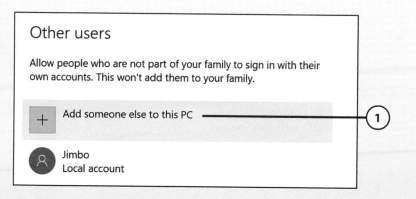

2. Enter the Microsoft account email address. (You can tap or click The Person I Want to Add Doesn't Have an Email Address if you don't have a Microsoft account.)

3. Tap or click Next.

4. Tap or click Finish.

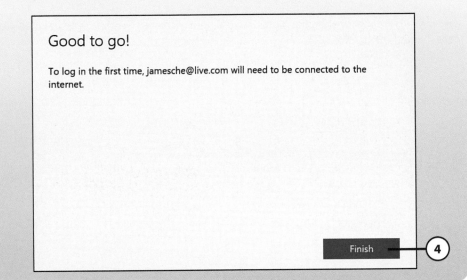

Removing a User Account

If you no longer want to allow an account access to your PC, you can remove the account. The user will need to be logged off before you can delete the account.

1. From the Family & Other Users screen, tap or click the account you want to remove.

2. Tap or click Remove to remove the account.

3. Tap or click Delete Account and Data to delete the account.

It's Not All Good

Removing an Account Removes Data Too

When you remove an account, it will also remove data for the account. In other words, if the user has stored documents, pictures, or other files, those files will be permanently deleted when you remove the account.

Changing an Account Type

You can change an account type and make an account an administrator account. An administrator account has full access to the PC.

1. From the Family & Other Users screen, tap or click the account for which you'd like to change the type.

2. Tap or click Change Account Type.

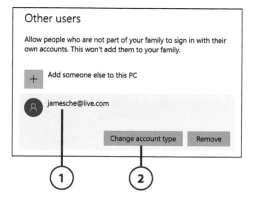

3. Tap or click Account Type.

4. Tap or click the desired account type.

5. Tap or click OK.

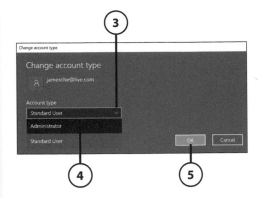

Setting an Account for Assigned Access

There might be times when you want to allow a user access to only one app on your tablet. Windows 10 enables you to do that using a feature called Assigned Access.

You can configure an account for Assigned Access and choose one app that the account can access. When the user signs in, he will be taken directly to the app that you have assigned to him. Access to any other apps or features on your tablet will be restricted.

It's Not All Good

Only Windows Store Apps

Assigned Access can only be assigned to Windows Store apps. Apps that run on your tablet's desktop cannot be controlled with Assigned Access.

Exiting Assigned Access

If you are logged in with a user who is restricted by Assigned Access, you can log in with another user by pressing Ctrl+Alt+Delete on your keyboard. If you don't have a keyboard attached, press and hold the Windows button on your tablet and press and release the power button.

1. From the Accounts screen, tap or click Family & Other Users.

2. Tap or click Set Up Assigned Access.

3. Tap or click Choose an Account.

4. Tap or click the account you want to configure for Assigned Access.

5. Tap or click Choose an App.

6. Tap or click an app to assign it to the user. (Only Windows apps are available.)

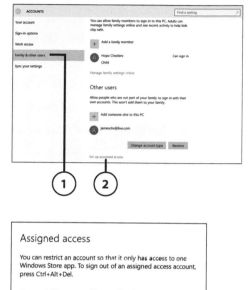

Rebooting for Assigned Access

Windows tells you that you must reboot for Assigned Access to take effect. That's actually not true when you're enabling Assigned Access. However, if you clear Assigned Access for a user, a reboot is required to return the user to an unassigned state.

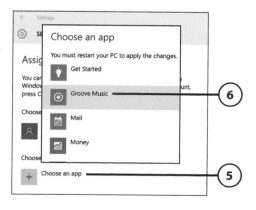

Clearing Assigned Access

If you want to clear assigned access for a user, you can easily do so. However, after going through these steps, you will need to reboot your tablet.

1. From the Family & Other Users screen, tap or click Set Up Assigned Access.

2. Tap or click the account you want to clear.

3. Tap or click Don't Use Assigned Access.

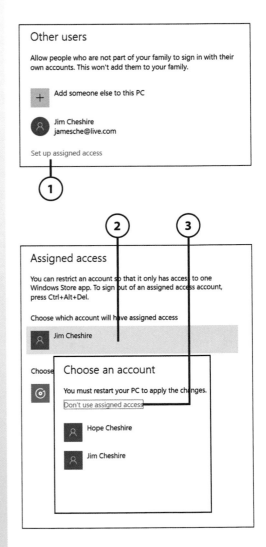

It's Not All Good

Login Loop

If you clear assigned access for an account and then try to log in on that account before rebooting your tablet, you'll get stuck in a login loop. To successfully log in with the user, you'll need to reboot your PC.

Switching Accounts

After you create a new account, you might want to switch to one of the other accounts while leaving the original account signed in. For example, you might be working on a Word document and the kids might ask to play a game. If you decide to take a break and indulge them, it's convenient to simply switch to the account used by the kids without having to close Word and sign out of your session.

1. From the Start menu, tap or click your name.

2. Tap or click the other account from the menu.

3. Enter the password for the other account, and press Enter to sign in.

Switching Users from the Login Screen

When you are on the login screen in step 3, you can tap or click another user in the lower-left corner to log in as that user.

Changing from a Local Account to a Microsoft Account

If you are using a local account, you might decide at some point that you want to enjoy the advantages of using a Microsoft account instead. You can easily switch your local account to a Microsoft account.

1. From the Accounts screen, tap or click Your Account.

2. Tap or click Sign In with a Microsoft Account Instead.

3. Enter your Microsoft account email address.

4. Enter your Microsoft account password.

5. Tap or click Sign In.

Moving to a Microsoft Account

When you switch to a Microsoft account, your files and settings will be transferred over to your Microsoft account so that you won't lose them.

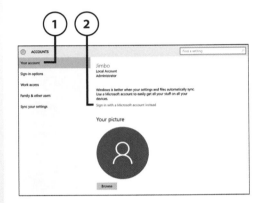

6. Enter the password for your local account.

7. Tap or click Next.

8. Tap or click Set a PIN to create a PIN for your account; otherwise, tap or click Skip This Step.

Creating a New Microsoft Account

If you don't already have a Microsoft account, you can create one by tapping Create One in the dialog box shown in step 2.

Trust Your PC

After you switch to a Microsoft account, you'll need to add the PC to your list of trusted PCs for your Microsoft account. You can do so by tapping Trust This PC from the Your Account screen.

Enter your old password one last time

From here on out, you'll unlock this device using the password or PIN you just set up.

Before we can say goodbye to your local password, you need to provide it one last time.

●●●●●●●●●

(leave blank if none)

Next

⑥ ⑦

Passwords are so yesterday

Using a PIN is faster and more secure than a password—we think you'll love it. How can a PIN be safer than a long password?

Skip this step

Set a PIN

⑧

Switching to a Local Account

You can switch from using your Microsoft account to a local account. Before you do this, you'll want to save anything you're working on and close your applications because Windows 10 requires you to log off your computer to complete this process.

1. From the Accounts settings screen, tap or click Your Account.

2. Tap or click Sign In with a Local Account Instead.

3. Enter your password.

4. Tap or click Next.

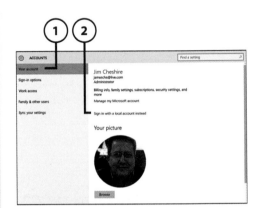

5. Enter a username. (This is the new username you will use when logging in.)

6. Enter a password.

7. Reenter the password.

8. Enter a password hint.

9. Tap or click Next.

10. Tap or click Sign Out and Finish.

5 **6**

← Switch to a local account

Enter the following information. You'll sign in to Windows with a local account from now on.

User name   JimCheshire

Password   ●●●●●●●●

Reenter password   ●●●●●●●●

Password hint   Which City Upper   ×

Next   Cancel

7   **8**   **9**

← Switch to a local account

Jimbo
Local account

You're almost done. Make sure you've saved your work, and use your new password the next time you sign in.

The information associated with your Microsoft account still exists, but apps might ask you to sign in before accessing that info.

Sign out and finish   Cancel

10

See detailed activity reporting
for children using all of your
Windows 10 PCs.

▪▪ Your family	×	+				—	□	×	

← → ○ | 🔒 Microsoft Corporation [US] account.**microsoft.com**/family#/settings/recent-activity/s/- ⬚ ☆ | ≡ ☑ ☁ ···

Recent activity

July 6 through today

Hope Cheshire
hopechesh@outlook.com

Activity reporting ● ⬤ On

Email weekly reports to me ⬤ On

Recent activity

Web browsing

Apps & games

Screen time

Web browsing

Settings

Recent searches (1)

coloring pages

Recent websites blocked (2) ●

› msn.com	Today 9:37 AM	Allow
2 visits		
› youtube.com	Today 10:04 AM	Allow
2 visits		

Control the days and times
when your children can use your
Windows 10 PCs.

Block websites and apps
you don't want your
children to see or use.

A computer is a wonderful tool for children, but it can also allow access to websites and apps that aren't appropriate for them. Microsoft Family is designed to help adults monitor and control what children can do on a PC. In this chapter, you learn about the following topics:

5

→ Adding and Removing Family Members

→ Controlling Website Access

→ Controlling App Access

→ Controlling PC Access

→ Configuring and Reviewing Reports

Using Microsoft Family

Microsoft Family (previously called Family Safety) provides a convenient way to help children that use your tablet (and your other PCs as well) from wandering into websites and apps that contain inappropriate material. You also can use Microsoft Family features to control the days and times that a child can use your computer. Finally, you can configure your tablet so that when a particular family member logs in, he or she can access only a specific app.

It's Not All Good

Only Windows 10

Microsoft Family features do not work on Windows 8.1 or earlier. You will have to upgrade to Windows 10 if you want to use these features.

Adding and Removing Family Members

To use Microsoft Family, you must add your family members to your account. You can add child accounts and adult accounts. Child accounts can be configured with restrictions on them, and adult accounts have the ability to monitor and configure these controls.

Microsoft Account Required

Your family members are associated with your Microsoft account, so you'll want to use your Microsoft account to sign in to your PC before you use Microsoft Family. For more information on using a Microsoft account, see "Managing User Accounts" in Chapter 4, "Security and Windows 10."

Adding a Family Member

You can easily add family members to your account. When you add a family member, you use their Microsoft account email address. If they don't have one, you can create one when you add them to your account.

1. From Settings, tap or click Accounts.

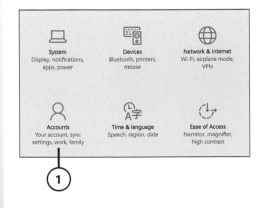

2. Tap or click Family & Other Users.

3. Tap or click Add a Family Member.

4. To add a child, tap or click Add a Child.

5. To add an adult, tap or click Add an Adult.

6. Enter the family member's Microsoft account email address. (If they don't have a Microsoft account, tap or click The Person I Want to Add Doesn't Have an Email Address, and you'll have the option to create one.)

7. Tap or click Next.

8. Tap or click Confirm.

9. Tap or click Close to complete the process.

Accepting an Invitation

The family member that you add will receive an email invitation in their Microsoft account email inbox. They will need to accept that invitation to be added to your Microsoft Family. If the invitation isn't accepted within 14 days, it will expire and you'll need to add the person to your Microsoft Family again. Any family members you invite must still be set up to log in to your tablet from the Accounts app.

Changing Type

You cannot change a family member from a child to an adult. If you unintentionally add an adult as a child account, or vice versa, you'll have to remove the account and then add it back using the correct account type.

Removing a Family Member

Family members can be removed from the Microsoft Family website. Once a family member is removed, he or she can no longer log in to your PC.

1. From the Family & Other Users screen in Settings, tap or click Manage Family Settings Online.

Invitation sent

You invited hopechesh@outlook.com to be added to your family as a child. Until they accept the invite from their email, they'll be able to log into this device without family settings applied to their account.

Let them know they'll need to be connected to the internet the first time they log into the device.

Close

Your family

You can allow family members to sign in to this PC. Adults can manage family settings online and see recent activity to help kids stay safe.

+ Add a family member

jamesche@live.com   Can sign in
Adult

hopechesh@outlook.com   Can sign in
Child

Manage family settings online

2. Tap or click Remove in the Child section to remove a child or in the Adults section to remove an adult.

3. Tap or click the family member you want to remove.

4. Tap or click Remove to confirm that you want to remove the family member.

It's Not All Good

No Confirmation Prompt

There's no confirmation prompt when you remove a family member. You can easily add a family member back to your account, but if you have configured Microsoft Family settings for the family member, those settings will be lost when you remove the family member and will have to be reconfigured if you add that family member back again.

Controlling Website Access

After you've added family members, you can configure child accounts to control their access to websites. You can automatically block access to adult websites (Microsoft decides what is and isn't an adult site), but you can also explicitly block or allow access to particular sites.

Requesting Access

Children can request access to websites that are blocked. You or another adult in your family will have the option to approve or deny such requests. See "Responding to Requests" later in this section for more information.

Blocking Inappropriate Websites

You can automatically block access to adult websites. Doing so will also block a child's ability to use InPrivate browsing and will also ensure that Bing SafeSearch is on so that inappropriate search results are not displayed in Bing searches.

InPrivate Browsing

InPrivate is a special mode in Microsoft Edge and Microsoft Internet Explorer that makes it possible to browse websites without any evidence stored on the PC of the site being visited.

1. Browse to https:// account.microsoft.com/family to access the Microsoft Family settings for your account. (You'll need to log in with your Microsoft account.)

2. Tap or click a child in your family.

3. Tap or click Web Browsing.

4. Tap or click Block Inappropriate Websites to turn on the setting.

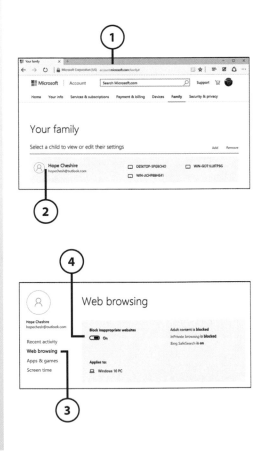

Changes Take Place Immediately

Changes you make on the Microsoft Family website take place immediately. Even if a child is currently using a PC, any changes you make will be immediately enforced.

Explicitly Allowing a Site

You might find that Microsoft Family blocks a site that you want to allow a child to access. You can explicitly allow access to a site so that it will always be allowed.

1. From the Web Browsing screen on the Microsoft Family website, swipe up or scroll down to access the Always Allow These section.

2. Enter a website URL in the Enter the URL of a Website You Want to Allow.

3. Tap or click Allow.

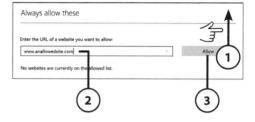

Removing an Allowed Site

If you want to remove access to a site that you've previously explicitly allowed, you can easily remove the site's URL.

1. From the Web Browsing screen on the Microsoft Family website, swipe up or scroll down to the list of allowed sites.

2. Tap or click Remove next to the URL that you no longer want to allow.

3. If you unintentionally remove the wrong site, tap or click Undo to add the URL back to the list of allowed sites.

Explicitly Blocking a Site

You might encounter websites that Microsoft Family allows but that you don't want your child to access. In these cases, you can explicitly block access to a site.

1. From the Web Browsing screen on the Microsoft Family website, swipe up or scroll down to Always Block These.

2. Enter the URL of a website you want to block.

3. Tap or click Block to add the site to the list of blocked sites.

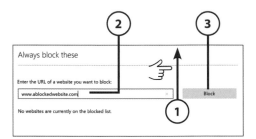

Removing a Blocked Site

If you want to remove the restriction on a website you've blocked, you can remove it from the list of blocked websites.

1. From the Web Browsing screen on the Microsoft Family website, swipe up or scroll down to Always Block These.

2. Tap or click Remove next to the website that you no longer want to block.

3. If you unintentionally removed the wrong site, tap or click Undo to add the URL back to the list of blocked sites.

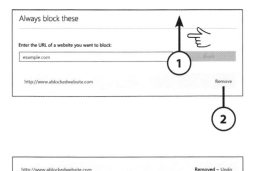

Responding to Requests

If a child attempts to browse to a website that is blocked, a message will let them know that they must ask for permission to access the website. If they click to ask for permission, an email message will be sent to all adults on the account asking for permission. You can then either approve or reject the request.

1. Open the email request that was sent to an adult in your family.

2. Review the requested URL to determine whether you want to allow access.

3. Tap or click Allow to allow access to the requested website.

4. If prompted, log in with your Microsoft account to confirm that you are allowing access.

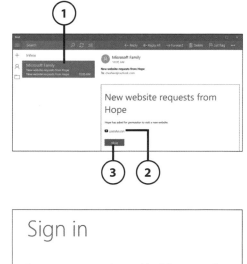

Allowed Websites

If you respond to a request and allow a website that you had previously blocked, the site will be moved from the Always Blocked list to the Always Allowed list. If you want to block the site again, you'll need to remove it from the Allowed list and add it back to the Blocked list.

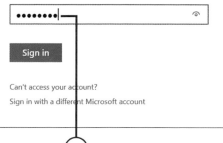

Denying a Request

If you want to deny a request, simply ignore the email requesting access. A request will be approved only if you take explicit action to approve it.

Controlling App Access

The Windows Store provides access to a wide assortment of apps, and some of them are not appropriate for children. All of the apps in the Windows Store are rated for the ages for which they are appropriate. Using Microsoft Family, you can control which apps your child can download and purchase. You can also block access to apps that have already been installed on the device, a useful feature if you want to block an app for a child but allow it for an adult.

Setting Age Restrictions on Windows Store Apps

You can configure Microsoft Family so that your child cannot download or purchase apps unless they are rated as appropriate for the age group you specify.

1. From the Microsoft Family website, tap or click the child for whom you want to set an age restriction.

2. Tap or click Apps & Games.

3. Tap or click Block Inappropriate Apps and Games to turn the setting to On.

4. Swipe up or scroll down to the Limit Apps and Games from the Windows Store section.

5. Tap or click Child Can Download and Purchase Apps and Games Appropriate For.

6. Tap or click the appropriate age for your child.

Age Ratings

The Microsoft Family website will display rating indicators based on the age you select. Your child will be able to download or purchase games with the ratings displayed.

It's Not All Good

Doesn't Block Installed Apps

If there is an app already installed on your tablet that is rated for ages older than the age you select, your child will still be able to use that app. Setting an age restriction will only block the purchase or download of apps from the Windows Store. If you want to stop a child from using an app that's already installed, follow the steps in "Blocking Specific Apps."

Blocking Specific Apps

You can block specific apps so that your child cannot use them. Note that the child must use the app first so that it appears in the Recent Activity list. If you would like, you can log in as the child and launch the app to satisfy this requirement.

It's Not All Good

Wait 4 Hours

There is a 4-hour window between the time a child uses apps on a PC and the time the activity shows up in Recent Activity on the Microsoft Family website.

1. From the Microsoft Family website, tap or click the child you want to block from using an app.

2. Tap or click Recent Activity.

3. Tap or click to ensure that Activity Reporting is turned on.

4. Swipe up or scroll down to Apps & Games.

5. Locate the app you want to block. Tap or click Show All to see all apps if the app you want isn't visible.

6. Tap or click to expand the app's entry and view the device on which the app was used if you're interested in knowing that information.

7. Tap or click Block to block usage of the app.

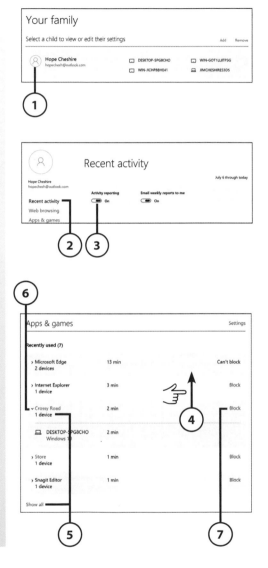

It's Not All Good

You Cannot Block Edge

Note that you cannot block the use of Microsoft Edge.

Unblocking an App

If you would like to allow the use of an app that you had previously blocked, you can remove it from the blocked app list.

1. After selecting the child from the Microsoft Family website, tap or click Apps & Games.

2. Swipe up or scroll down to the Blocked Apps & Games section.

3. Tap or click Remove next to the blocked app.

4. If you unintentionally unblock the wrong app, tap or click Undo to add the app back to the blocked app list.

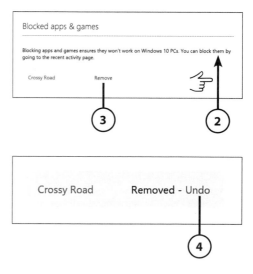

Enabling Assigned Access

You can configure your tablet so that your child (or whatever account you specify) can use only one specific app. When that user logs in to your tablet, the app you specify will be launched full-screen and the user will not be able to close it or switch to another app.

It's Not All Good

Administrator Access Required

To enable or disable Assigned Access, you must be logged in using an account with administrator access.

Kiosk Mode

You will sometimes hear Assigned Access referred to as "kiosk mode." That's because it's an ideal way to use a Windows 10 tablet in a kiosk situation where you don't want users to be able to mess with settings or otherwise change the PC.

It's Not All Good

Only Windows Store Apps

Assigned Access works only with Windows Store apps.

1. From the Accounts screen in Settings, tap or click Family & Other Users.

2. Tap or click Set Up Assigned Access.

3. Tap or click Choose an Account.

4. Tap or click the account you want to use for Assigned Access.

5. Tap or click Choose an App.

6. Tap or click the app you want to allow the user to access on the machine.

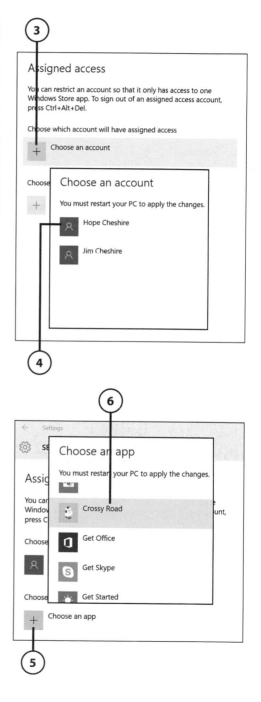

7. From the Start menu, tap or click Power.

8. Tap or click Restart to restart your tablet.

Accessing Other Users

Even when Assigned Access is in use, you can press Ctrl+Alt+Delete on your keyboard to access the Windows login screen and log in as another user. If you don't have a keyboard connected, press the Windows logo and the power button on your tablet at the same time.

Disabling Assigned Access

You can turn off Assigned Access for a user so that he or she can use more than one app on the PC. After making this change, you will need to restart your computer.

1. From the Family & Other Users settings screen, tap or click on Set Up Assigned Access.

2. Tap or click the user who has Assigned Access.

3. Tap or click Don't Use Assigned Access.

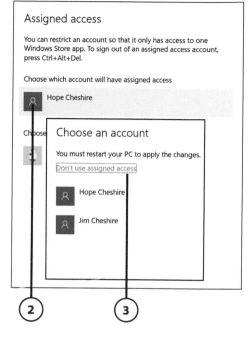

Controlling PC Access

You can block a child from signing in to your tablet. You also can control how long and at what times your child is able to use your tablet (and other PCs running Windows 10) each day.

Blocking a Child from Signing In

You can block your child from ever signing in to your tablet. This setting is specific to the device where you configure it, so you can use it to control which of your Windows 10 computers your child is allowed to access.

1. From the Family & Other Users section in Settings, tap or click the child you want to block from signing in to your PC.

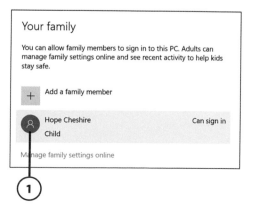

2. Tap or click Block.

3. Tap or click Block to block the child from signing in.

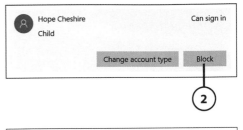

Unblocking a Child from Signing In

You can unblock a child whom you've previously blocked from signing in.

1. From the Family & Other Users section in Settings, tap or click the child who is blocked from signing in.

2. Tap or click Allow.

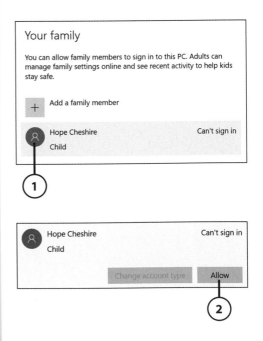

3. Tap or click Allow to allow the child to sign in.

Allow this person to sign in?

Allow this person to sign in?

    Hope Cheshire
    hopechesh@outlook.com

They'll be able to sign in and use this PC.

Allow   Cancel

Setting Time and Day Restrictions on Usage

You can control how long and at what times a child is allowed to use your Windows 10 computers. Unlike blocking a child from signing in, these settings apply to all of your Windows 10 PCs and not just the one you are using when you configure the settings.

1. From the Microsoft Family website, tap or click the child you want to configure.

2. Tap or click Screen Time.

3. Tap or click Set Limits for When My Child Can Use Devices to change the setting to On.

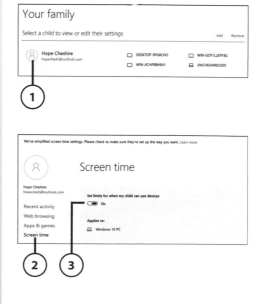

Your family

Select a child to view or edit their settings   Add Remove

Hope Cheshire
hopechesh@outlook.com

DESKTOP-SPG8CHO   WIN-GOT1LL8TP3G

WIN-8CHP8BHE41   JMCHESHIRES3DS

We've simplified screen time settings. Please check to make sure they're set up the way you want. Learn more

Screen time

Hope Cheshire
hopechesh@outlook.com   Set limits for when my child can use devices

On

Recent activity

Web browsing   Applies to:

Apps & games   Windows 10 PC

Screen time

4. Swipe up or scroll down to choose days and times when your devices can be used.

5. Tap or click As Early As on each day to choose the earliest time that your child can use your Windows 10 PCs.

6. Tap or click No Later Than on each day to choose the latest time that your child can use your Windows 10 PCs.

7. Tap or click Limit Per Day, Per Device to set the time limit each day per device.

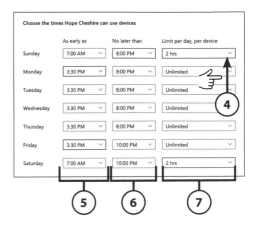

It's Not All Good

Time Limit Per Device

Notice that the time limit is per day, per device. That means that if you set a time limit of 2 hours and you have two Windows 10 PCs, your child will be able to use your PCs for a total of 4 hours, provided he or she uses the PCs within the timeframes you specify.

Configuring and Reviewing Reports

In addition to controlling how your child can use your PCs, you can also review details on what your child is doing on your PCs. You can view report data on the Microsoft Family website. You also can configure Microsoft Family to send you a weekly report on your child's activities in an email message.

Enabling Activity Reporting and Weekly Reports

To see your child's activities on the Microsoft Family website, you will need to make sure that Activity Reporting is enabled. (Activity Reporting is enabled by default, so these steps apply only if you've previously disabled it.) Once you enable Activity Reporting, you can also enable a weekly email report of the child's activities.

Activity Reporting Is Per User

The Activity Reporting setting is configured separately for each child; therefore, you can choose to have it enabled for one child and not another. It's your choice.

---

1. From the Microsoft Family website, tap or click the child you want to configure.

2. From the Recent Activity page, tap or click to set Activity Reporting to On.

3. If you want to receive a weekly email report of your child's activities, tap or click Email Weekly Reports to Me to set it to On.

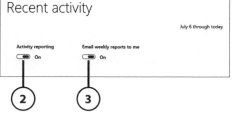

Reviewing Website Activity

You can view your child's website activity, including searches that were performed, websites that were blocked, and websites that were visited.

1. While viewing the Recent Activity for your child, swipe up or scroll down to the Web Browsing section.

2. Review the web searches your child performed in the Recent Searches section. Note that clicking a web search link will show you the results for that search.

3. Review the websites that were blocked in the Recent Websites Blocked section.

4. Tap or click to expand a website and see the pages on the site that your child attempted to visit.

5. Tap or click Allow next to a page or site to remove it from the blocked URL list.

6. Swipe up or scroll down if necessary to see more items on the page.

Web browsing   Settings

Recent searches (1)

coloring pages

Recent websites blocked (2)

⌄ msn.com   Today 9:37 AM   Allow
   2 visits

   MSN.com - Hotmail, Outlook, Skype, Bing, Latest News, Ph...   Today 9:37 AM   Allow
   2 visits

   › youtube.com   Today 10:04 AM   Allow
     2 visits

Recent websites visited (16)

   › msn.com   Today 11:37 AM   Block
     98 visits

   › microsoft.com   Today 11:38 AM   Block

7. Review the websites your child visited in the Recent Websites Visited section.

8. Tap or click to expand a site and see the pages that were visited on the site.

9. Tap or click Show All to see additional sites that were visited.

10. Tap or click Block to add a site or page to the blocked URL list.

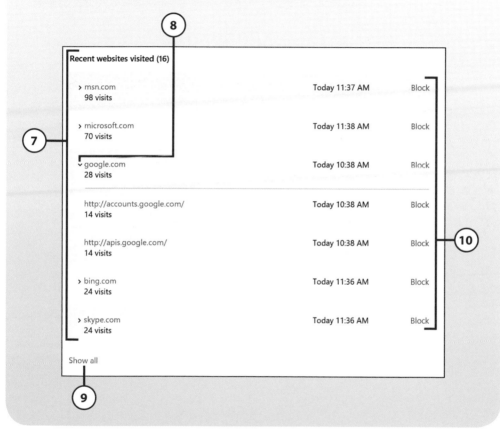

Reviewing App Activity

You can review your child's app activity (including games). In addition to seeing which apps were used, you can see what devices they were used on and how long they were used.

1. While viewing a child's recent activity, swipe up or scroll down to the Apps & Games section.

2. Tap or click to expand an app and see which devices it was used on.

3. Tap or click Show All to see a full list of apps that were used.

4. Tap or click Block to block usage of an app.

Apps & games		Settings
Recently used (7)		
⌄ Microsoft Edge 2 devices	16 min	Can't block
🖥 DESKTOP-SPG8CHO Windows 10	13 min	
🖥 JIMCHESHIRE53D5 Windows 10	2 min	
› Internet Explorer 1 device	3 min	Block
› Crossy Road 1 device	2 min	Block
› MSN Weather 1 device	2 min	Block
› Music 1 device	1 min	Block
Show all		

Reviewing Device Usage

You can view details of your child's usage of each of your Windows 10 PCs. You can see how long each PC was used along with a breakdown of usage on each day for the past 7 days.

1. While viewing a child's recent activity, swipe up or scroll down to the Screen Time section.

2. Review the time spent on each device in total for the past 7 days.

3. Review the daily breakdown of usage for each device. (Note that each device is indicated in a unique color.)

Screen time	Settings

On these devices

🖵	DESKTOP-SPG8CHO Windows 10	23 min
🖵	JIMCHESHIRE53D5 Windows 10	4 min

Total   **28 min**

							28 m

| Time | 0 m | 0 m | 0 m | 0 m | 0 m | 0 m | |

| Date | Mon
Jul 6 | Tue | Wed | Thu | Fri | Sat | Today
Jul 12 |

Restore backed up files easily.

Control how long files are saved and more.

Back up to local and network disks.

In this chapter, you learn how to back up your data using the File History feature in Windows 10. You learn about

Backing Up Your Data with File History

Your tablet uses a solid-state hard drive. That means it has no moving parts and, because of that, it's faster and more mechanically reliable than a traditional hard drive. However, solid-state drives don't even approach 100% reliability; therefore, the chances of losing data stored on your tablet at some point is higher than you might think. Because most of us store irreplaceable data on our PCs these days (things such as priceless photographs), the importance of a good backup strategy simply cannot be overstated.

Configuring and Starting File History

File History is a feature originally introduced in Windows 8 that makes it easy to automatically save backups of critical files to an external drive or a network drive. If something happens to damage your critical files, you can easily restore them from the backed-up source.

Starting Your First Backup

You start your first backup by opening File History in Control Panel and pointing it to a removable drive.

Quickly Backing Up to a Removable Drive

When you insert a removable drive, such as a USB thumb drive, Windows 10 displays a notification asking you to tap to choose what to do when the removable drive is inserted. If you tap that notification, you can then choose to use the drive to back up your files in one step.

Note that the option to use the drive for File History backups appears only if File History is turned off when the drive is connected.

1. Make sure you have a removable drive inserted. Press Winkey+W and enter **File History** in the search box.

Removable Drives

Your removable drive can be an SD card, a USB hard drive, or any other removable storage device.

2. Tap or click File History in the search results.

3. After your drive is found, tap or click Turn On to enable File History and back up your files.

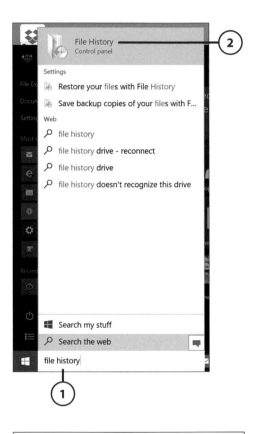

4. If you are a member of a HomeGroup, Windows will prompt you if you want to recommend this backup location to other members of your workgroup. Tap or click Yes or No.

5. Wait until the first backup of your files is complete before you remove the drive.

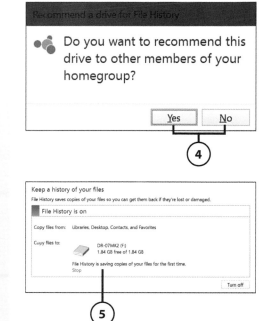

Recommending Drives

If you choose to recommend a drive to others on your HomeGroup, members of your HomeGroup will see your recommended drive as an option when they enable File History on their PC.

Selecting a Different Drive

After you've set up File History for the first time, you can change to a different drive for your backups. For example, you might want to back up to another machine on your network.

1. From File History in Control Panel, tap or click Select Drive.

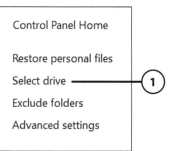

2. Select a drive from the list if your desired drive appears.

3. To add a new network location for backup, tap or click Add Network Location.

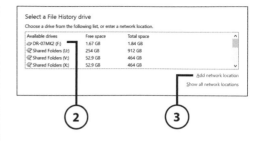

4. Browse to the network location or enter a network path.

5. Tap or click Select Folder.

Existing Backups

If a backup already exists on the drive you choose, you will have an option to choose an existing backup. If you do, files backed up on the original drive will remain on that drive.

6. Tap or click OK to confirm the new drive.

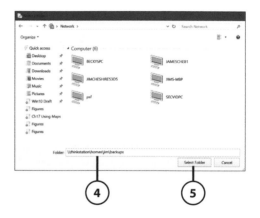

7. Tap or click Yes to move your previously backed up files to the new drive; otherwise, tap or click No. (If your selected drive contains a previous backup, this step will be skipped.)

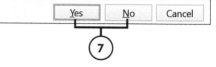

Do you want to move your existing files, too?

We found some files you previously copied using File History. We can move them to your new drive so they'll still be available.

Yes   No   Cancel

⑦

Unavailable Drives

File History is designed to accommodate situations in which a backup drive becomes unavailable. If you unplug a removable drive, shut down the PC you're backing up to, put your PC to sleep, and so on, File History will recognize that and will quietly wait until the drive is available again. When it sees the drive again, it will pick up right where it left off.

Excluding Folders

You might want to exclude some folders from being backed up. For example, if you have temporarily saved some videos to your Videos library, you might want to exclude them from being backed up to save space in your backup drive.

1. From File History, tap or click Exclude Folders.

2. Tap or click Add.

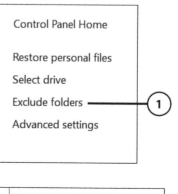

Control Panel Home

Restore personal files

Select drive

Exclude folders ——— ①

Advanced settings

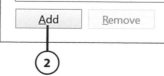

Add   Remove

②

3. Select the folder you want to exclude.

4. Tap or click Select Folder.

5. Tap or click Save Changes.

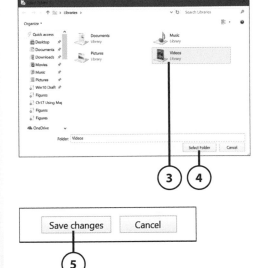

Choosing When Backups Happen

By default, your backups happen once per hour. You can change how often backups occur so that they occur more frequently or less frequently.

1. From File History, tap or click Advanced Settings.

2. Tap or click the Save Copies of Files drop-down and select a time interval for backups.

3. Tap or click Save Changes.

Backups Only When Changes Happen

File History backs up a file only if the file has changed since the last time it was backed up.

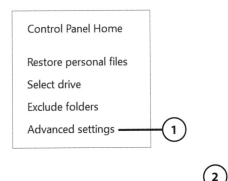

Controlling How Long Backups Are Kept

By default, File History saves your backups forever; however, this can quickly fill up your backup drive. You can control how long File History saves backups.

1. From the Advanced Settings screen, tap or click the Keep Saved Versions drop-down.

2. Choose a new value to set how long File History keeps your backups.

3. Tap or click Save Changes.

Advanced settings

Choose how often you want to save copies of your files, and how long to keep saved versions.

Versions

Save copies of files: Every 3 hours

Keep saved versions: Forever (default)

Until space is needed
1 month
3 months
6 months
9 months
1 year
2 years
Forever (default)

HomeGroup

This PC can't share with others in the homegroup.
View homegroup settings

Event logs

Open File History event logs to view recent events or errors

Save changes   Cancel

Restoring Files

File History makes it easy to locate the backed-up copies of your files and restore them. You can restore files to the same folder where they were located when File History backed them up, but you can also choose to restore files to a different location if you prefer.

Restoring Files to the Original Location

You can browse your backed-up files and easily restore one or more of them to the original file location.

1. From File History, tap or click Restore Personal Files.

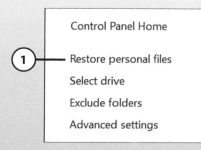

Control Panel Home

Restore personal files

Select drive

Exclude folders

Advanced settings

2. Double-tap or double-click a folder to browse files inside the folder.

3. Tap or click the up arrow to go back to the parent folder.

4. Select a previous path from the drop-down to quickly navigate to that path.

5. Tap or click Options, and then tap or click the View menu to change the view.

6. Tap or click Previous Version to see an earlier version of backed-up files.

7. Tap or click Next Version to see later versions of backed-up files.

8. Select one or more files or folders, and tap or click Restore to restore them to the original location.

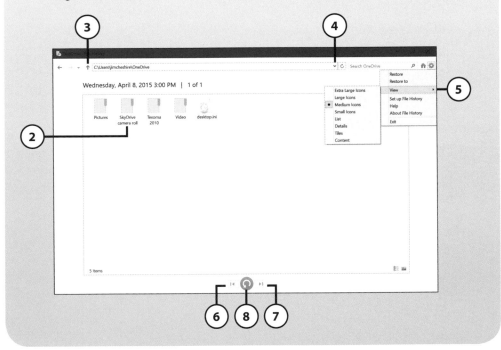

Resolving File Conflicts

If you attempt to restore a file to your local drive and that file already exists in the same location, File History enables you to overwrite the existing file, skip the file restore, or view information about the original file and the backed-up file so that you can decide what you would like to do.

1. Tap or click Restore to restore one or more existing files.

2. Tap or click Replace to overwrite the existing file or files.

3. Tap or click Skip to skip the file or files.

4. Tap or click Compare Info for Both Files if only one conflict exists or Let Me Decide for Each File if multiple conflicts exist to compare the files and select those you want to keep.

5. Check a location to keep all files in that location. (Files from the backup are listed on the left.)

6. Check individual files to keep specific files.

7. Check Skip to skip all files that have the same date and size.

8. Tap or click Continue to perform the actions you selected.

Resolving Conflicts

File History tries to help you resolve conflicts by bolding differences in file attributes. If one version of a file has a larger file size than another, File History displays the larger size in a bold font. If one file has a later date than another, the one with the later date appears bolded.

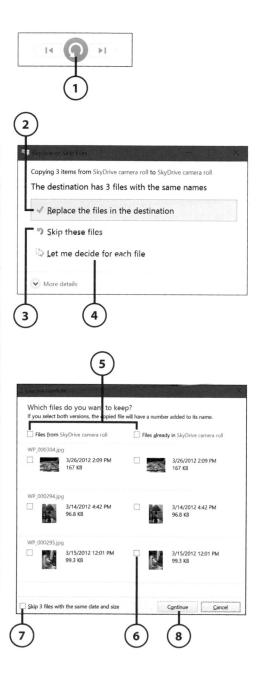

Restoring to a Different Location

If you would like to restore files to a location other than their original location, you can easily do that. This is useful in cases where you want an additional copy of a file on your local machine or if you want to restore files to a USB thumb drive or another removable device.

1. Select the files or folders you want to restore.

2. Tap or click Options, and then tap or click Restore To.

3. Select a location where you would like to restore the files or folders.

4. Tap or click Select Folder to restore the files.

Cleaning Up Files

By default, File History saves your backed-up files forever. In many cases, you will want to keep all versions of your files, but if you have files that change often, keeping all versions might mean that your backups use more disk space than you would like. Fortunately, you can clean up backed-up files so that you can free disk space on your backup drive.

Performing a Cleanup

When you clean up file versions, you can specify to clean up files older than a certain timeframe, or you can clean up all versions except the most recent version. In no cases will cleaning file versions remove the latest version of a file.

1. From the Advanced Settings dialog in File History, tap or click Clean Up Versions.

2. Select an option from the Delete Files drop-down. By default, a cleanup will remove all files older than one year, but you can modify that as desired.

3. Tap or click Clean Up to delete the file versions in the backup as per your selection.

File History Might Not Find Files to Delete

If File History cannot find any files in your backups that are old enough to be deleted given your selected timeframe, it will notify you and ask you to choose a shorter period of time.

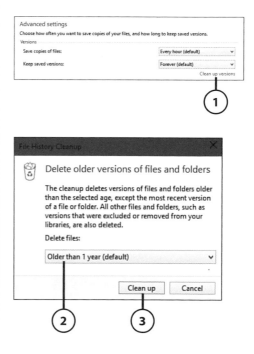

It's Not All Good

Grab a Snack

If your backups are on a network location, it could take quite a while for File History to parse through your files and clean things up. Start the process, and then go grab a snack.

Troubleshooting File History

If you see error messages that don't provide enough detail for you to figure out what went wrong, or if you notice that files you expect to be backed up aren't getting backed up, you can view detailed logs from the Windows Event Viewer.

Viewing File History Event History

You can view details of all File History events in the Windows Event Viewer.

1. From the Advanced Settings screen in File History, tap the Open File History Event Logs link.

2. Select an event to see more details about it.

HomeGroup

This PC can't share with others in the homegroup.
View homegroup settings

Event logs

🛡 Open File History event logs to view recent events or errors

(1)

(2)

File History backup log	Number of events: 1			
Level	Date and Time		Source	Even
⚠ Warning	4/8/2015 5:21:11 PM		FileHistory-Core	

Event 204, FileHistory-Core   ×

General | Details

Unusual condition was encountered during finalization of a backup cycle for configuration C:
\Users\jamesche\AppData\Local\Microsoft\Windows\FileHistory\Configuration\Config

Log Name:	Microsoft-Windows-FileHistory-Engine/File History backup log		
Source:	FileHistory-Core	Logged:	4/8/2015 5:21:11 PM
Event ID:	204	Task Category:	None
Level:	Warning	Keywords:	
User:	SYSTEM	Computer:	jwccarbon
OpCode:	Info		
More Information:	Event Log Online Help		

It's Not All Good

File History Events

File History will likely log plenty of events that make no sense to you. Don't worry about them. The Event Viewer logs are really intended to be used by advanced users. However, if you do see an error that looks serious and you need more information on it, a search of Microsoft's Knowledge Base at support.microsoft.com might give you the information you need.

Use Reading View for a cleanly formatted reading experience.

Save your favorite sites and save articles for reading later.

Browse the modern Internet with a new browser.

Windows 10 comes with Microsoft Edge, a brand-new browser designed for the modern Internet. In this chapter, you learn how to use Microsoft Edge. You learn about

→ Browsing and Searching Websites

→ Configuring Edge

→ Using Cortana with the Web

→ Using Web Notes

Finding Information on the Internet

It should come as no surprise to you if I say that the Internet is the greatest single source of information that man has ever known. Windows 10 has some great features that are designed to bring that information to your fingertips quickly and easily.

Along with Microsoft Edge, a new web browser that's designed for today's Internet, Microsoft added *Cortana* integration into the web browser experience. Cortana is a digital personal assistant, and she can offer some amazing assistance to you while you're browsing the Internet.

More on Cortana

You'll learn more about Cortana in the next chapter, "Using Cortana."

Browsing and Searching Websites

Windows 10 introduces Microsoft Edge, a brand new web browser built for the modern web. Edge adds quite a few nice features to the web browsing experience, all of which you will learn about in this section.

Browsing to a Website

You can browse directly to a website if you know the website's address. Later you'll learn how you can use Favorites to store your favorite website addresses for faster access.

1. Tap or click the Edge button on the Taskbar.

2. Tap or click inside the address bar. (If a site's address already appears there, it will be selected so that typing a new address will delete it.)

3. Enter the address for the website you want to visit and press Enter.

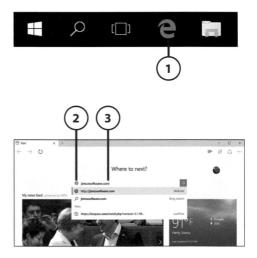

Suggested Addresses and Information

As you enter addresses and other information in the address bar, suggested information from Bing may pop up below the address bar. You can always tap or click one of these suggestions to use it.

Opening a Link in a New Tab

As you read through a web page, you will encounter links that you can click to visit other web pages. These links usually replace the page you're currently reading with a new page. If you'd prefer, you can open a link in a new tab so that you can easily return to the original page.

1. Locate a link that you want to open in a new tab.

2. Tap and hold or right-click on the link, and then tap or click Open in New Tab.

3. Tap or click the new tab to activate it.

4. Tap or click the original tab to switch back to the original page.

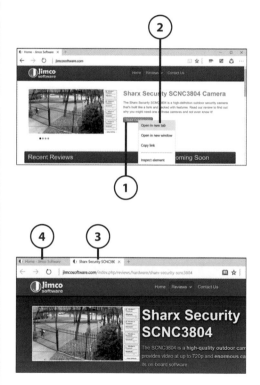

Opening a Link in a New Window

Instead of opening a link in a new tab, you can choose to open a link in an entirely new window. This is especially useful if you want to view two windows side-by-side for comparison.

1. While browsing a page, tap and hold or right-click on a link, and then tap or click Open in New Window.

2. Tap the original window to reactivate it.

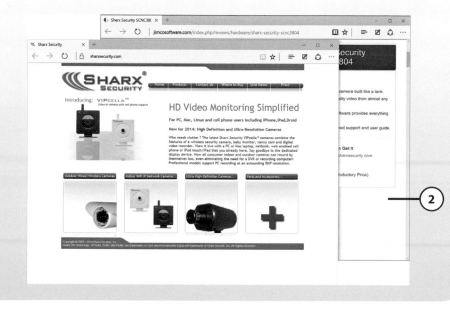

Adding a Favorite

If you visit a particular website often, you may want to add it to your Favorites. Once you've added a site to your Favorites, you can quickly and easily return to the site without having to remember the website's address.

1. While viewing the website that you want to add to your Favorites, tap or click Add to Favorites or Reading List.

2. Edit the name if you want to or accept the default.

3. Tap or click Create In if you want to choose another existing folder for the Favorite.

4. Tap or click Create New Folder to create a new folder.

5. Tap or click Create Folder In and choose a new parent folder if you want to create the new folder inside of another folder.

6. Enter the name for your new folder.

7. Tap or click Add.

Folders in Favorites

Folders are a great way to organize your Favorites. You can think of folders just like you think of the folders in a file cabinet.

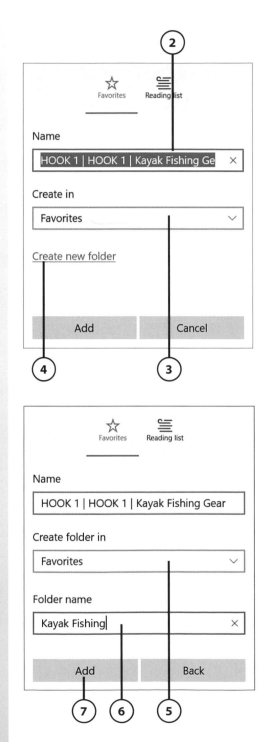

Browsing to a Favorite

You can easily browse to a website that you've saved as a Favorite.

1. In Edge, tap or click Hub.

2. Tap or click the folder that contains your Favorite.

3. Tap or click your Favorite to browse to the site.

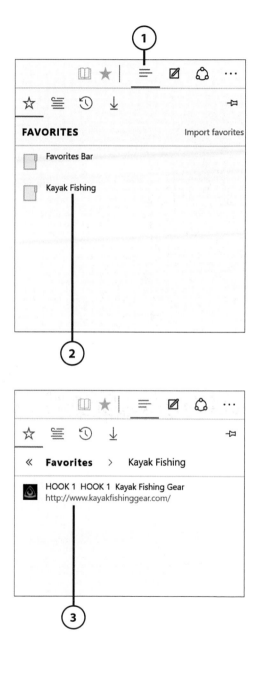

Deleting a Favorite

You might find that you want to delete a Favorite you've added. For example, you might have been saving Favorites for a project you were working on. When the project is completed, you might want to delete those Favorites.

1. Tap or click Hub.

2. Tap and hold or right-click on the Favorite or folder you want to delete.

3. Tap or click Remove.

Faster Deletion

If you are saving some Favorites temporarily, it's always a good idea to save them in their own folder. By doing that, you can delete all the Favorites in one quick step when you no longer need them.

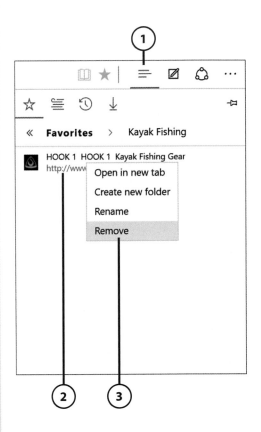

Viewing Browsing History

As you browse the Internet, Edge stores a list of all the websites you've viewed in your browsing history. You can access that list if you need to revisit a website that you visited at some point in the past.

1. Tap or click Hub.

2. Tap or click History.

3. Tap or click a timeframe to see history for that time period.

4. Tap or click a link in your history to go to the link.

Recommendations Based on History

As you are entering website addresses into the address bar, Edge will recommend sites you've visited before. You can always recognize these recommendations because they are associated with an icon that looks like a clock.

HISTORY   Clear all history

Last hour   ×

HOOK 1 | HOOK 1 | Kayak Fishing Gear   2:55 PM
kayakfishinggear.com

Bass fishing - Pensacola Blue Angels Bass   2:55 PM
hook1.com

Sharx Security   2:52 PM
sharxsecurity.com

Sharx Security SCNC3804 - Jimco Software   2:44 PM
jimcosoftware.com/index.php/reviews/har

Home - Jimco Software   2:44 PM
jimcosoftware.com

IIS 7.0 Detailed Error - 404.0 - Not Found 2:35 PM
jimcosoftware.com/admin

Reason 8 - Jimco Software   2:32 PM
jimcosoftware.com/index.php/reviews/auc

Today - 7/6   ×

Yesterday - 7/5   ×

Last week - 6/28 to 7/4   ×

Saving Websites for Reading Later

As you're browsing the Internet, you might come across one or more articles that you'd like to read, but the timing isn't convenient. In these cases, you can add the article to Edge's reading list. You can then read the article at your leisure.

1. While viewing the article you want to read later, tap or click Add to Favorites or Reading List.

2. Tap or click Reading List.

3. Edit the name if you want to.

4. Tap or click Add.

Reading Later

You can return to the Reading List at any time and tap or click an item to read it.

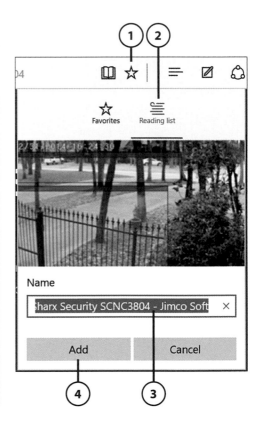

It's Not All Good

No Offline Reading

You will need to be online to read items in your Reading List. The Reading List is not designed to enable you to read items offline.

Using Reading View

Many websites are cluttered with advertisements, banner links to other content, and more. This clutter can sometimes make it hard to read items such as news articles. Reading View is designed to make reading such articles much easier.

Reading View takes all the relevant content (text and images) from a web page and presents it in a clean and uncluttered view for easy reading.

1. While viewing a web page, tap or click Reading View.

2. Swipe up or scroll down to see more of the article.

3. Tap or click Reading View again to return to normal mode.

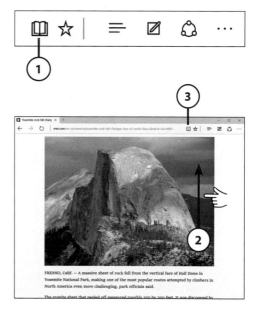

It's Not All Good

Not Always Available

Reading View isn't always available. Some web pages are too complex or not configured in a way that enables Reading View to display the content. Microsoft is always working to improve this feature, so the amount of content supported by Reading View should continue to grow.

Changing Reading View Options

You can change the background color and size of the text in Reading View. This is a great benefit when the web page you are viewing has small type that is difficult to read. It's also helpful for those pages that use light gray text on a white background.

1. Tap or click More Actions.

2. Tap or click Settings.

3. Swipe up or scroll down to the Reading section.

4. To change the background color in Reading View, tap or click Reading View Style, and tap or click the desired color.

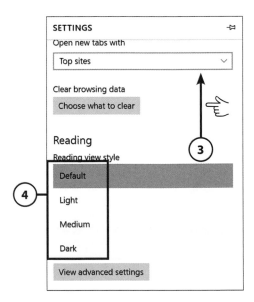

5. To change the text size in Reading View, tap or click Reading View Font Size, and tap or click the desired size.

SETTINGS

Open new tabs with

Top sites ⌄

Clear browsing data

Choose what to clear

Reading

Reading view style

Default ⌄

Reading view font size

Small

Medium

Large

Extra Large

About this app

Microsoft Edge 20.10162.0.0

© 2015 Microsoft

Searching the Internet

Edge makes it easy to search the Internet. Microsoft's own search engine Bing is used by default. The next section shows you how you can change your default search engine.

1. Enter a search term in the address bar.

2. Tap or click a suggested search term or press Enter.

3. Tap or click a search result to visit that page.

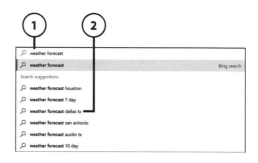

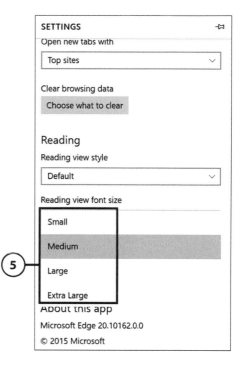

Configuring Edge

Edge offers several settings you can use to configure it the way you want it. You can change the startup page, your search engine, a pop-up window blocker, and more.

Changing the Page Edge Opens With

When you launch Edge, the Start Page is displayed by default. The Start Page shows some curated news content, weather content, and other content based on your location. You can change what page Edge opens with.

1. Tap or click More Actions.

2. Tap or click Settings.

New window

New InPrivate window

Zoom   — 150% +

Find on page

Print

Pin to Start

F12 Developer Tools

Open with Internet Explorer

Send feedback

Settings

3. If you want Edge to start with a new tab, tap or click New Tab Page.

4. If you want Edge to start with the pages that were open when you last closed it, tap or click Previous Pages.

5. To start with a specific page, tap or click A Specific Page or Pages.

6. Tap or click the page drop-down, and select Bing or MSN to set the startup page to Bing or MSN.

7. Tap or click Custom to specify a custom startup page.

SETTINGS

Choose a theme

Light

Show the favorites bar
Off

Import favorites from another browser

Open with
- Start page
- New tab page
- Previous pages
- A specific page or pages

Open new tabs with

Top sites

SETTINGS

Choose a theme

Light

Show the favorites bar
Off

Import favorites from another browser

Open with
- Start page
- New tab page
- Previous pages
- A specific page or pages

MSN

Bing

Custom

Clear browsing data
Choose what to clear

Reading

8. Enter the address of the site you want to use for the startup page.

9. Tap or click Save.

10. Enter a second address if you want another page to open at startup.

11. Tap or click + to add additional startup pages.

Blank Page and Shortcuts to Recent Sites

If you use **about:blank** for the address in step 8, Edge will use a blank page for the startup page. If you use **about:tabs** for the address, Edge will show tiles that link to your most recently visited websites. You can also use **about:Start** to use the Start Page.

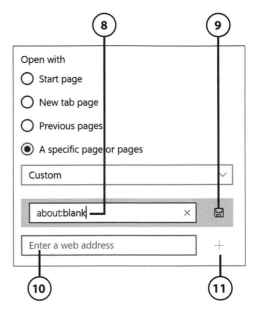

Clearing Browser Data

As you browse the Internet, Edge stores information on the sites you visit to make your browsing experience faster. Edge also saves a history of where you've been, along with other data. You can delete this information if you want to.

Why Clear?

I do a lot of shopping on the Internet for gifts on birthdays and other special occasions. To keep family members from finding out what I'm buying, I'll regularly clear my browser history so that no one can see where I've been.

1. From the Settings pane, tap or click Choose What to Clear.

2. Tap or click to check Browsing History to clear your history.

3. Tap or click to check Cookies and Saved Website Data to clear any cookies or site data.

4. Tap or click to check Cached Data and Files to clear cached files from websites you've visited.

5. Tap or click to check Download History to clear the history of all files you've downloaded.

6. Tap or click to check Form Data to clear any data you are storing that is used to automatically fill in forms on web pages.

7. Tap or click to check Passwords to clear saved passwords.

8. Tap or click Show More to see additional items you can clear.

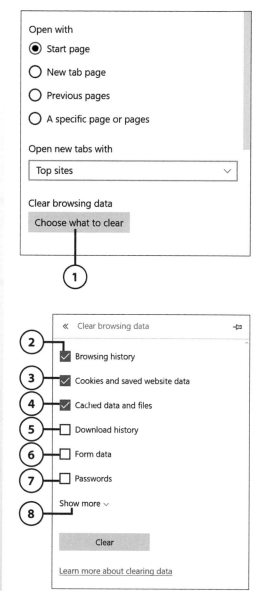

9. Tap or click Media Licenses to clear any licenses for media content.

10. Tap or click Pop-Up Exceptions to reset any pop-up window exceptions.

11. Tap or click Location Permissions to remove any permissions granted to websites for your location information.

12. Tap or click Full Screen Permissions to remove any permissions granted to websites to switch to full-screen mode.

13. Tap or click Compatibility Permissions to reset any sites that are currently configured to always open in Internet Explorer instead of Edge.

14. Tap or click Clear.

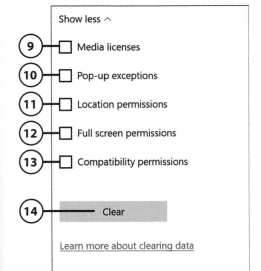

Disabling the Pop-Up Blocker

Some websites will pop open windows automatically, often so that they can show you advertisements. Edge will block most of these pop-up windows by default. If you want to, you can disable the pop-up window blocker.

1. From the Settings pane, swipe up or scroll down to the Advanced Settings section.

2. Tap or click View Advanced Settings.

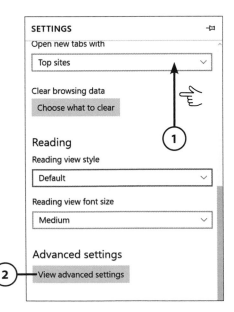

3. Tap or click Block Pop-Ups to turn off the pop-up blocker.

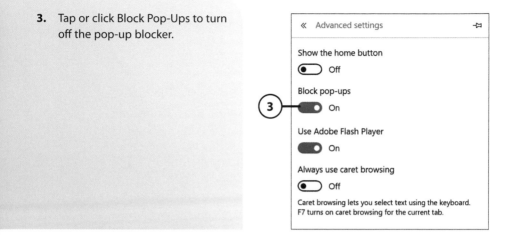

Using Cortana with the Web

As I mentioned earlier, Cortana is what Microsoft calls a "digital personal assistant." Some of the features that Cortana brings to Edge certainly fulfill that description. Cortana sits in the background, watching what you're doing on the Internet. If she has any helpful information to share, she'll pop up and let you know.

More Info on Cortana
For more information on using Cortana, see Chapter 8, "Using Cortana."

Getting Restaurant Directions and Reviews

If you're browsing the web for a restaurant, Cortana can offer you directions, restaurant reviews, and more.

1. While browsing a restaurant website, tap or click the Cortana symbol.

2. Tap or click Detailed Directions to open Bing Maps in a new tab with directions to the restaurant.

3. Tap or click Parking Suggestions to open ParkMe.com in a new tab with parking information for the area.

4. Tap or click Menu for a restaurant menu.

5. Swipe up or scroll down for more information.

6. Tap or click See All Photos to open Bing in a new tab with photos and more.

7. Tap or click Recent, Favorable, or Critical to view reviews from Yelp.

I've got the details.

Photos

⑥ — See all photos

Reviews

yelp⁑

⑦ — Recent | Favorable | Critical

★★★★☆ Apr 04, 2015
This place is great for breakfast! It is a hidden gem in Keller. The place feels a little more upscale than most places, yet not stuffy. The restaurant itself is ... Full review

Reviewing Cortana Search Results

As you enter search terms in the address bar, Cortana might offer to show you information she thinks you might be interested in. In this example, I'll show you how Cortana might offer you a weather forecast.

1. Tap or click inside the address bar.

2. Enter **weather dallas**, and Cortana displays the current weather for Dallas, Texas.

① ②

| DeVivo Bros Eatery | + | — □ × |

← → ↻   🔍 weather dallas

≡ ✎ ○ ⋯

🔍 Dallas, Texas ALERT - Flood - Warning   Bing search
☁ 81 °F Mostly cloudy
          Wind 8 MPH

🔍 **weather dallas**   Bing search

Search suggestions

🔍 **weather dallas** tx

Home
▾ About the Eatery
   Contact Us
Hook & Ladder Pizza
▾ Menus
   Bakery Menu
   Catering Menu
   Eatery Menu
   Gluten Friendly Menu
   Kids Menu
Testimonial and Awards

🔍 **weather dallas** texas 10 day

🔍 **weather dallas** texas hour by hour

🔍 **weather dallas** radar live

🔍 **weather dallas** tx hourly

🔍 **weather dallas** texas 7 day forecast

🔍 **weather dallas** tx metroplex map

The DeVivo Bros. Eatery is a locally owned and operated family business that takes enormous pride in

More Info

Cortana can also show you stock prices. For example, if you enter **MSFT stock** in the address bar, Cortana will show you the current Microsoft stock price.

Asking Cortana for More Information

As you're reading a web page, you can find more information about something on that page by asking Cortana.

1. Select something on a web page that you want to know more about.

2. Tap and hold or right-click, and then tap or click Ask Cortana.

Meteorite

From Wikipedia, the free encyclopedia

This article is about debris from space that survives impact with the ground. For Meteor (disambiguation). For popular applications, see Falling star. For the fictio universe, see Meteorite (comics).

See also: Meteoroid and Meteor

A **meteorite** is a solid piece of debris from a source such as an asteroid or a comet, which originates in outer space and survives its impact with the Earth's surface. It is called a meteoroid before its impact. A meteorite's size can range from small to extremely large. When a meteoroid enters the atmosphere, friction, pressure, and chemical interactions with the atmospheric gases cause it to heat up and radiate that energy, thus forming a fireball, also known as a meteor or shooting/falling star. A bolide is either an extraterrestrial body that collides with the Earth, or an exceptionally bright, fireball-like meteor _____ r it ultimately impacts the surface.

Ask Cortana

More generally, a meteorite on the surface of any c les object that has come from outer space. Meteorites ave ___ oon[1][2] after being observed as they transit the atmosphere or i ___ alled m as *finds*. As of February 2010, there are approxima ely ___ having are more than 38,660 well-documented meteorite f ds.

Select all

Copy

Inspect element

Meteorites have traditionally been divided into three broad categorie : stony meteor

3. Tap or click links in the panel to see additional information.

4. Tap or click outside the panel to dismiss it.

Using Web Notes

Edge makes it easy to add notes and other markup to a website and share those notes with others using a feature called Web Notes.

Adding Web Notes to a Web Page

You can use a stylus to add sketches, handwritten notes, and more to a page.

1. While browsing a page, tap or click Make a Web Note.

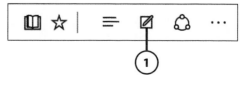

2. Tap the pen to activate it. The pen is used to draw and write on the page.

3. Tap the pen again, and tap a color to change ink color.

4. Tap a size to change the size of the pen's tip.

5. Tap the highlighter to activate it. The highlighter is used to high-light content on the page.

6. Tap the highlighter again, and then tap a color to change the highlighter color.

7. Tap a shape to change the shape of the highlighter tip.

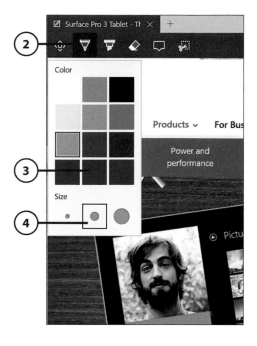

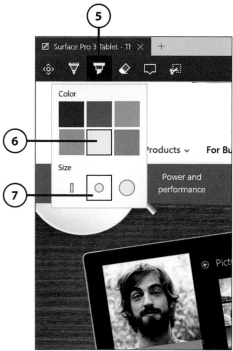

8. Tap the eraser to activate it. Web Notes can be erased by using the eraser.

9. Tap the eraser again, and tap Clear All Ink to remove all Web Notes.

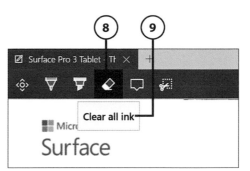

10. Tap the note to activate it.

11. Tap the page where you want to add a note.

12. Enter your note.

13. Tap the note icon to display notes.

14. Tap the note icon again to hide a note.

15. Tap the Delete button to delete a note.

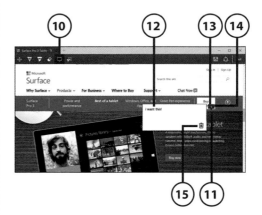

Saving Web Notes to OneNote

You can save Web Notes to OneNote so that you can access them later or share them with other users of your OneNote notebook.

1. Add a Web Note to a page.

2. Tap or click Save.

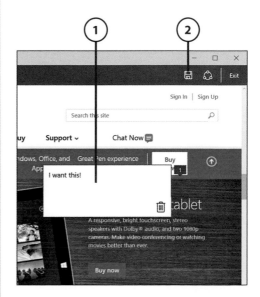

3. Tap or click OneNote.

4. Tap or click Send.

5. Tap or click View Note to open OneNote and view your Web Note.

Using OneNote

For more information on using OneNote notebooks, see Chapter 21, "Organizing Notes with Microsoft OneNote."

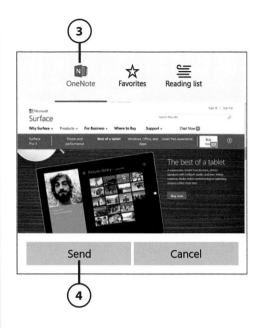

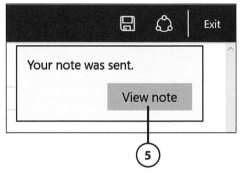

It's Not All Good

Cannot Edit Saved Web Notes

When you save a Web Note, it is saved as an image; therefore, you cannot retrieve a saved Web Note and edit it.

Saving a Web Note to Favorites or Reading List

You can also save Web Notes to your Favorites or to Reading List.

1. Add a Web Note to a page.

2. Tap or click Save.

3. Tap or click Favorites to save the Web Note to Favorites or Reading List to save the Web Note to Reading List.

4. Edit the name if you want to.

5. If saving to Favorites, select a folder, or tap or click Create New Folder to create a new folder.

6. Tap or click Add to save the Web Note.

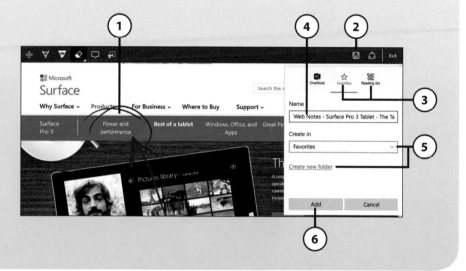

Tell Cortana what you're interested in and let her keep you up to date.

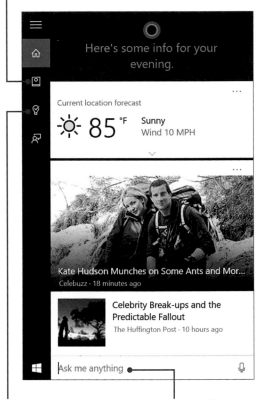

Here's some info for your evening.

Current location forecast

☀ 85 °F Sunny
Wind 10 MPH

Kate Hudson Munches on Some Ants and Mor...
Celebuzz · 18 minutes ago

Celebrity Break-ups and the Predictable Fallout
The Huffington Post · 10 hours ago

Ask me anything

Let Cortana remind you of important things at certain times, when you interact with a contact, or when you arrive at or leave a place.

Search for your stuff and on the Web for anything you need to know.

Cortana is a powerful and flexible tool that can help you get the most from your Windows tablet. In this chapter, you learn how to get the most from Cortana. You learn about the following:

→ Configuring Cortana

→ Using the Notebook

→ Searching with Cortana

→ Using Reminders

Using Cortana

Cortana is what Microsoft calls an "intelligent personal assistant." If you've ever used Siri on an iPhone or iPad, you already have some idea of what Cortana can do for you, but Cortana takes things a step further than Siri. Up until now, only Windows Phone users have been able to enjoy using Cortana. Windows 10, however, brings Cortana to everyone else.

Who Is Cortana?
Cortana actually began as an artificial intelligence character in the Halo series of video games. When Microsoft added a personal assistant to Windows Phone, it only made sense to name her Cortana.

Cortana's voice is actually the voice of Jen Taylor, the same actress who voiced Cortana in the Halo games.

Cortana can help you find things on your tablet or on the Internet, she can help you keep track of what you need to do each day, and she can help you get around by informing you of traffic issues. Cortana also has a powerful, location-based reminder feature that's unique and remarkable.

Configuring Cortana

Cortana is turned off by default, so you'll need to enable the feature before you can use it. You'll also want to let Cortana know what she should call you.

Microsoft Account Required

To use Cortana, you will need to sign in to your tablet with your Microsoft account. If you're not sure how to do that, see Chapter 4, "Security and Windows 10."

Enabling Cortana

Before you can take advantage of Cortana, you'll need to turn on the feature. (It's off by default.)

1. Tap or click the Start button.

2. Tap or click inside the Search box.

3. Tap or click Next.

4. Tap or click I Agree.

5. Enter the name you would like Cortana to use when talking to you.

6. Tap or click Next to complete the setup and enable Cortana.

Cortana Settings

If you have the Search box or Search icon enabled on the Taskbar, you can access Cortana settings by tapping or clicking it and searching "Cortana." You can access Cortana's Notebook settings from the Cortana menu.

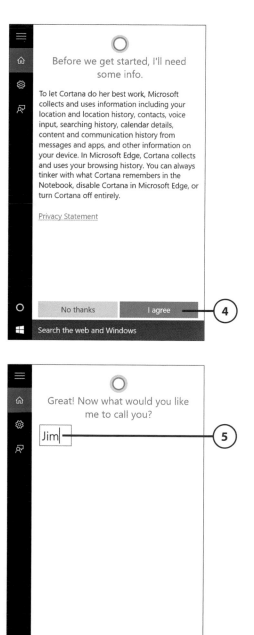

Changing Your Name

If you decide that you would like
Cortana to call you by a different name,
you can change your name.

1. Tap or click inside the Search box,
   or tap or click the Search icon.

2. Tap or click Notebook.

3. Tap or click About Me.

4. Tap or click Change My Name.

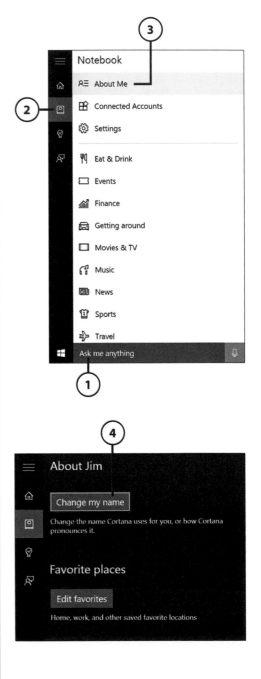

5. Enter the new name you would like Cortana to use.

6. Tap or click Enter.

Adjusting Cortana Settings

Cortana can help you by looking up flight information and other tracking information based on emails you receive. She can also help you when you call on her by saying "Hey Cortana." You can enable or disable these features easily.

1. After activating Cortana, tap or click Notebook.

2. Tap or click Settings.

3. Tap Let Cortana Respond To "Hey Cortana" to enable or disable voice activation for Cortana.

4. Tap or click Detect Tracking Info, Such as Flights, in Messages on My Device to turn tracking info detection on or off.

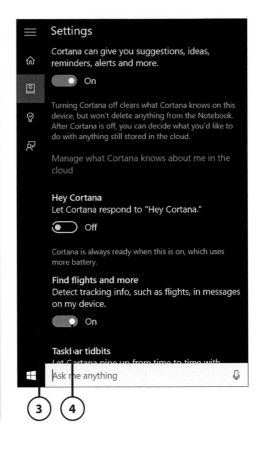

Using the Notebook

Cortana stores information about what you want to see and other information about you in her Notebook. When you activate Cortana, she'll display relevant information based on what she has stored in her Notebook about you. Each item you see is based on settings that Cortana has stored for you.

You can configure settings for different categories stored in Cortana's Notebook to tell her more about yourself.

Changing Category Settings

Cortana uses *cards* to display information on various categories. You can configure the cards in Cortana's Notebook to make the information she provides to you more relevant.

1. After activating Cortana, tap or click Notebook.

2. Tap or click a category.

3. Make the desired changes to the category's settings, and then tap or click Save.

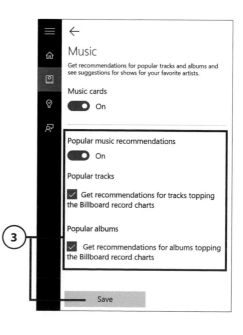

Turning Off a Category's Cards

You can turn off the cards for a category if you are not interest in seeing them. Turning off a category's cards causes Cortana to stop displaying information based on that category. You can always open the Notebook later and turn the cards back on again and keep all of your settings.

1. After activating Cortana, tap or click Notebook.

2. Tap or click the category whose cards you want to turn off.

3. Tap or click the slider to turn off the category's cards.

4. Tap or click Save.

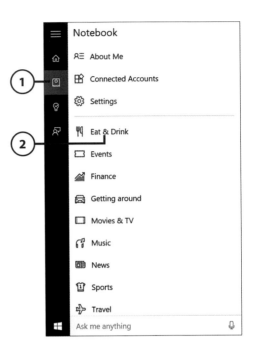

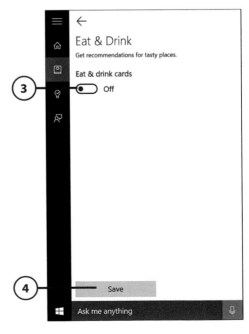

Turning On a Category's Cards

If you've previously turned off a category's cards, you can turn them back on from inside the Notebook.

1. From the Notebook, tap or click the category you want to turn back on.

2. Tap or click the slider to turn the cards on.

3. Tap or click Save.

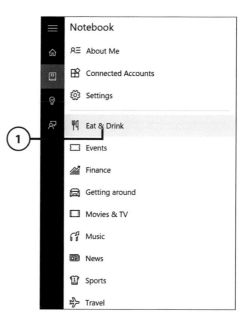

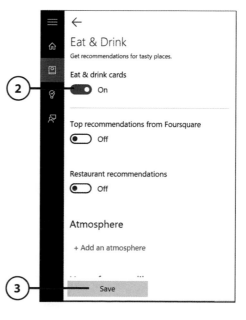

Searching with Cortana

Cortana makes it easy to find things that are stored on your tablet or on the Internet. She can find apps and documents and search the Web.

It's Not All Good

Your Music Collection

Cortana cannot find music that's in your music collection in the Groove Music app. However, she can play music in your collection if you ask her.

Searching Your Tablet

Cortana will display some results from your tablet if you simply enter a search term into the Search box, but she'll give you much more if you tell her that you want her to search only your stuff.

1. Tap or click inside of the Search box.

2. Enter a search phrase.

3. Tap or click My Stuff.

Fishing Tournament Rules.rtf
Rich Text Document
Last modified: 7/10/2015

Store

Dynamite **Fishing** World Games

Real **Fishing** Ace Pro Wild Trophy Catch 3D

Web

🔍 **fishing** rod carrying case

🔍 **fishing** games

🔍 **fishing** galveston

🔍 **fishing** tackle unlimited

🔍 **fishing** license texas

🔍 **fishing** kayaks

🔍 **fishing**

🔍 **fishing** cabins in texas

🪟 My stuff   🔍 Web

fishing

① ② ③

4. Swipe up or scroll down to see more search results.

5. Tap or click a Sort drop-down to change the sort order of results.

6. Tap or click the Show drop-down to filter search results.

7. Tap or click a search result to open the item.

Searching the Web

Cortana can search the Web for you. She'll display the most common web searches when you enter a search term. She can then open your browser and enter your search term into your search engine for you.

1. Enter a search term into the Search box.

2. Tap or click a suggested search term.

3. To search the Web for your exact search term, tap or click Web.

Using Reminders

Cortana has a powerful reminders feature that can remind you of something not only at a particular time, but also when you next speak to someone or when you arrive or leave a particular place.

Setting a Reminder for a Specific Time

You can have Cortana remind you of something at a specific time of day. You can configure your reminder to repeat every day or on particular days.

1. After activating Cortana, tap or click Reminders.

2. Tap or click + to add a new reminder.

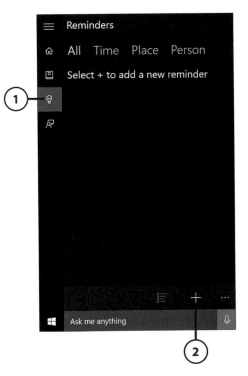

3. Enter a message for your reminder.

4. Tap or click Time to select a time.

5. Tap or click an hour, minute, and AM or PM to select the desired time for your reminder.

6. Tap or click the check mark to save your time selection.

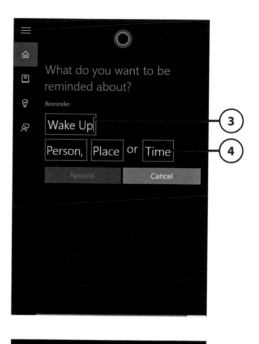

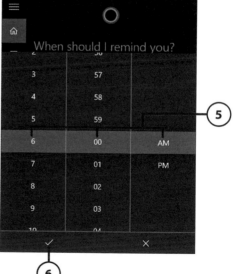

7. Tap or click the Date box to change the date for your reminder if necessary.

8. Tap or click Only Once if you want your reminder to repeat daily or on a specific day of the week.

9. Tap or click Remind to set your reminder.

Setting a Place Reminder

Cortana can remind you to do something when you arrive at or leave a specific place. She can also remind you when you arrive at or leave a kind of place, such as a grocery store.

1. From the Reminders pane, tap or click + to add a new reminder.

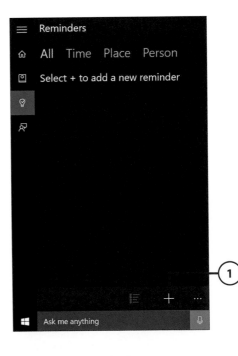

2. Enter the text for your reminder.

3. Tap or click Place.

4. By default, Cortana uses your current location for the reminder. Enter a new location or the kind of place if you want to.

5. Tap or click a suggested location.

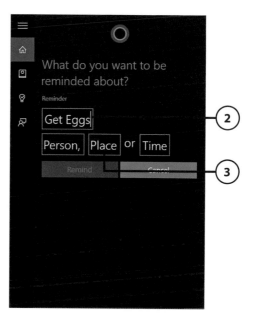

6. Tap or click Arrive to be reminded when you arrive at the location you specified.

7. Tap or click Depart to be reminded when you depart the location you specified.

8. Tap or click Done.

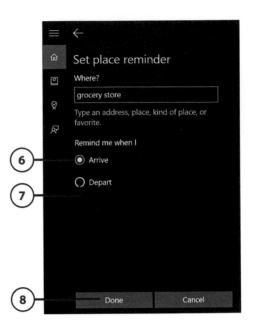

Setting a People Reminder

Cortana can remind you when you interact with a particular person. For example, she can remind you to do something when you send an email to or receive an email from one of your contacts.

1. From the Reminders pane, tap or click + to add a new reminder.

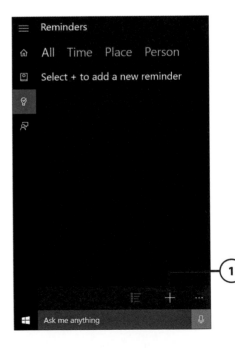

2. Enter the text for your reminder.

3. Tap or click Person.

4. Enter a contact name or tap or click one of your contacts.

5. Tap or click Remind.

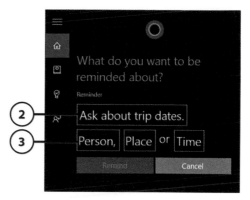

Organize and edit
your contacts.

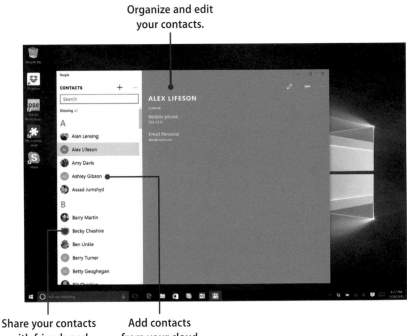

Share your contacts
with friends and
family.

Add contacts
from your cloud
accounts.

Windows 10 can access contacts you have stored in the cloud, making it easy to interact with the people you know and to share information about your contacts with others. In this chapter, you learn about the People app. You find out about

→ Working with Contacts

→ Sharing Contact Information

Connecting with People

You likely have a core group of friends and family with whom you interact. Windows 10's People app makes interacting with friends and family easy and convenient.

Working with Contacts

Before you can connect with your friends and family on Windows 10, you must add them as contacts. You have several ways to go about doing that. You can manually add each person, but you also can let Windows 10 automatically add your contacts from your Microsoft account, Exchange and Office 365, Google, iCloud, and more.

Contacts in the Cloud

Cloud is the buzzword of the day, and for good reason. By using contacts in the cloud (which really just means that it's on the Internet), you'll be able to maintain only one copy of your contacts. When you update a contact in one place, the update is automatically available everywhere else that contact is shared.

Adding Contacts from the Cloud

Contacts in Windows 10 are managed using the People app. The People app can pull in your contacts from many different cloud providers.

1. From the Start menu, tap or click the People app. (If it doesn't appear here, search "People" in the Cortana search box.)

2. While in the People app, tap or click on See More.

3. Tap or click Settings.

4. Tap or click Add an Account.

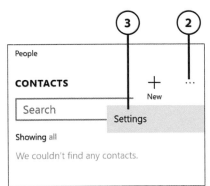

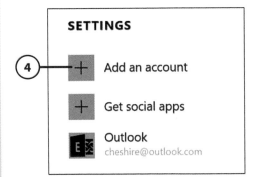

5. Tap or click an account type that you want to add.

6. Enter any information the service requires, and tap or click Sign-In.

7. Tap or click Done.

Adding Services

The information required to add a particular service might differ from the example I provided. Each service defines its own requirements.

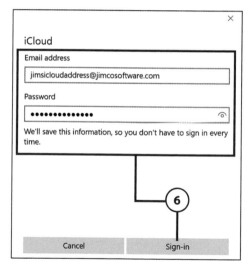

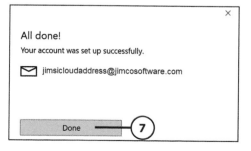

It's Not All Good

How Long?

After you configure a connection with one of your services, you might need to wait for several minutes before the People app synchronizes with the service and updates its content.

Changing Contact Sort Order

You might notice that, by default, the People app sorts your contacts by first name. If you would prefer, you can change this so that your contacts are sorted by last name.

1. From the Settings screen in the People app, tap or click Last Name to sort by last name.

2. Tap or click First Name to sort by first name.

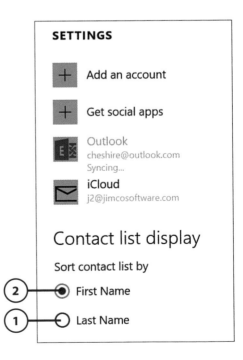

Filtering Your Contacts

You can filter your contacts so that only those contacts from the services you choose are displayed. You can also choose to hide any contacts that don't have a phone number.

1. From the Settings screen for the People app, tap or click Filter Contact List.

2. Tap or click Hide Contacts without Phone Numbers to hide any contacts without a phone number.

3. Tap or click a service to uncheck it and hide contacts from that service.

4. Tap or click Done.

Linking Contacts

If you add contacts from more than one service, you might have some contacts that appear twice in your list. In most cases, Windows 10 is smart enough to display duplicate contacts as one contact, but if the name is slightly different, you might need to manually link duplicates.

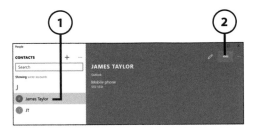

1. Tap or click one of the contacts you want to link from your list of contacts.

2. Tap or click Link Contacts.

3. Tap or click Choose a Contact to Link.

4. Tap or click on a contact you want to link.

5. To select more than one contact to link, tap or click Select.

6. Tap or click the contacts you want to link.

7. Tap or click Done.

8. Tap or click Back to return to the list of contacts.

Linked Contacts

When you link two or more contacts, your contact list displays one contact entry for the contacts you select to link together. Contact information for that single entry will be consolidated from all the linked contacts.

1 contact selected

J

☐ Jerry Hunter

☐ Jim Cheshire

☐ (JD) Jimmie Dickey

☐ (JD) Joe Dupuy

☐ (JS) Joe Smith

☐ Joel Williams

☐ John Cooper

☐ John Mitchell

☑ (J) JT

K

☐ (KC) Keller Bass Club

☐ (KD) Kevin Davis

☐ Kim Dillard

✓   ✕   ⋯

← People

LINKS FOR JAMES TAYLOR

Linking multiple profiles for this contact lets you see all their info in one place.

Linked profiles

(JT) **James Taylor**
       Outlook

Choose a contact to link

Unlinking Contacts

If you no longer want two or more contacts to be linked, you can unlink the contacts.

1. Tap or click the linked contact.

2. Tap or click Link Contacts.

3. Tap or click the contact or contacts you want to unlink.

4. Tap or click Unlink.

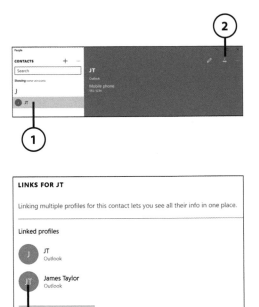

Creating a New Contact

You can create new contacts on your tablet. When you create a contact, you can choose an online service for the contact. Any device that synchronizes with the selected online service will have access to the contact you create.

1. From the People screen, tap or click New.

2. Tap or click Save To and select the account to use for the new contact. (This will not be visible if you have only one account configured.)

3. Enter the contact's name.

4. Tap or click Edit Name to add additional name information.

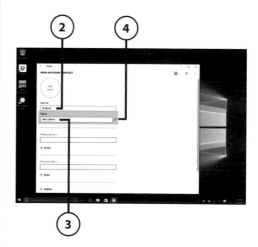

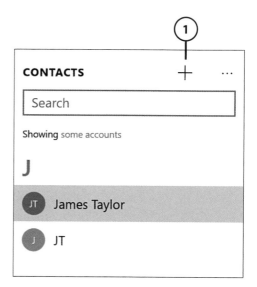

5. Enter additional name information, such as a nickname.

6. Tap or click Done.

7. Enter additional contact information.

8. Tap or click the plus sign to add a new field, such as a new phone number or a business address.

9. Tap or click Add Photo if you want to add a photo of the contact.

10. Tap or click Save to save the new contact.

Contacts Are Not Local

It's important for you to realize that when you add a contact on your tablet, that contact isn't specific to your tablet. You are actually adding an online contact for the service you select, and that contact will be available to all devices that use the service, not just your tablet.

Edit name

First name

Alex

Last name

Lifeson

Middle name

Nickname

⑤ Lerxst

Title

Suffix

Phonetic first name

Phonetic last name

⑥ | Done | Cancel |

⑨ ⑩

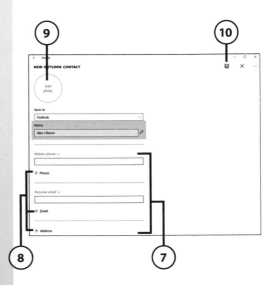

NEW OUTLOOK CONTACT

Add photo

Save to

Outlook

Name

Alex Lifeson

Mobile phone ∨

+ Phone

Personal email ∨

+ Email

+ Address

⑧ ⑦

Deleting a Contact

You can delete a contact from the contact list in the People app. Deleting a contact removes the contact from all devices that synchronize with the service that originally contained the contact.

1. Tap or click the contact you would like to delete.

2. Tap or click See More.

3. Tap or click Delete.

4. Tap or click Delete to confirm that you want to delete the contact.

It's Not All Good

Take Care When Deleting Contacts

Contacts in Windows 10 come from one or more online services. If you delete a contact from your tablet, you are actually deleting the contact from the online service, and if you have other computers or devices (such as your smartphone) that use the same online service for contacts, the contact will be removed from those devices as well.

Removing All Contacts from a Service

As you've seen, when you add a connection to a service, any contacts for that service are added to your contact list. If you want to remove those contacts from your tablet without deleting the contacts from the service, you can simply remove the connection with the service containing the contacts.

1. From the Settings screen, tap or click the service that you want to remove.

2. Tap or click Delete Account.

3. Tap or click Delete to confirm you want to delete the account.

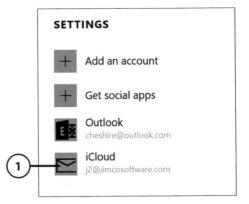

SETTINGS

➕ Add an account

➕ Get social apps

Outlook
cheshire@outlook.com

iCloud
j2@jimcosoftware.com

---

iCloud account settings

✉ j2@jimcosoftware.com

Password

●●●●●●●●●●●●●●●●

Account name

iCloud

Change mailbox sync settings
Options for syncing email, contacts, and calendar.

Delete account
Remove this account from your device.

Delete this account?

✉ j2@jimcosoftware.com

If you delete this account, all content associated with it will be removed from this device.

Are you sure you want to continue?

| Delete | Cancel |

Editing a Contact

You can edit a contact in cases where information has changed or where you want to add additional information for a contact.

1. Tap or click a contact that you would like to edit.

2. Tap or click Edit.

3. Edit the contact's existing information, if necessary.

4. To add additional information, tap or click a plus sign.

5. To change the name for a field, tap or click the current field name and select a new name from the list.

6. Tap or click Save to save the contact.

Sharing Contact Information

You can share a contact with someone as a vCard. Because vCard is a standard for sharing contact information, the person with whom you share a contact can open the contact and add it to her contact list easily.

Sharing a Contact

You can share a contact using email right within the People app.

1. Tap or click the contact you want to share.

2. Tap or click See More.

3. Tap or click Share Contact.

4. Tap or click Confirm.

5. Tap or click a recent email recipient, or tap or click Mail to share the contact with someone else. (You might not see a recent recipient.)

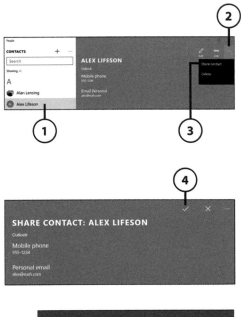

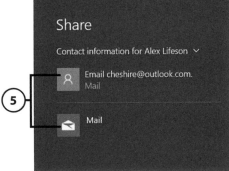

6. Tap or click the email account you want to use to send the contact. (If you have only one email account, you won't need this step.)

7. Add additional recipients if you want to.

8. Add a message if you want to.

9. Tap or click Send.

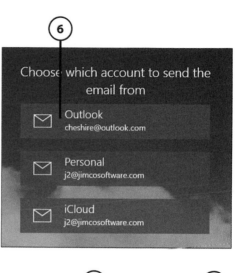

Accepting a Shared Contact

If you are sent a shared contact, you can add it to your contacts easily.

1. Tap or click the vCard file attached to your mail message (it will have a .vcf file extension) to open it.

2. If prompted, choose the People app to open the vCard.

3. Tap or click OK.

4. Tap or click Save to save the contact.

5. Tap or click Save To and choose the account you want to add the contact to.

6. Make any other desired changes to the contact.

7. Tap or click Save.

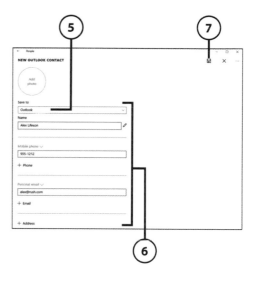

Send and receive email from all of your email accounts.

Send automatic replies and use other advanced features.

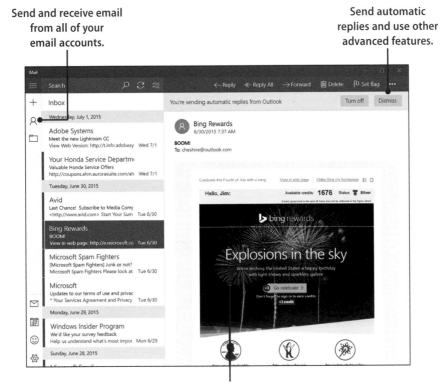

Send emails with rich content and formatting.

Most people use their computer to send and receive email. Windows 10 includes the Mail app so that you can use your email on your tablet. In this chapter, you learn all about the Mail app, including the following:

→ Adding and Managing Email Accounts

→ Reading and Organizing Email

→ Composing and Sending Email

→ Setting Mail Options

Using Mail

The Mail app included in Windows 10 is a full-featured mail app that makes it easy to read, send, and organize your email. It supports many different types of email accounts, including Exchange, Google, iCloud, and more.

Adding and Managing Email Accounts

If you sign in to your tablet using your Microsoft account, Mail automatically configures itself for your Microsoft email. You can easily add your other email accounts as well.

Adding a Microsoft Account

If you logged in to your tablet with your Microsoft account, that email address is automatically added to Mail. You can add additional Microsoft accounts to Mail, too.

1. From the Start menu, tap or click Mail to launch the Mail app.

2. Tap or click Settings.

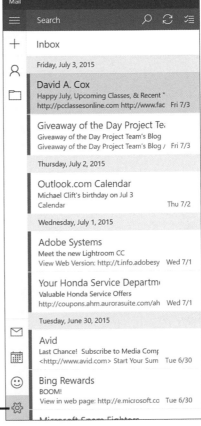

3. Tap or click Accounts from the Settings pane.

4. Tap or click Add Account in the Accounts pane.

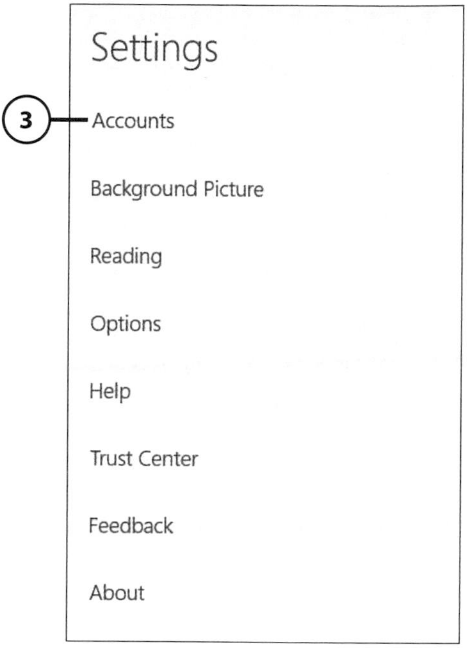

Settings

(3)— Accounts

Background Picture

Reading

Options

Help

Trust Center

Feedback

About

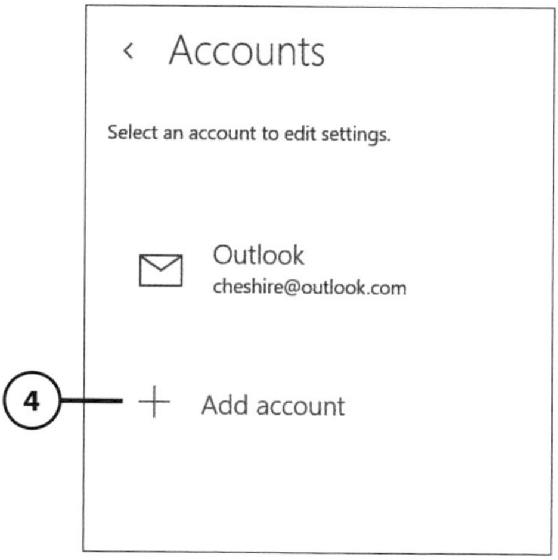

‹ Accounts

Select an account to edit settings.

✉ Outlook
cheshire@outlook.com

(4)— + Add account

5. Tap or click Outlook.com.

6. Enter your Microsoft account email address.

7. Enter your Microsoft account password.

8. Tap or click Sign In.

9. Tap or click Done.

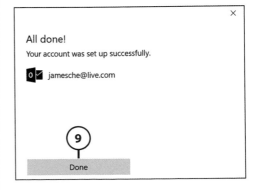

Choose an account

Outlook.com
Outlook.com, Live.com, Hotmail, MSN — 5

Exchange
Exchange, Office 365

Google

Yahoo! Mail

iCloud

Other account
POP, IMAP

Close

Add your Microsoft account

Sign in with your Microsoft account. You can use this account with other apps on this device. Learn more.

jamesche@live.com — 6

•••••••• — 7

Forgot my password

No account? Create one!

Microsoft privacy statement

8 — Sign in   Cancel

All done!
Your account was set up successfully.

jamesche@live.com

9

Done

Adding an Exchange or Office 365 Account

You can add your Exchange account or an Office 365 account so that you can read your work or school email.

1. From the Choose an Account dialog in Mail, tap or click Exchange.

2. Enter your email address.

3. Tap or click Next.

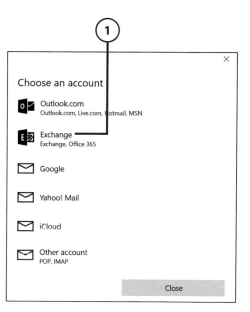

4. Enter your password.

5. Tap or click Sign-In.

6. Tap or click Done.

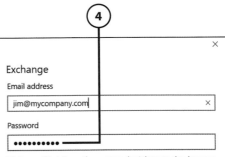

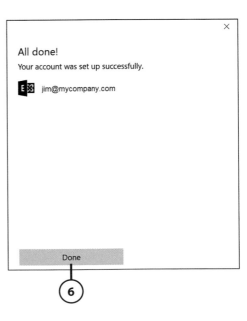

Adding a Google Account

You can add a Google account so that you can read your Gmail in Mail.

1. From the Choose an Account dialog in Mail, tap or click Google.

2. Enter your email address.

3. Tap or click Next.

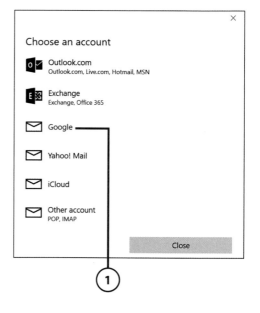

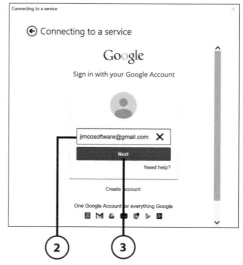

4. Enter your password.

5. Tap or click Sign In.

6. Tap or click Accept.

7. Tap or click Done.

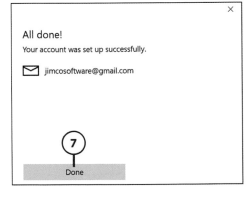

Adding an iCloud Account

If you have an iCloud email account, you can add it to Mail.

1. From the Choose an Account dialog box, tap or click iCloud.

2. Enter your email address.

3. Enter your password.

4. Tap or click Sign-In.

5. Tap or click Done.

Yahoo! Mail

You can add a Yahoo! Mail account by selecting Yahoo! Mail from the Choose an Account screen. The rest of the steps are the same as those for an iCloud account.

Choose an account

☒

Outlook.com
Outlook.com, Live.com, Hotmail, MSN

Exchange
Exchange, Office 365

✉ **Google**

✉ **Yahoo! Mail**

① ✉ **iCloud**

✉ **Other account**
POP, IMAP

Close

✕

iCloud

Email address

② jim@icloud.com

Password

③ ●●●●●●●●●●●●●● 👁

We'll save this information, so you don't have to sign in every time.

Cancel   Sign-in ④

✕

All done!

Your account was set up successfully.

✉ jim@icloud.com

⑤ Done

Adding a POP or IMAP Account

If you want to add a POP or IMAP mail account, you can also do that. If you don't know some of the information that Mail needs to add your account, check with your email provider.

IMAP and POP Email

Most IMAP and POP email accounts are ones that are provided by your Internet service provider. However, if you happen to have your own domain name for a website you run, you might also have an IMAP or POP mail account for that domain.

1. From the Choose an Account dialog, tap or click Other Account.

2. Enter your email address.

3. Enter your password.

4. Tap or click Sign-In.

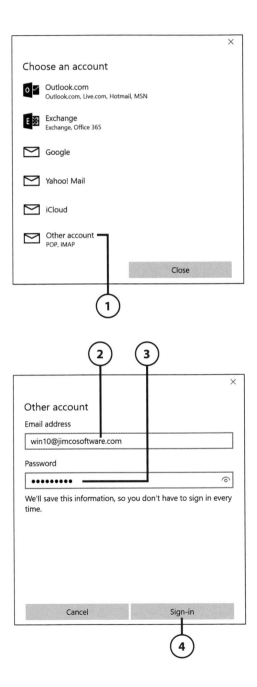

5. If your account settings don't work, tap or click Try Again. Continue to tap or click Try Again three more times if necessary.

Why Retries?

The Mail app attempts to discover all of your mail settings using your email address. In some cases, Mail cannot figure out what your settings are using your email address. In those cases, it will retry a few times before it finally just gives up.

6. If info for your account could not be found, tap or click Advanced.

Other account

Email address

win10@jimcosoftware.com

Password

•••••••••

We couldn't find info for that account. Make sure that the email address is correct and then try again.

Cancel   Try again

5

Other account

Email address

win10@jimcosoftware.com

Password

•••••••••

We couldn't find info for that account. Make sure that the email address is correct and then try again.

To add account info manually, select Advanced.

Cancel   Advanced

6

7. Enter an account name. (This can be anything you want it to be.)

8. Enter your name.

9. Enter the address for your incoming mail server.

10. Tap or click Account Type and select an account type.

11. Swipe up or scroll down to see additional settings.

12. Enter your username.

13. Enter a password if necessary. (This field should already contain the password you entered in step 3.)

14. Enter an address for your outgoing mail server.

15. If your outgoing mail server requires authentication, leave the Outgoing Server Requires Authentication box checked. Otherwise, tap or click it to uncheck it.

16. If your outgoing username and password match your incoming username and password, leave the Use the Same User Name and Password for Sending Email box checked. Otherwise, tap or click it to uncheck it.

17. Swipe up or scroll down for additional settings.

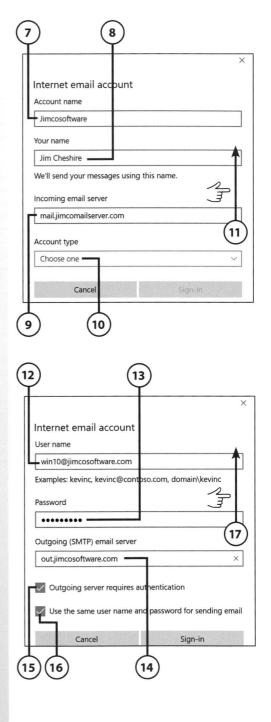

18. If you don't require SSL for incoming mail, tap or click the Require SSL for Incoming Email box to uncheck it.

19. If you don't require SSL for outgoing mail, tap or click the Require SSL for Outgoing Email box to uncheck it.

20. Tap or click Sign-In.

21. Tap or click Done.

Internet email account

Password

••••••••

Outgoing (SMTP) email server

out.jimcosoftware.com

☑ Outgoing server requires authentication

☑ Use the same user name and password for sending email

☑ Require SSL for incoming email

☑ Require SSL for outgoing email

Cancel   Sign-in

All done!

Your account was set up successfully.

✉ win10@jimcosoftware.com

Done

Setting When and How Much Email Is Downloaded

By default, Mail downloads new emails as they arrive on the mail server and downloads all email from the last three months. You can modify how often Mail downloads email and how much email it retrieves as well.

1. From the Accounts pane, tap or click an account to change the settings for the account.

2. Tap or click Change Mailbox Sync Settings.

‹ **Accounts**

Select an account to edit settings.

✉ Outlook
cheshire@outlook.com

✉ Live
jamesche@live.com

① ✉ Gmail
jimcosoftware@gmail.com

✉ Jimcosoftware
win10@jimcosoftware.com

＋ Add account

×

Gmail account settings

✉ jimcosoftware@gmail.com

Account name

Gmail

Change mailbox sync settings
Options for syncing email, contacts, and calendar.

Delete account
Remove this account from your device.

②

3. Tap or click Download New Email and select how often you want Mail to retrieve new email.

4. Tap or click Download Email From and select how many days of email you want Mail to download.

5. Tap or click Done.

Changing an Account Name or Password

You can change an account's name in the dialog box that is displayed in step 2.

Based on My Usage

Mail can automatically set the Download New Content setting based on how often email arrives and how often you check your email. By selecting "Based on My Usage" in step 3, you can tell Mail to set the option automatically to be as efficient as possible with your battery life and data usage.

Removing an Account

If you decide you no longer want to synchronize with an account, you can remove the account from Mail.

1. From the Accounts pane, tap the account you would like to remove.

2. Tap or click Delete Account.

< Accounts

Select an account to edit settings.

Outlook
cheshire@outlook.com

Live
jamesche@live.com

Gmail
jimcosoftware@gmail.com

1 — Jimcosoftware
win10@jimcosoftware.com

\+   Add account

✕

Jimcosoftware account settings

win10@jimcosoftware.com

Password

••••••••••••••••

Account name

Jimcosoftware

Change mailbox sync settings
Options for syncing email, contacts, and calendar.

Delete account ———————— **2**
Remove this account from your device.

Save   Cancel

3. Tap or click Delete to confirm that you want to delete the account.

> ×
>
> Delete this account?
>
> ✉ win10@jimcosoftware.com
>
> If you delete this account, all content associated with it will be removed from this device.
>
> Are you sure you want to continue?
>
> | Delete | Cancel |
> |---|---|

③

It's Not All Good

Deleting an Account Can Delete Data

When you delete an email account, any data associated with that email account will be deleted from your tablet. For example, if you have downloaded email attachments that are still stored within email messages, those attachments will be deleted from your device. However, they will still remain attached to the email messages so that you can access them from another device or from your tablet if you add the account back later.

Reading and Organizing Email

The Mail app displays email from one account at a time. You can choose between any of the accounts you have configured in Mail. While viewing email, you can use folders to keep everything organized.

Reading an Email

The Mail app supports HTML emails as well as plain text emails. HTML is the technology used to create websites, and emails created in HTML can contain pictures along with richly formatted text.

1. Tap or click All Accounts.

2. Tap or click the desired email account.

3. Tap or click All Folders.

4. Tap or click the desired folder.

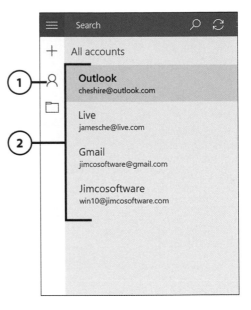

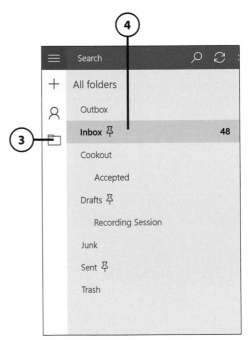

5. Tap an email from the list to view the email in the reading pane.

Unread Emails

The number of unread messages in the folder is shown immediately to the right of the folder name. Unread emails in the email list have a blue subject line.

6. Swipe up and down to scroll in the reading pane.

7. If necessary, you can also swipe right and left to view wider emails.

8. Tap a link in an email to launch your web browser and navigate to the link.

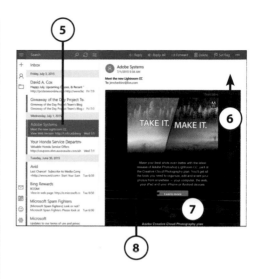

Viewing or Saving Email Attachments

You can save an attachment sent to you in email to your tablet so that you can view it later.

1. Select an email that includes an attachment. Emails with an attachment display a paperclip icon.

2. Tap or click the attachment to download it to your tablet.

3. Tap or click the attachment again to open it.

4. To save the attachment, tap and hold or right-click the attachment and tap Save.

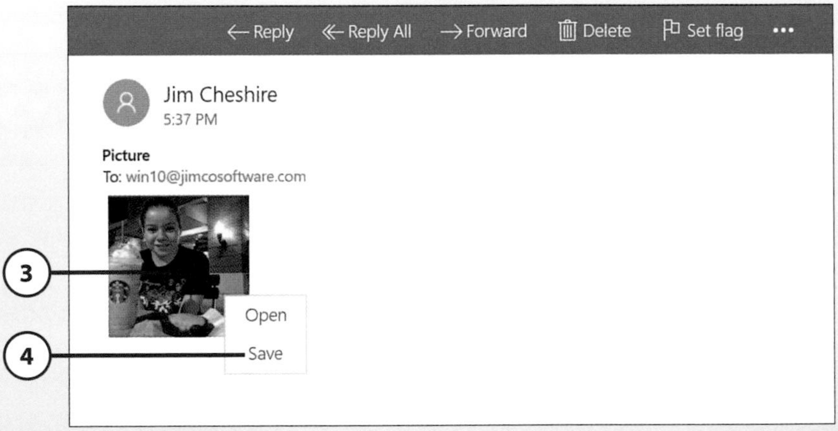

5. Browse to the location where you want to save the file.

6. Enter a name for the file.

7. Tap or click Save.

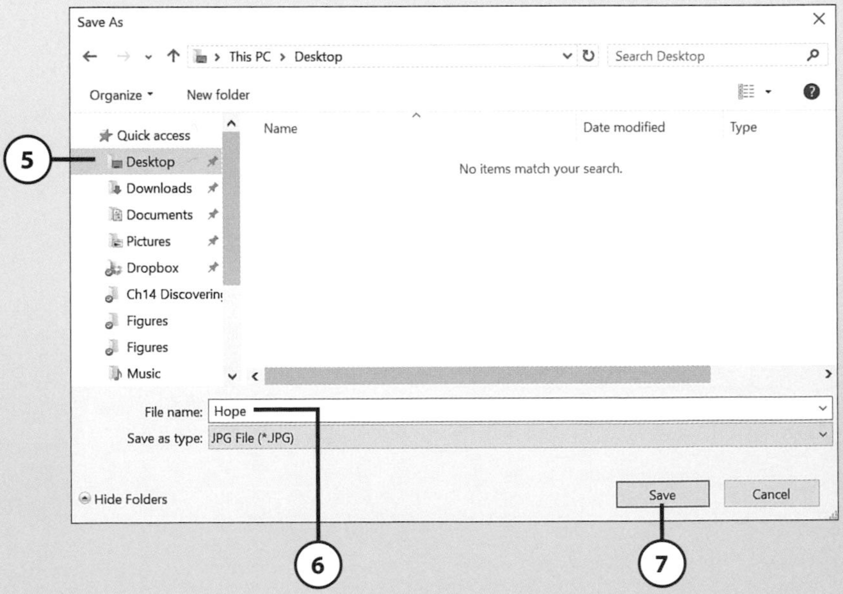

Deleting Email Messages

You can delete email messages easily using a mouse or touch. When you delete emails, they are moved to the Trash folder. If you delete emails from within the Trash folder, they are deleted permanently.

Trash Folder

Deleted mail goes into a folder called Trash for a Microsoft account email address. Other email account types may use a different name for the Trash folder.

1. To delete a message with your mouse, click the email message and then click Delete.

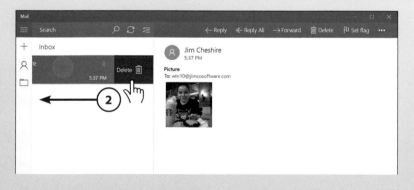

2. To delete a message using touch, tap and slide the email message left.

Deleting with the Keyboard

You can also press the Delete key or Ctrl+D on your keyboard to delete selected email messages.

Undeleting Email Messages

If you've unintentionally deleted one or more mail messages and you would like to restore them, you can undelete them.

1. Tap or click All Folders.

2. Tap or click Deleted Items.

Deleted Items

My email account uses a folder called Deleted Items for the trash. Your account might use a different name. For example, a Microsoft account uses a folder named Trash.

---

3. Tap or click the email you want to undelete.

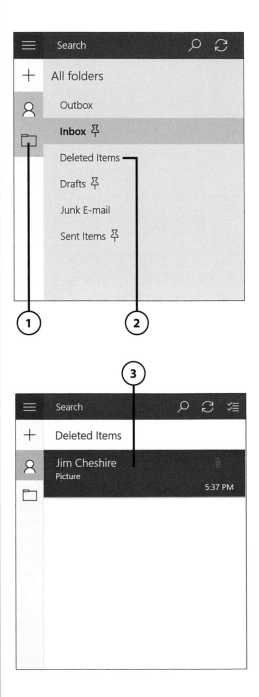

4. Tap or click Actions.

5. Tap or click Move.

6. Tap or click Inbox to move the email back to the Inbox. (You can also select a different folder if you want to.)

Composing and Sending Email

The Mail app provides tools for basic editing of email messages. You can also attach files to an email and share parts of an email with someone easily.

Creating a New Email Message

You can create a new, blank email message.

1. Tap or click All Accounts, and tap the account you want to use to send the email.

2. Tap or click the + button in the upper-left corner of the Mail app.

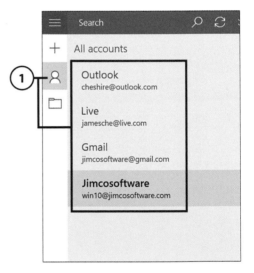

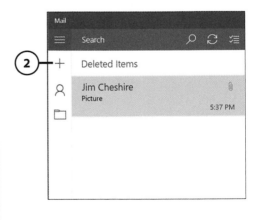

3. Enter one or more email addresses. Multiple email addresses should be separated by a semicolon.

Entering Email Addresses

As you enter email addresses, you will see a pop-up of people who are in your contact list. You can choose one from the list by tapping or clicking it.

4. Tap or click Cc & Bcc to enter an email address that should be copied or blind copied.

5. Enter a subject for your email.

6. Enter your email message.

7. Spelling errors are underlined with a red, squiggly line. Tap and hold or right-click the word to see a menu of corrections.

8. Tap a correctly spelled word from the list to change the misspelled word.

9. Tap the word with a plus sign next to it to add the word to your dictionary so that it won't be marked as misspelled again.

10. Tap Ignore All to ignore the spelling error for this mail message only.

11. Tap Send to send your mail message.

12. Tap Discard to delete your message without sending it.

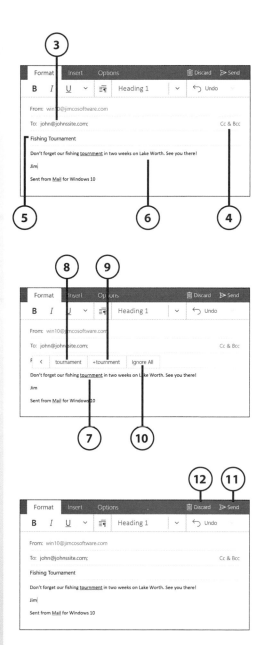

Replying to Email

You can reply to the sender of an email, reply to everyone who received the email, or forward an email to someone else.

1. With the email message selected, tap or click Reply to respond only to the sender of the email.

2. Tap or click Reply All to respond to everyone who received the message, except for those who were blind copied.

3. Tap or click Forward to forward the email message to someone else.

4. If you're forwarding the message, enter a recipient's email address.

5. Enter your message text.

6. Tap Send.

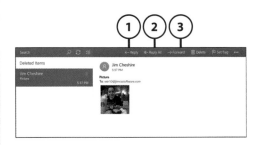

Formatting Text in an Email

You can apply special formatting to text when creating email messages.

1. Select text in your email message to which you would like to apply formatting.

2. Tap or click Bold, Italic, or Underline to format the text as you want.

3. Tap or click Font Formatting to access additional formatting options.

4. Tap or click Font and select a new font to apply a different font.

5. Tap or click Font Size and select a new size for the selected text.

6. Tap or click Strikethrough to format the text as strikethrough text.

7. Tap or click Subscript or Superscript to format the selected text as subscripted or superscripted.

8. Tap or click Highlight to highlight the selected text.

9. Tap or click Font Color, and then tap or click a new color to recolor the text.

10. Tap or click Clear Formatting to clear any formatting applied to the selected text.

11. Tap or click Paragraph Formatting to access additional formatting options.

12. Tap or click Bullets to select a bulleted list style.

13. Tap or click Numbering to select a numbering style.

14. Tap or click Decrease Indent or Increase Indent to change the indentation.

15. Tap or click Special Indent to format the selected text with a hanging indent or a first-line indent.

16. Tap or click a paragraph alignment option to align the paragraph.

17. Tap or click Line Spacing to specify line spacing.

18. Tap or click Add Space Before Paragraph to add additional space above the paragraph.

19. Tap or click Add Space After Paragraph to add additional space below the paragraph.

20. Tap Insert to insert a table, picture, or a link in your email.

Attaching Files to a Email

You can attach files to an email.

1. While composing your mail message, tap or click Insert.

2. Tap or click Attach.

3. Navigate to the folder that contains the file (or files) you would like to attach.

4. Tap or click the file that you would like to attach to your message.

5. Tap or click Open.

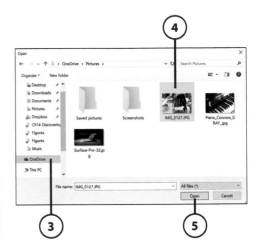

Setting Mail Options

The Mail app has many options you can set that control the behavior of the application. You can also configure options such as an email signature for each mail account you have configured in the Mail app.

Setting a Background Picture

When no email messages are selected, the Mail app uses an image of a blue sky and a cloud in the background. You can change this picture to one of your own to make the Mail app more personalized.

1. From the Settings pane, tap or click Background Picture.

2. Tap or click Browse.

3. Browse to the folder where your picture is located.

4. Tap or click a picture to select it.

5. Tap or click Open.

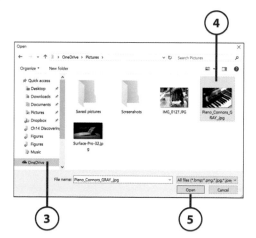

Setting Reading Options

You can configure whether the next email message is opened automatically after you delete a message. You can also configure when the Mail app marks a mail message as being read.

1. From the Settings pane, tap or click Reading.

2. To configure the mail app to automatically open the next message in the list after a message is deleted, tap or click Auto-Open Next Item to change the slider to On.

3. Tap or click When Selection Changes to configure the Mail app to mark messages as read when you select another message.

4. Tap or click Don't Automatically Mark Item As Read to prevent the Mail app from automatically marking mail messages as read. You will have to tap or click Mark As Read on the Actions menu to mark messages as read when this option is selected.

5. Tap or click When Viewed in the Reading Pane and enter a number of seconds to configure the Mail app to mark messages as read after being displayed for a particular number of seconds.

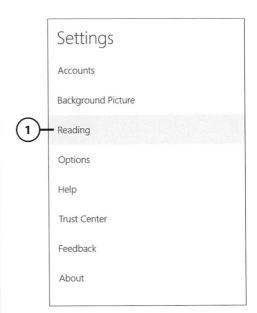

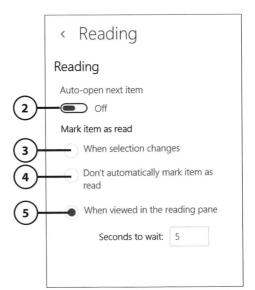

Configuring Quick Actions

As you saw earlier, you can delete a message by swiping to the left on the mail message. You can also set a flag on a message by swiping to the right. These swiping actions are called Quick Actions, and you can configure them so that you can quickly access your most often used actions.

1. From the Options pane, tap or click the Account drop-down and choose the account you want to configure.

2. Tap or click Swipe Actions to turn on the feature. (It's on by default.)

3. Tap or click Swipe Right/Hover and select an action from the drop-down.

4. Tap or click Swipe Left/Hover and select an action from the drop-down.

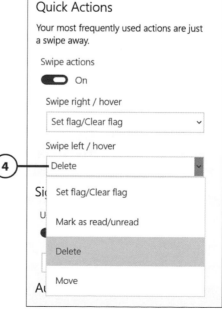

Sending Automatic Replies

You can send automatic replies in situations where you might not be able to respond to people who send you email. Note that the Mail app must be running for automatic replies to be sent and that not all account types support this feature.

1. From the Options pane, tap or click the Account drop-down and choose the account you want to configure.

2. Swipe up or scroll down to the Automatic Replies section.

3. Tap or click Send Automatic Replies to turn on automatic replies.

4. Enter a message to be automatically sent to people sending you email.

5. If you want automatic replies to be sent only to those in your contact list, tap or click Send Replies Only to My Contacts.

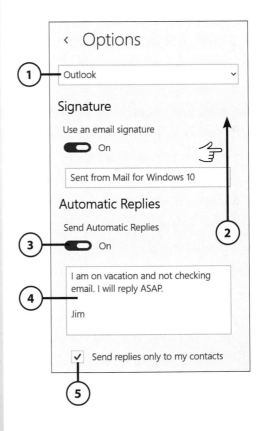

Configuring Notifications

By default, the Mail app does not notify you when new emails arrive. You can configure the Mail app to display a notification banner, play a sound, or both.

1. From the Options pane, tap or click the Account drop-down and choose the account you want to configure.

2. Swipe up or scroll down to reveal the Notifications section.

3. Tap or click Show in Action Center to change the setting to On.

4. Tap or click Show a Notification Banner to check the box if you want to see a notification banner when new mail arrives.

5. Tap or click Play a Sound to check the box if you want a sound played when new mail arrives.

< Options

1 ── Outlook

Signature

Use an email signature

● On

Sent from Mail for Windows 10

Automatic Replies

Send Automatic Replies

● On

I am on vacation and not checking email. I will reply ASAP.

Jim

2

✓ Send replies only to my contacts

Notifications

Show in action center

3 ── ● On

4 ── ✓ Show a notification banner

✓ Play a sound

5

Using an Email Signature

You can enter a signature for your email
account that will be automatically
added to the end of all your email messages sent from that account.

1. From the Options pane, tap or
   click the Account drop-down and
   choose the account you want to
   configure.

2. Swipe up or scroll down to the
   Signature section.

3. Tap or click the Use an Email
   Signature slider to change the setting to On.

4. Enter your desired email signature
   in the text box.

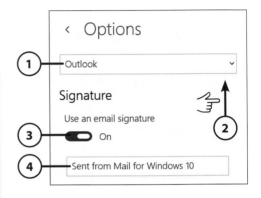

Create calendar
events with
reminders and more.

Calendar   — □ ×

☰   📅 Day   🗓 Work week   📅 Week │📋 Month   📅 Today

+ New event

July 2015

								Sunday	Monday	Tuesday	Wednesday	Thursday	Friday	Saturday
July 2015						∧ ∨		6/28	29	30	7/1	2	3	4
Su	Mo	Tu	We	Th	Fr	Sa				Troy Kirchenba			Michael Clift's	Independence
28	29	30	1	2	3	4								
5	6	7	8	9	10	11		5	6	7	8	9	10	11
12	13	14	15	16	17	18			Katherine Mos			John Mitchell':	Vince Felchle's	
19	20	21	22	23	24	25								
26	27	28	29	30	31	1		12	13	14	15	16	17	18
2	3	4	5	6	7	8		Gregg Wilson'		Jon Elder's bir				
								Kage Njaka's I						

∧ Search   19   20   **21**   22   23   24   25

☑ Reminders

∧ iCloud

☑ Home   26   27   28   29   30   31   8/1

☑ Home

☑ Family

∧ Outlook

✉ 📅   ☺   ⚙

Add calendars
from multiple
online sources.

View your calendar
events easily.

The Calendar app makes it easy to keep up with what's going on in your hectic life. You can connect the Calendar app to an Exchange or Office 365 calendar, a Microsoft account calendar, a Google calendar, an iCloud calendar, and more. In this chapter, you learn about

→ Connecting Calendars

→ Viewing Calendars

→ Working with Events

→ Calendar Settings

11

Using Calendar

There's nothing new about a calendar on your computer, but there is something new about Calendar in Windows 10. As with other apps in Windows 10, Calendar is a cloud-enabled app that makes it easy to keep track of multiple calendars in one place.

Connecting Calendars

I use a couple different calendars. I have a work calendar on my company's Exchange server, and we keep a family calendar in Google. Fortunately, I don't have to re-create all the appointments in these calendars on my tablet. Instead, I simply connect both of these calendars to the Calendar app, and all my appointments are immediately available to me.

You can add your Outlook.com calendar (which includes Outlook.com, Live.com, Hotmail and MSN calendars), Exchange and Office 365 calendars, a Google calendar (Gmail), and an iCloud calendar.

Adding an Outlook.com Calendar

You can add a calendar from your Outlook.com, Hotmail.com, or Live.com account.

1. From the Start menu, tap or click Calendar to launch the Calendar app.

2. Tap or click Settings.

3. Tap or click Accounts.

4. Tap or click Add Account.

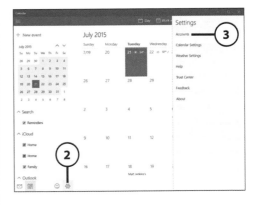

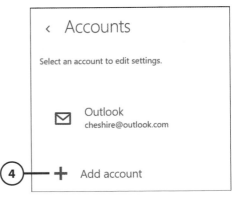

5. Tap or click Outlook.com.

6. Enter the email address for your account.

7. Enter your password.

8. Tap or click Sign In.

9. Tap or click Done.

Exchange and Office 365

You can also add an Exchange or Office 365 calendar. Simply tap or click Exchange in step 5 and enter the information for your Exchange server or Office 365 account.

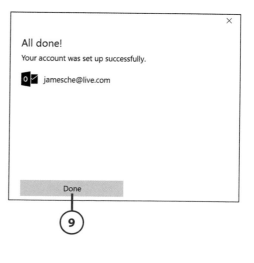

Adding a Google (Gmail) Calendar

You can add your Google calendar so that you can see appointments and create new appointments on your Google calendar.

1. From the Choose an Account screen, tap or click Google.

2. Enter your Google username.

3. Tap or click Next.

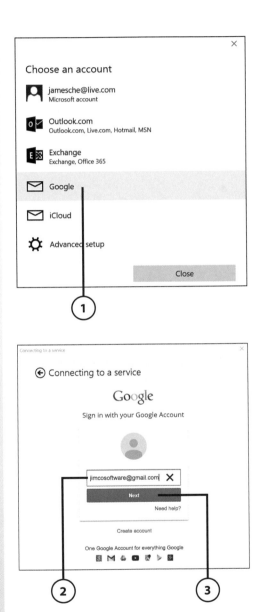

4. Enter your Google password.

5. Tap or click Sign In.

6. Tap or click Accept.

7. Tap or click Done.

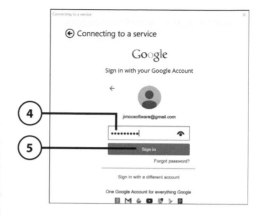

Adding an iCloud Calendar

You can add the calendar from your iCloud account so that you can use the Calendar app to manage your iCloud calendar.

1. From the Choose an Account screen, tap or click iCloud.

2. Enter your iCloud email address.

3. Enter your password.

4. Tap or click Sign In.

5. Tap or click Done.

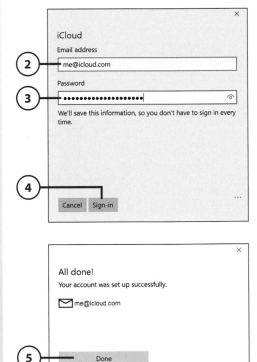

Viewing Calendars

You can choose which calendars to display in Calendar, the color used for each calendar, and which view you would like to see for your events.

Hiding a Calendar

By default, after you connect a calendar to the Calendar app, events from that calendar are displayed. If you don't want to see events from a particular calendar, you can hide it.

1. If the sidebar isn't visible, tap or click the Expand button.

2. Tap or click a calendar to uncheck it and hide that calendar.

Birthday and Holiday Calendars

Note that the Calendar app automatically displays a birthday calendar and a holiday calendar. The birthday calendar displays an event when one of your contacts in the People app has a birthday.

Changing a Calendar's Display Color

The Calendar app chooses a different color for each calendar you connect. This makes it easy to tell at a glance which calendar contains a specific event. You can customize the color used for each of your calendars.

1. Tap and hold or right-click the calendar whose color you want to change.

2. Tap or click the color you want to use for that calendar.

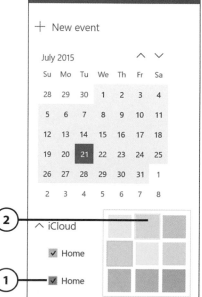

Viewing Events

You can choose between viewing your calendar events in Day view, Work Week view, Week view, or Month view.

1. Tap or click Day, and then tap the number of days to view events for multiple days.

2. Tap or click Work Week to view only days in your work week.

Work Week

You learn how you can configure the days in your work week later in this chapter.

3. Tap or click Week to view the entire week's events.

4. Tap or click Month to view the entire month.

5. Tap or click Today to make today's date visible.

6. Tap or click an event to view details on that event.

Working with Events

Events in Calendar are automatically synchronized from your online calendars. If you add or modify an event on your smartphone or another computer, Calendar reflects that change automatically. Additionally, events you create or modify in Calendar synchronize with your other devices.

Adding a Basic Event

A basic event is one without any recurrences and that uses the default reminder time and other options.

1. In the Calendar app, tap or click New Event.

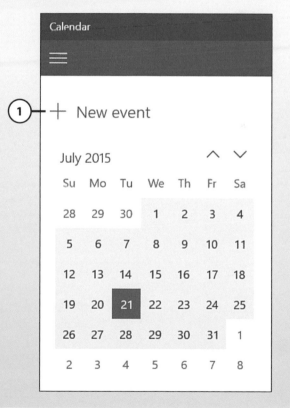

2. Enter a description for the event.

3. Enter a location.

4. Enter a start date, or tap or click the calendar icon and select a start date.

5. Select a start time.

6. Enter an end date, or tap or click the calendar icon and select an end date.

7. If the event is an all-day event, tap or click All Day to make the event an all-day event, or select an ending time.

8. Tap or click the calendar and select a different calendar if you want to.

9. Enter any additional information you want to add for the event.

10. To invite other people, enter a contact's name in the People box.

11. Tap or click the contact's name to add them to the event.

12. Tap or click Save and Close. (If you've invited others to the event, the Save and Close button changes to a Send button.)

Quickly Creating an Event

You can more quickly create an event by tapping the date or time for the event. (You won't see times if you are in Month view.)

1. Tap a date or time for the event.

2. Enter a name for the event.

3. Enter a start time for the event.

4. Tap or click All Day to make the event an all-day event, or enter an end time for the event.

5. Enter a location.

6. Select a different calendar if you want to.

7. Tap or click More Details to access the full screen for adding a new event.

8. Tap or click Done.

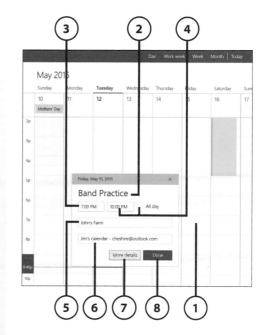

Adding a Recurring Event

You can create an event that recurs at a regular interval.

1. While creating your event, tap or click Repeat.

2. Select a recurrence timeframe for the event.

3. If you want the recurring event to have an end date, enter it or tap or click the calendar icon and select the end date.

Repeat

Start: August 21, 2015

Weekly

Every 1 ∨ week(s) on

☐ Sun ☐ Mon ☐ Tue ☐ Wed

☐ Thu ✔ Fri ☐ Sat

End: Never

③

Setting Reminders

Windows 10 notifies you of events using the Notifications pane. By default, you will be reminded of events 15 minutes prior to the start time, but you can choose a different reminder time or choose not to be reminded.

② ①

1. While creating your event, tap or click Reminder.

2. Tap or click the desired time-frame prior to the event for your reminder or select None to turn off the reminder.

Specifying an Event Status

You can specify a status for your event of Free, Busy, Tentative, or Out of Office. Calendar displays a unique colored left edge for the event based on the status you select. Free displays a light-colored edge, Busy displays a light purple edge, Tentative displays a hashed edge of alternating colors, and Out of Office displays a dark purple edge.

1. While creating an event, tap or click Show As.

2. Tap or click the status for the event.

Creating a Private Event

You might want to create an event that only you can see. You can do that by marking an event as private. When you do, the event is actually created only as a local event on the device you are using. You (or others) will not be able to see the event on other devices that synchronize with your calendar.

1. While creating your event, tap or click Private to make the event private.

2. Tap or click Private again to make the event non-private.

Editing an Event

If you would like to make a change to an event, you can edit it and then resave it.

1. Tap or click the event you would like to edit.

2. Make any changes you want to the event. (If necessary, click More Details.)

3. Tap or click Save and Close to save the edited event.

Save or Send

If the event you are editing includes invites to others, you will tap Send to save the edited event and send it to those with whom you've shared the event.

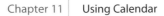

Deleting an Event

If an event has been canceled, you can delete it from your calendar.

1. Tap or click the event you would like to delete.

Canceling Events with Attendees

If you have invited others to the event you are deleting, you will be asked to enter a cancellation message. The invited people will then receive a cancellation email from you.

2. Tap or click Delete to delete the event. (Click More Details, if necessary.)

Calendar Settings

You can configure the settings for the Calendar app so that your work week and work hours appear correctly and so that Calendar recognizes which day of the week starts your week.

Changing the First Day of the Week

By default, the Calendar app uses Sunday as the first day of the week. You can change the first day of the week if a different day marks your first day of the week.

1. Tap or click Settings.

2. Tap or click Calendar Settings.

3. Tap or click First Day of Week and select a new first day of the week.

< Calendar Settings

Week

First Day of Week

Sunday ⌄ ——(3)

Sunday

Monday

Tuesday

Wednesday

Thursday

Friday

Saturday

☐ Saturday

Changing Days in Your Work Week

By default, Calendar uses Monday through Friday as the days in the work week. You can change the days in your work week if you work different days.

1. From the Settings screen, tap or click Calendar Settings.

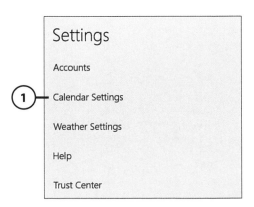

Settings

Accounts

(1)— Calendar Settings

Weather Settings

Help

Trust Center

2. Tap or click to check a day to add it to your work week.

3. Tap or click to uncheck a day to remove it from your work week.

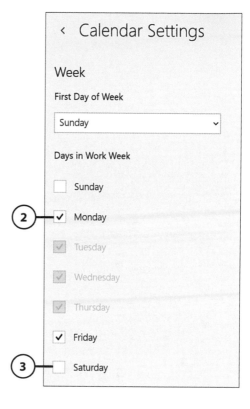

< Calendar Settings

Week

First Day of Week

Sunday

Days in Work Week

☐ Sunday

2 — ☑ Monday

☑ Tuesday

☑ Wednesday

☑ Thursday

☑ Friday

3 — ☐ Saturday

Changing Working Hours

Nonworking hours are shaded in the Calendar app so that you can quickly see the hours you work. You can change your working hours to accurately reflect when you are working.

1. From the Working Hours section in Calendar Settings, tap or click to select a start time for your working day.

2. Tap or click and select an end time for your working day.

Working Hours

Start time

1 — 8:00 AM

End time

2 — 5:00 PM

Week Numbers

Off

Calendar Color Options

⦿ Light Colors

◯ Bright Colors

Read news from your
local news sources.

Add your own interests to
see news that you want.

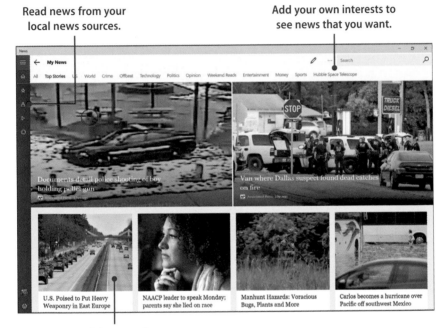

Read the news that
interests you.

In this chapter, you learn how to use the News app to keep up with news. You'll learn about

→ Reading the News

→ Adding and Removing News Interests

12

Keeping Up to Date with News

It's becoming more common for people to turn to computers instead of newspapers, radio, and television to keep up with the news. Using the News app on your tablet, you can keep track of news and read Internet articles that interest you in an attractive interface optimized for a tablet.

Reading the News

The News app keeps track of news from sources all around the world. Articles are categorized for easy browsing. When you start the News app, you'll see a synopsis of news from many sources, but you can choose from many categories and even add your own interests so you can view news about the things that interest you.

Reading an Article

News provides a convenient one-stop way for you to get up to date on all the latest news. You can read top news stories as well as stories from several different categories of news.

1. From the Start menu, tap or click the News tile to launch the News app.

2. Tap or click an interest to see all news stories in that category.

3. Tap or click a news story to read the entire story.

4. Swipe up or scroll down to read more of a story.

5. Tap or click the left-arrow button to move to the previous article.

6. Tap or click the right-arrow button to move to the next article.

7. Tap or click Back to return to the previous screen.

News Interests

The categories that you see in the News app are called Interests. You can customize what you see there, and you can add your own Interests based on a search term. I'll show you how in the "Adding and Removing News Interests" section later in this chapter.

Sharing News

You can share news articles with friends and family. News articles are shared using email, so you'll need to have an email account set up on your tablet.

Using Email

For more information on how to set up an email account on your tablet, see Chapter 10, "Using Mail."

It's Not All Good

Only Curated News

You can share only curated news in the News app; you can't share a news article that appears in the News app because of an interest that you have configured. However, you do have the option of copying a link to news stories that are based on your interests. You can then mail that link to someone to share the article.

1. While reading a news article that you want to share, tap or click Share.

2. In the Share pane, tap or click Mail.

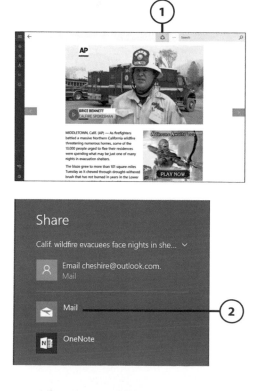

3. If you have more than one email account configured, tap or click on the account you want to use to share the article.

4. Enter one or more email addresses of the people with whom you want to share the article.

5. Enter a message if you want to.

6. Tap or click Remove Attachment if you want to remove any attachments that were automatically added to the mail message.

7. Tap or click Send.

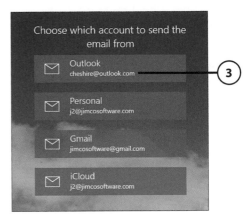

Reading Local News

News makes it easy to catch up on news from your local area. Depending on where you live, News may offer multiple news sources for your area.

1. Tap or click Local.

2. If prompted, tap or click Yes to allow News to use your location.

3. Tap or click a news source to see news articles from that source.

4. Tap or click an article to read it in the News app.

5. Tap or click Back to return to the previous view.

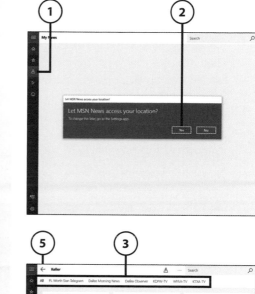

Watching Videos

The News app makes it easy to watch news videos because it has one view that shows you only videos.

1. Tap or click Videos.

2. Tap or click a video to watch it.

3. Tap or click Back to return to the News app home screen.

Adding and Removing News Interests

The News app comes with a predefined set of news topics. These topics are called Interests, and you can customize them so that you see only the news that interests you most. You can choose from Interests that are included with the News app or add your own Interests based on a search term that you provide.

Reading Topics

News Interests come from websites all over the Internet. When you tap on a news story in an Interest, the News app displays the web page associated with the news story.

Adding or Removing Included News Interests

You can add a news Interest from a list of Interests that come preconfigured in the News app.

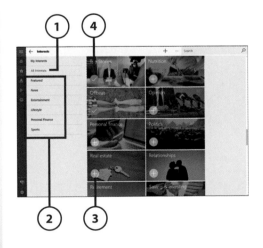

1. Tap or click All Interests.

2. Tap or click an Interest category.

3. Tap or click the plus sign to add an Interest to News.

4. Tap or click the check sign to remove an Interest from News.

My Interests

The My Interests category contains all the Interests that you've added to the News app.

Adding a Custom News Interest

If you want to add an Interest that isn't listed, you can create your own. When you're adding a custom Interest, you might see that Microsoft already has an Interest that you can add. However, if not, you can also add an Interest based purely on a search term.

1. Tap or click All Interests.

2. Tap or click inside the Search box and enter a search term.

3. If a suggested Interest appears, tap or click it from the list; otherwise, press Enter on your keyboard.

4. Tap or click on Add Interest to add the Interest to the News app.

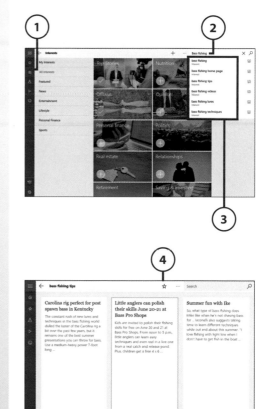

Back up files to
OneDrive.

Share files with
friends and family.

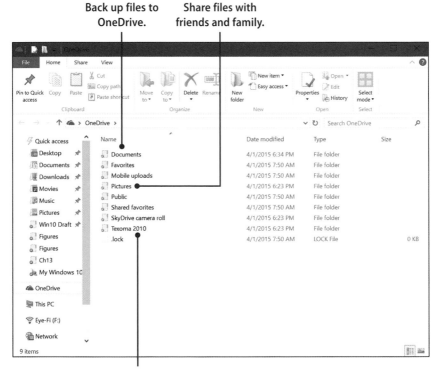

Sync OneDrive files
to your local PC.

In this chapter, you learn how you can use HomeGroups and OneDrive to share files with other people and to back up data on your tablet. You learn about

→ Using HomeGroups

→ Using OneDrive

HomeGroups and OneDrive

As you might have realized by now, a big component of Windows 10 is the capability to share files and content with friends and family. Both HomeGroups and OneDrive make that possible, but in different ways. HomeGroups enable you to see files that others have shared on your home network. OneDrive enables you to share files with anyone who has Internet access, and you can use OneDrive to share files among all your devices as well. OneDrive can also be used as a backup device for your tablet.

Using HomeGroups

Using HomeGroups is a convenient way to share files with others on your network. You can create a HomeGroup on a Windows 7, Windows 8, Windows 8.1, or Windows 10 PC. You then choose what you want to share on the HomeGroup. When that basic setup is complete, you can join the HomeGroup from your tablet and you'll be able to see any files that have been shared. You can also share printers or stream media between PCs in the HomeGroup.

Creating a HomeGroup

A HomeGroup is created on one PC in your home or office. Other users can then join your HomeGroup, and you can share files, printers, and media among PCs.

1. Tap and hold or right-click the Start button.

2. Tap or click Control Panel.

3. In the Network and Internet section, tap or click Choose HomeGroup and Sharing Options.

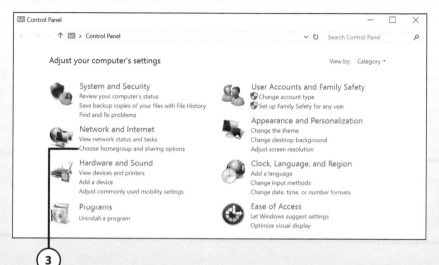

4. Tap or click Create a HomeGroup.

5. Tap or click Next.

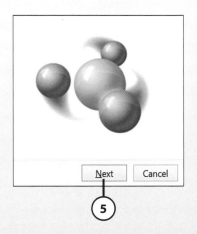

5

6. Choose what you want to share by selecting either Shared or Not Shared from the drop-downs.

7. Tap or click Next.

Share with other homegroup members

Choose files and devices you want to share, and set permission levels.

Library or folder	Permissions
Pictures	Shared ⌄
Videos	Shared ⌄
Music	Shared ⌄
Documents	Not shared ⌄
Printers & Devices	Shared ⌄

Next   Cancel

6   7

8. Write down the HomeGroup's password in a safe place.

9. Tap or click Finish.

Use this password to add other computers to your homegroup

Before you can access files and printers located on other computers, add those computers to your homegroup. You'll need the following password.

Write down this password:

2hQ9TC44yq ———— ⑧

Print password and instructions

If you ever forget your homegroup password, you can view or change it by opening HomeGroup in Control Panel.

Finish ——— ⑨

Joining a HomeGroup

To see the shared items in a HomeGroup, you first must join the HomeGroup on your tablet.

1. In the Network and Internet section of Control Panel, tap or click Choose HomeGroup and Sharing Options.

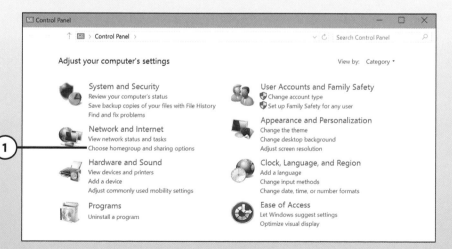

2. Tap or click Join Now to join the HomeGroup.

Share with other home computers

  Jim Cheshire on JIMCHESHIRE53D5 has created a homegroup on the network.

With a homegroup, you can share files and printers with other computers on your home network. You can also stream media to devices.

The homegroup is protected with a password, and you'll always be able to choose what you share.

Change advanced sharing settings...

Start the HomeGroup troubleshooter

                                                           Join now   Close

(2)

---

3. Tap or click Next.

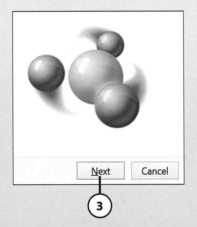

                Next   Cancel

(3)

4. Choose what you want to share with other members of the HomeGroup by selecting either Shared or Not Shared from the drop-downs.

5. Tap or click Next.

Share with other homegroup members

Choose files and devices you want to share, and set permission levels.

Library or folder	Permissions
Pictures	Shared ⌄
Videos	Shared ⌄
Music	Shared ⌄
Documents	Not shared ⌄
Printers & Devices	Shared ⌄

④   **⑤**

Next   Cancel

6. Enter the HomeGroup password.

7. Tap or click Next.

— ☐ ✕

🖳 Join a Homegroup

Type the homegroup password

A password helps prevent unauthorized access to homegroup files and printers. You can get the password from Jim Cheshire on JIMCHESHIRE53D5 or another member of the homegroup.

Type the password:

⑥   2hQ9TC44yq

Next   Cancel

⑦

8. Tap Finish.

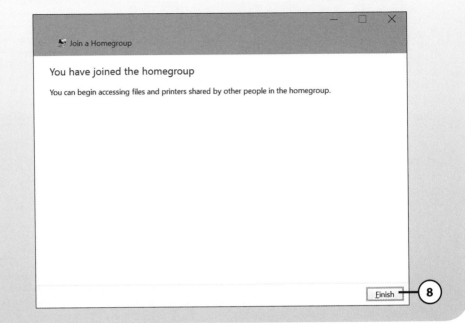

Leaving a HomeGroup

If you no longer want to be a member of a HomeGroup, you can leave it. When you do, you will no longer be able to see files shared on that HomeGroup. If the creator of a HomeGroup leaves the HomeGroup, the HomeGroup is removed from the network.

1. From the HomeGroup Settings screen, tap or click Leave the HomeGroup.

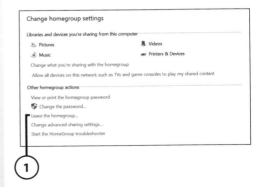

2. Tap or click Leave the HomeGroup.

3. Tap or click Finish.

Changing Your Mind

If you change your mind, you can always rejoin a HomeGroup at any time.

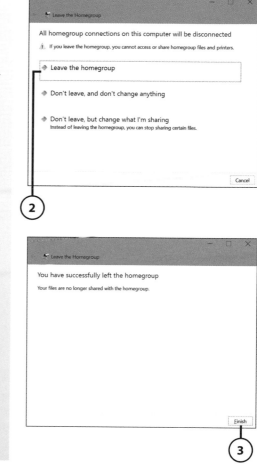

Accessing Shared Files

You can access files that are shared in your HomeGroup from any app that enables you to browse for files. For example, you can open a Word document shared on your HomeGroup, or you can open a picture shared on your HomeGroup. You also can save files back to shared folders on your HomeGroup.

Ensuring That Files Are Available

For you to access a file on your HomeGroup, the computer where the file is saved must be powered on. If it's not, you'll be able to see the computer when browsing for files, but Windows 10 won't be able to connect to it.

In this step-by-step, I will open a document in WordPad that is shared on my HomeGroup. The steps used are essentially the same in any app.

1. Within WordPad, tap or click File and then tap or click Open.

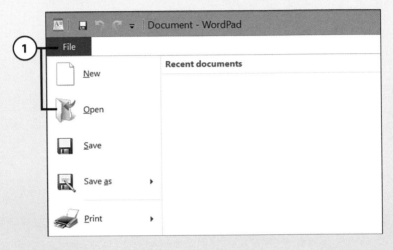

2. In the Open dialog, tap or click your HomeGroup.

3. Double-tap or double-click the library where the file is shared (in this case, Documents).

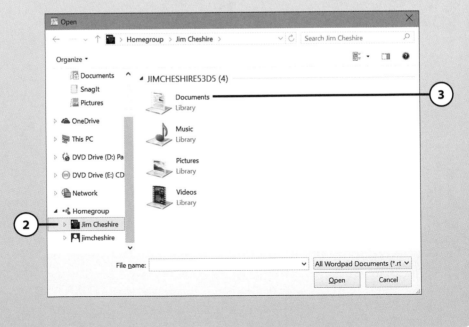

4. Tap or click the file you want to open.

5. Tap or click Open to open the file.

Using OneDrive

OneDrive is Microsoft's cloud storage service. By signing up for a Microsoft account, you get 15GB of OneDrive storage for free, and if you back up your camera roll, Microsoft will give you another 15GB free. You can purchase additional storage for a small fee from OneDrive.live.com.

Microsoft Account Required

These steps require a Microsoft account to be used. For more information on using a Microsoft account, see "Managing User Accounts" in Chapter 4, "Security and Windows 10."

Syncing Folders with OneDrive

You can choose to synchronize all your OneDrive folders with your PC, or you can selectively choose which folders are synced.

Choosing Folders

When you first sign in to your tablet with a Microsoft account, OneDrive will offer to let you choose which folders to sync. The steps I give here show you how you can choose folders to sync after you've gone through the initial launch of OneDrive.

1. Tap and hold or right-click the OneDrive icon in the Windows system tray.

2. Tap or click Settings.

3. Tap or click the Choose Folders tab.

4. Tap or click Choose Folders.

Open your OneDrive folder
Go to OneDrive.com
View sync problems
Manage storage
Settings
Help
Exit

6:43 PM
4/1/2015

Microsoft OneDrive

Settings | Choose folders | Performance | About

Your folders syncing on this PC

If you don't want to keep everything on your OneDrive on this PC, you can choose to sync only some folders by clicking "Choose folders."

Choose folders

OK   Cancel

5. Tap or click Sync All Files and Folders in My OneDrive to sync all files to your local PC.

6. Tap or click Sync Only These Folders to choose which folders to sync.

7. Tap or click a checked folder to uncheck it and turn off syncing for that folder.

8. Tap or click an unchecked folder to sync that folder to your local PC.

9. Tap or click OK.

10. Tap or click OK.

Microsoft OneDrive

Choose what you want to sync

To save space on your PC, sync only the files you need.

○ Sync all files and folders in my OneDrive
Everything but files shared with you will sync on this PC

● Sync only these folders
☑ Files not in a folder
☑ Documents
☑ Favorites
☑ Mobile uploads
☑ Music
☑ Pictures
☑ Files in "Pictures"
☑ Public
☑ Shared favorites
☑ SkyDrive camera roll
☑ Texoma 2010

OK   Cancel

Microsoft OneDrive

Settings | Choose folders | Performance | About

Your folders syncing on this PC

If you don't want to keep everything on your OneDrive on this PC, you can choose to sync only some folders by clicking "Choose folders."

Choose folders

OK   Cancel

It's Not All Good

Stopping Syncing Deletes Files

If you stop syncing a folder, any files that previously synced from that folder to your local PC will be removed from your local PC.

Accessing Your Files Remotely

OneDrive makes it easy to access all the files on your PC from another PC that you own. You can access these files by browsing to the OneDrive website.

1. From the Settings dialog in OneDrive, tap or click on the Settings tab.

2. Tap or click to check the Let Me Use OneDrive to Fetch Any of My Files on this PC check box.

3. Tap OK.

4. Open a web browser and browse to https://onedrive.live.com.

5. If you're not automatically logged in, tap or click Sign In.

6. Enter your Microsoft account email address.

7. Tap or click Next.

8. Enter your password.

9. Tap or click Sign In.

10. In the list of PCs, tap or click the PC whose files you want to access.

11. Tap or click a folder or drive to access your files.

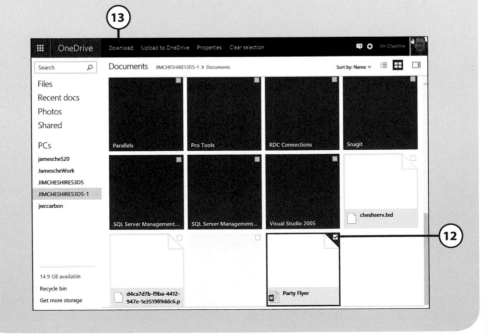

12. Tap or click the check box in the upper-right corner of a file you want to download.

13. Tap or click Download to download the file to your PC.

It's Not All Good

Sharing Files

You can share files that are stored in OneDrive with others. Sharing files is a great way to collaborate among multiple people or to share pictures or video with friends and family. You can even share content with people who don't have a Microsoft account.

1. Tap and hold or right-click the OneDrive icon in the Windows system tray.

2. Tap or click Open Your OneDrive Folder.

Faster OneDrive Folder Access

You can access your OneDrive folder faster by double-tapping or double-clicking the OneDrive icon in the system tray.

3. Tap and hold or right-click the folder you want to share, and then tap or click More OneDrive Sharing Options.

4. If prompted for a confirmation, tap or click Share this Folder.

5. Enter an email address for the people you want to share your folder with.

6. Enter a message to share with the invitees.

7. If you want people you're sharing the folder with to be able to edit files, tap or click Recipients Can Only View.

Invite people to "Pictures"

Enter contacts to send an email or Facebook message with a link to this item. You can **manage** your Facebook connection at any point.

To

(5) — cooldude@hook1.com ✕

(6) — Check out these great pics!

(7) — Recipients can only view

Share   **Close**

8. Tap or click Recipients Can Only View and tap or click Recipients Can Edit if you want to allow people you're sharing with to edit your files.

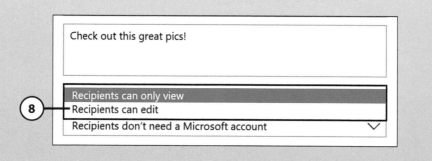

Check out this great pics!

Recipients can only view
(8) — Recipients can edit
Recipients don't need a Microsoft account   ∨

9. Tap or click Recipients Don't Need a Microsoft Account and tap or click Recipients Need to Sign In with a Microsoft Account to require users to use a Microsoft account to access and/or edit your files.

10. Tap or click Share.

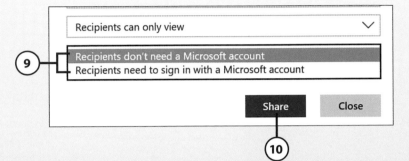

11. If you want to change the access level, tap or click the down arrow and choose the new access level.

12. Tap or click Close.

How Others Access Shared Files

When you share files with others, they will receive an email link to the files. Clicking the link opens the files. If you've selected the option to require a Microsoft account in step 9, the user will first need to sign in to a Microsoft account before he or she can access your files.

Browse your favorite
music artists.

Play music from your collection, or
choose from almost anything in the
Music Store using a Groove Music Pass.

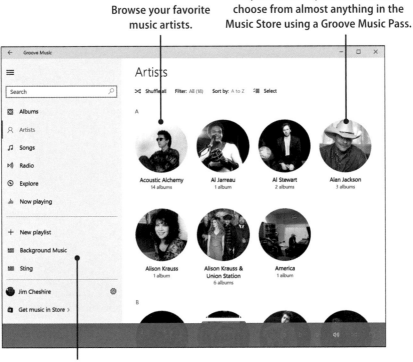

Create and edit
playlists.

In this chapter, you learn how you can use the Groove Music app in Windows 10 to discover new music and to listen to your favorite music. You learn about

→ Managing Your Music Library

→ Browsing Your Music Collection

→ Using Groove Music Pass

→ Music Playlists

→ Using Radio

Discovering and Playing Music

Your Windows 10 tablet comes with the Groove Music app. Using the Groove Music app, you can discover music, listen to your own music collection, or listen to an astounding number of songs using a Groove Music Pass.

Managing Your Music Library

You probably have some digital music stored on another computer in your house or on an external hard drive or other device. You can add that music to your Music library on your tablet and it will appear in the Groove Music app. You also can purchase music from the Windows Store to add music to your library. Finally, if you have a Groove Music Pass, you can download many songs in the Store to your library. (I cover using a Groove Music Pass later in this chapter.)

Adding Music to OneDrive

You can add music to the Music folder in your OneDrive folder and it will be available in the Groove Music app on all your PCs without you having to download the music to each PC. If you have a Groove Music Pass, Microsoft will even give you 100GB of extra OneDrive storage so you can store all of your music.

Adding a Folder to Your Collection

The Groove Music app looks in the Windows Music library to find music on your tablet. You can add additional folders, and any music in those folders will be automatically added to your collection in Groove Music.

1. From the Groove Music app, tap or click the Settings button.

2. Tap or click Choose Where We Look for Music.

3. Tap or click Add Folder.

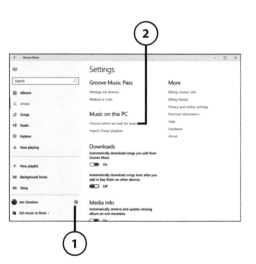

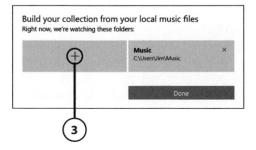

4. Browse to the location you want to add. This can be a local folder, a folder in your HomeGroup, a network folder, or a folder on your OneDrive.

5. Tap or click the folder you want to add.

6. Tap Add This Folder to Music.

7. Tap Done.

HomeGroups

If you would like information on joining a HomeGroup and accessing files on a HomeGroup, see Chapter 13, "HomeGroups and OneDrive."

Build your collection from your local music files
Right now, we're watching these folders:

| | Music |
| | D:\Music |

Music
C:\Users\Jim\Music

Done

It's Not All Good

Network Folders

Adding a network location to your collection has the benefit of not using any of the memory on your tablet. However, there is a disadvantage to using this method: You must be on your network to access your music. It also requires the computer where the music files reside to be turned on for you to access the music files there.

If you have a large music collection, you might be better off using a microSD memory card for your music so that it's available no matter where you take your tablet.

Controlling Album Art and Metadata

The Groove Music app automatically downloads album art that is displayed when you are browsing and playing your music. It also updates album and track titles to reflect what is in the Store. If you'd prefer, you can turn off this feature.

1. Tap or click Settings.

2. Swipe up or scroll down to see additional settings.

3. Tap or click Automatically Retrieve and Update Missing Album Art and Metadata to set the slider to Off.

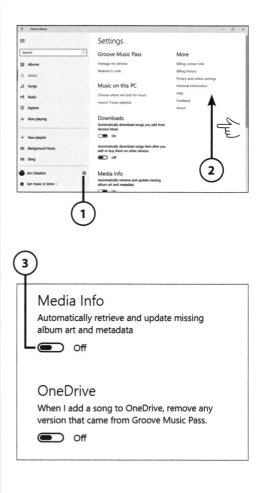

Deleting Music from Your Collection

You can delete music from your music collection. Be careful when doing so because unless the music is backed up somewhere, deleting it from your tablet deletes it permanently. Music that you delete from within the Groove Music app does not get moved to the Windows Recycle Bin.

Purchased Music
If you delete music from your PC that you originally purchased from the Store, you can download that music again from the Store.

It's Not All Good

Don't Delete Cloud Music

The Groove Music app will enable you to delete music that's in the cloud. If you don't have another copy of your music and you delete it from the cloud, the only way to get it back is to buy it again. Be very careful when you are deleting music.

1. From within the Groove Music app, tap or click Albums.

2. Tap or click the album that contains the music you want to delete.

3. To delete the entire album, tap or click More, and then tap or click Delete.

4. Tap or click Delete to confirm the deletion.

5. To delete one or more songs, tap or click Select.

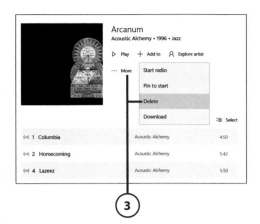

6. Tap or click the checkbox to select the songs you want to delete.

7. Tap or click Delete to delete the songs.

8. Tap or click Delete to confirm the deletion.

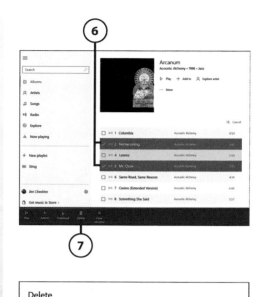

It's Not All Good

Deleting Is Permanent

I've already said this, but it's worth repeating because I don't want you to miss it. If you delete music from the Groove Music app, it deletes the music permanently. Make absolutely sure that you want to delete a music file before you do so.

Browsing Your Music Collection

After you've configured the Groove Music app so that you have a music collection populated with your music, you can use the features within the Groove Music app to browse and easily locate the music that you want to listen to.

Browsing Albums

The Groove Music app can organize all of your music by album. This makes it easy to play all songs on a particular album.

1. Tap or click Albums.

2. Tap or click Filter, and tap or click a filter option to filter your albums.

3. Tap or click Sort By, and tap or click a sort option to sort your albums.

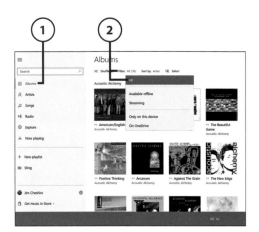

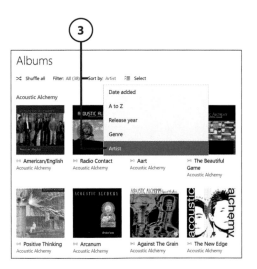

4. Swipe up or scroll down to see additional albums.

5. Tap or click an album to see all the tracks on the album.

6. Tap or click Back to return to the previous screen.

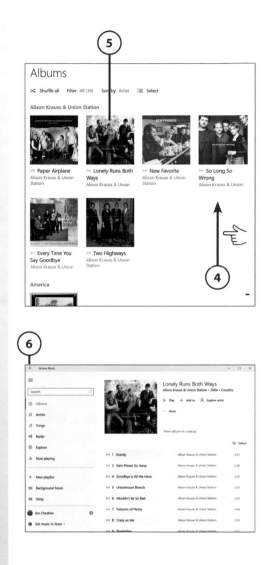

Browsing Artists

If you prefer to see all songs by a certain artist, you can easily browse the artists in your collection.

1. Tap or click Artists.

2. Tap or click Filter, and tap or click a filter option to filter artists.

3. Swipe up or scroll down to see additional artists.

4. After tapping on an artist, swipe up or scroll down to see additional songs and albums by the artist.

5. Tap or click Songs View to see all songs by the selected artist.

6. Tap or click Back to return to the previous screen.

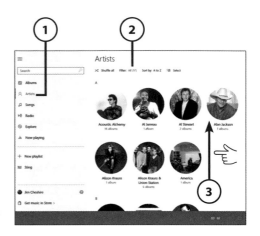

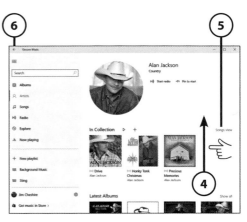

Cannot Sort Artists

You cannot change the sort order of artists. They will always be sorted in ascending alphabetical order.

Quickly Browsing

If you want to quickly browse in the Groove Music app, pinch in the list of albums, artists, or songs to access buttons that will enable you to easily jump to the music you want based on your sort order. For example, if you are viewing a list sorted in alphabetical order, pinching the screen will display buttons for each letter of the alphabet so that you can quickly jump to music that starts with a particular letter.

Browsing Songs

You can view a list of all your songs and sort or filter them to quickly access the songs you want to hear.

1. Tap or click Songs.

2. Swipe up or scroll down to see more songs.

3. Tap or click Filter to filter the song list.

4. Tap or click Sort By to change the sort order.

5. Tap or click a song to select so that you can play it or add it to a playlist.

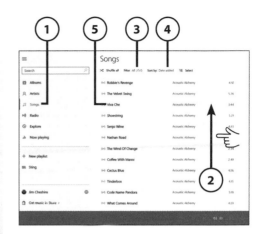

Playlists

I cover how to create and manage playlists later in this chapter in the "Music Playlists" section.

Searching for Music

If you can't locate the music you're interested in by browsing your collection, you can search your music. You can search for an artist name, an album name, or a song name.

1. Tap or click in the Search box and enter a search term.

2. Swipe up or scroll down to see more results.

3. Tap Show All to see all artists, albums, or songs that match your search.

4. Tap an item to see details on it.

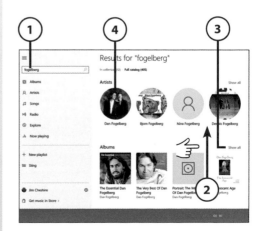

Using Groove Music Pass

Groove Music Pass is Microsoft's music subscription service. For $9.99 a month (or $99.90 for a year), you can stream or download a large number of songs from the Music Store. Microsoft has made a huge investment in the Groove Music Pass experience, and you can stream your Groove Music Pass music on your PC, your Xbox console, your Windows Phone, your Android phone, or your iOS device.

In this section, I show you how to sign up for a Groove Music Pass and how you can add Groove Music Pass music to your library by downloading it. In the section that follows, I explain how you can play Groove Music Pass music along with other music in your library.

It's Not All Good

No Holy Grail Here

Not all artists and/or record labels allow their music to be played using Groove Music Pass; therefore, some songs and albums won't be available. Even worse, record labels can pull songs from Groove Music Pass whenever they choose, and if they do, you will no longer be able to stream those songs. If you've downloaded a song or album and the record label pulls it, that song or album will simply disappear from your library. It's there one day, gone the next. This has happened to me on numerous occasions.

Groove Music Pass is still a great feature, and it's one that distinguishes Microsoft's music store from anyone else's. Microsoft will allow you to use the service free for 30 days, so it's worth trying out. The catalog of music consists of millions of songs, so you might find that all the music you want is available with Groove Music Pass.

Purchasing a Groove Music Pass Subscription

You can purchase Groove Music Pass directly from your tablet. (You can also sign up for a trial of the Groove Music Pass service.) In this example, I will use a PIN to purchase Groove Music Pass. For more information on PINs, see "Using PINs" in Chapter 4, "Security and Windows 10."

1. From the Settings panel in the Groove Music app, tap or click Get a Groove Music Pass.

2. Tap or click the Groove Music Pass plan you want to purchase.

3. Enter your PIN.

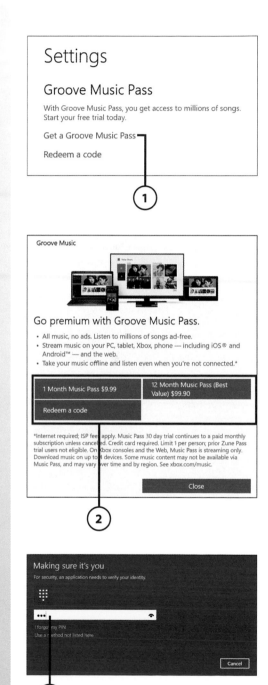

Settings

Groove Music Pass

With Groove Music Pass, you get access to millions of songs. Start your free trial today.

Get a Groove Music Pass

Redeem a code

①

Groove Music

Go premium with Groove Music Pass.

- All music, no ads. Listen to millions of songs ad-free.
- Stream music on your PC, tablet, Xbox, phone — including iOS® and Android™ — and the web.
- Take your music offline and listen even when you're not connected.*

1 Month Music Pass $9.99	12 Month Music Pass (Best Value) $99.90
Redeem a code	

*Internet required; ISP fees apply. Music Pass 30 day trial continues to a paid monthly subscription unless cancelled. Credit card required. Limit 1 per person; prior Zune Pass trial users not eligible. On Xbox consoles and the Web, Music Pass is streaming only. Download music on up to 4 devices. Some music content may not be available via Music Pass, and may vary over time and by region. See xbox.com/music.

Close

②

Making sure it's you

For security, an application needs to verify your identity.

•••

I forgot my PIN
Use a method not listed here

Cancel

③

4. If you don't want to have to sign in every time you make a purchase or change your account, tap or click the slider to change it to Off.

5. Tap or click Next.

6. Tap or click Confirm to confirm your purchase.

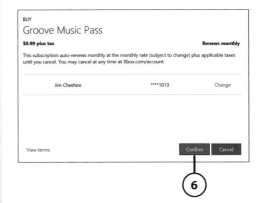

Billing Information

If you have not already provided your billing information for your Microsoft account, you are required to enter your billing name, address, and phone number at this point.

Automatic Renewal

Your Groove Music Pass automatically renews, so if you signed up for the trial and you don't want to continue using the service when your trial expires, be sure you cancel your subscription before your trial ends. You can cancel at any time and your Groove Music Pass will still be active through the entire 30-day trial period.

Automatically Downloading Groove Music Pass Music

If you like to listen to music when you're not connected to Wi-Fi, you can configure the Groove Music app to automatically download your Groove Music Pass music after you add it to a playlist.

1. From the Preferences screen in Groove Music, tap or click the Automatically Download Songs You Add from Groove Music to set the slider to On.

2. If you also want music that you add or buy on other devices to download to your tablet, tap or click the slider to automatically download music added or purchased from other devices to turn it on.

Playlists

I show you how to use playlists in Groove Music in the "Music Playlists" section, later in this chapter.

---

①

Music on this PC

Choose where we look for music

Import iTunes playlists

Downloads

Automatically download songs you add from Groove Music

 On

Automatically download songs here after you add or buy them on other devices

 Off

②

Downloading Groove Music Pass Music

You can manually download Groove Music Pass music to your tablet so that you can play it even when you're not connected to the Internet.

1. Browse or search to locate an album or song.

2. Tap or click Select.

3. Tap or click the albums or songs that you want to download.

4. Tap or click Add To.

5. Tap or click Collection.

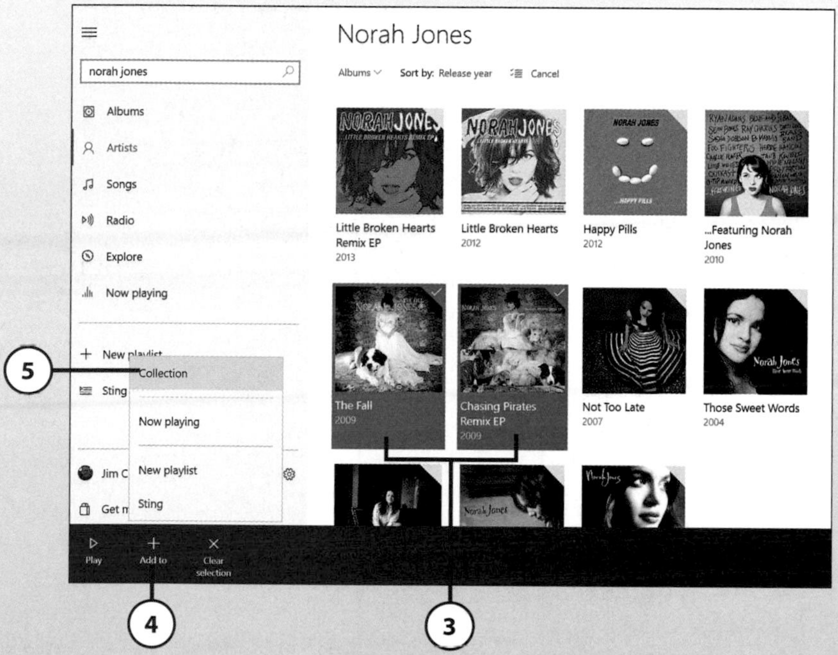

Music Playlists

Music playlists are a great way to play through a series of songs that you choose. For example, if you're having a party, you might want to play a certain type of music for your guests. A playlist makes it possible to do so easily.

Adding Songs to the Now Playing Playlist

The Groove Music app auto-creates a playlist called Now Playing when you start playing any music. Think of the Now Playing playlist as a queue of songs to which you can add songs.

1. Tap or click a song, an artist, or an album to select it.

2. Tap or click Add To.

3. Tap Now Playing to add the item and start playing.

Adding Music

You can add to the Now Playing queue (or any other playlist) wherever you see the Add To button.

Creating a Playlist

You can create your own playlists using songs from the Music Store, your collection, and Groove Music Pass.

1. After selecting the song, album, or artist that you want to add to the new playlist, tap or click Add To.

2. Tap or click New Playlist from the menu.

3. Enter a name for your playlist.

4. Tap or click Save.

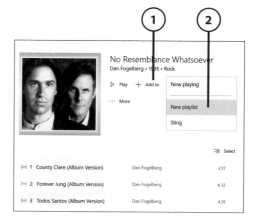

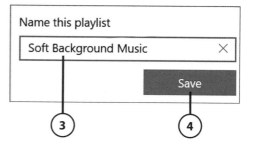

Adding Songs to a Playlist

You can add songs to a playlist you've already created. As you've already seen, you can add a single song, an entire album, or all songs by a particular artist.

1. While viewing an album, artist, or song that you want to add to your playlist, tap or click Add To.

2. Tap or click the name of the playlist to which you would like to add your songs.

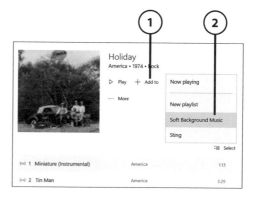

Editing a Playlist

You can edit a playlist by removing songs from it or by changing the order of songs. Note that deleting a song from a playlist only removes the song from the list. It doesn't actually delete the song from your collection.

1. Tap or click the playlist you want to edit.

2. Tap or click Select.

3. Tap or click a song in the playlist to select it.

4. To move a song up in the play order, tap or click Move Up.

5. To move a song down in the play order, tap or click Move Down.

6. To move a song to the top of the playlist, tap or click Move to Top.

7. To move a song to the bottom of the playlist, tap or click Move to Bottom.

8. To remove a song from the playlist, tap or click Remove from Playlist.

Cannot Change Play Order of Multiple Songs

If you select multiple songs in step 3, you won't be able to change the play order. You can only edit the play order if you select a single song.

Renaming a Playlist

You can rename a playlist if you want to change the name.

1. Tap or click the playlist you want to rename.

2. Tap or click Rename.

3. Enter a new name for the playlist.

4. Tap or click Save.

Deleting a Playlist

If you want to delete a playlist entirely, you can do so. Keep in mind that there isn't a way to restore a playlist after you delete it. Note that deleting a playlist does not delete the songs in your collection.

1. Tap or click the playlist you would like to delete.

2. Tap or click More.

3. Tap or click Delete.

4. Tap or click the Delete button to confirm that you want to delete the playlist.

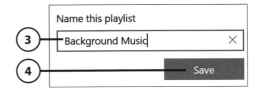

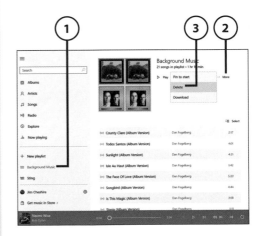

Seeing What's Playing

While you are playing songs on a play-list, you can see the songs that have already played, the song that's currently playing, and what's coming up.

1. Tap or click Now Playing while playing music.

2. Slide or scroll up and down to scroll through the songs.

Cannot Change Song Order

Although you can shuffle the songs in the Now Playing playlist, you cannot change the order so that songs are played in a specific order of your choosing.

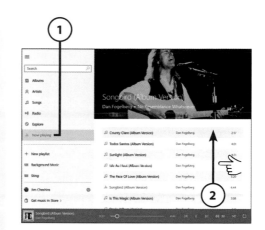

Shuffling or Repeating Songs in a Playlist

If you want to mix things up, you can shuffle the playback order of songs in your playlist. (This also applies to the Now Playing playlist.) You can also turn on Repeat mode so that playback will repeat until you explicitly stop it.

1. While your playlist is playing, tap or click Shuffle to toggle shuffle on and off.

2. Tap or click Repeat to toggle repeat on and off.

Using Radio

If you have a hard time deciding what to listen to, you can let the Groove Music app choose for you by using Radio. Radio chooses music that is similar to an artist you select.

Creating a Radio Station

To use Radio, you must first create a Radio station.

1. Tap or click Radio.

2. Tap or click Start a Radio Station.

3. Enter an artist.

4. Tap or click the artist name from the results, or tap or click the Radio button.

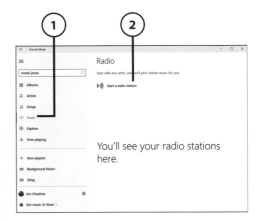

You'll see your radio stations here.

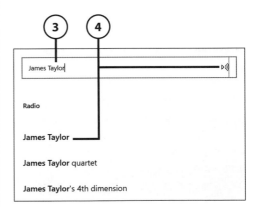

Playing a Radio Station

You can play any of your Radio stations from within the Groove Music app.

1. Tap or click Radio.

2. Tap or click the Radio station you want to play.

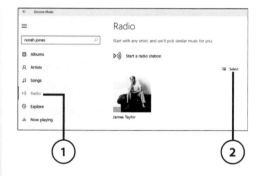

Deleting a Radio Station

If you no longer want to listen to a station, you can delete it.

1. Tap or click Radio.

2. Tap or click Select.

3. Tap or click the radio station you want to delete.

4. Tap or click Delete.

Pinning Radio Stations

Note that you can also pin a radio station to the Start menu by tapping or clicking on Pin to Start so that you can access it more quickly.

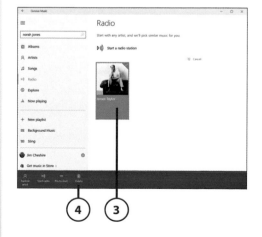

Rent and purchase the latest blockbuster movies.

Purchase single TV show episodes or an entire season to watch when you want to.

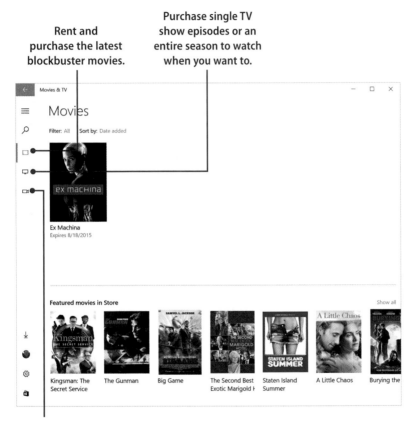

Watch videos in your personal video collection.

The Movies & TV app in Windows 10 makes it easy to organize your videos and to buy or rent movies and TV shows. In this chapter, you learn about

→ Managing Videos

→ Exploring, Buying, and Renting Videos

→ Playing Videos

15

Watching Video

The Movies & TV app makes a huge library of movies and TV shows available to you for rent or purchase. You can also use the Movies & TV app to build a collection of personal videos.

Managing Videos

The Videos section of the Movies & TV app contains videos that are in your video collection. You can add videos to your video library to add them to Videos. To remove a video from Videos, delete the video from your video library.

Adding Videos to the Movies & TV App

To add videos to the Movies & TV app, you can point the Movies & TV app to one or more folders where your videos are stored.

Playing Videos

I walk you through how to play videos in the "Playing Videos" section later in this chapter.

1. From the Start menu, tap or click the Movies & TV app to launch it.

2. Tap or click the Settings button.

3. Tap or click Choose Where We Look for Videos.

4. Tap or click + to add a new folder.

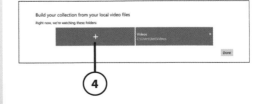

5. Browse to the folder that contains your videos. This can be on your PC or on your network.

6. Tap or click Add This Folder to Videos.

7. Tap or click Done.

Updating Might Be Slow

If you add a network folder to Videos, it might take a few minutes before videos start appearing.

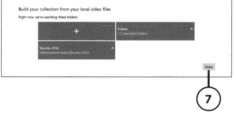

It's Not All Good

Video over Networks

If the folder you add to the Movies & TV app is a network folder on another computer, you might experience choppy performance when playing videos from that folder. If you want to use a network folder for video, make sure you test playback. If playback isn't as good as you would like, you can copy the video files to a local drive for better performance.

Exploring, Buying, and Renting Videos

In addition to watching your own videos, you can watch movies and television shows from the Store. You can purchase or rent videos.

Browsing Movies and TV Shows

Finding something to watch is sometimes a challenge—not because of a limitation on content in the Store, but simply because so much good content is available. Some features of the Store make it easy to find a video to fit your current mood.

This section describes how to browse the Store for Movies or TV shows.

1. If you aren't already in the Store, tap or click Shop for More.

2. Swipe up or scroll down to see additional movies and TV shows.

3. Tap or click Show All in a section to see more movies or TV shows.

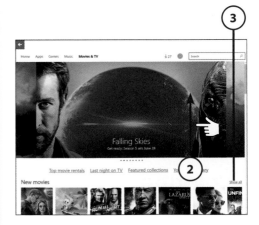

4. Swipe or scroll up and down to see more movies.

5. If you are viewing movies or TV shows that are new or are top-rated, top-selling, or top rentals, tap or click the Chart drop-down and tap a chart to refine the list.

6. Tap or click a genre to see only videos in that genre.

7. Swipe up or scroll down to see additional genres.

8. Tap or click a studio to see only movies from that studio. (TV shows will enable you to refine by network instead.)

9. Swipe up or scroll down to see additional studios.

10. Tap or click a movie to see details on the movie.

11. Tap or click Watch Trailer to watch a movie trailer.

12. Tap or click Show All to view all reviews for the movie.

13. Swipe up or scroll down for more information about the movie.

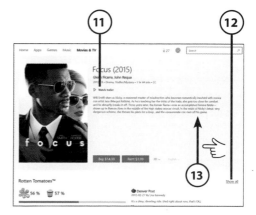

14. Tap or click Show All to see a full list of similar movies.

15. Tap or click Back to return to the list of movies and TV shows.

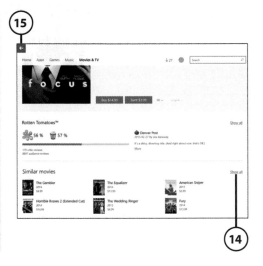

Renting Movies

Rented movies expire after 14 days or 24 hours from the time you start watching your rental. Options are available for both streaming and downloading, and many movies enable you to choose between standard and high-definition versions.

In these steps, I use a PIN to rent a movie. If you don't have a PIN configured, you will be asked for your Microsoft account password instead. I find a PIN to be more convenient. If you want details on how to configure a PIN, see "Using PINs" in Chapter 4, "Security and Windows 10."

1. After selecting a movie, tap or click SD to choose between SD and HD.

2. Tap or click Rent to rent the movie.

Rental Options

Not all rental options are available for all movies, and not all movies can be rented. New movies typically don't offer the option of renting.

Renting in Standard Definition

Keep in mind that the screen resolution of your tablet is most likely higher than the resolution of an SD movie, so movies in HD will look much better.

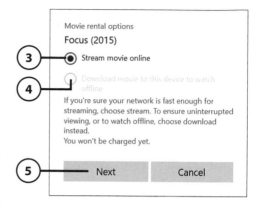

3. Tap or click Stream Movie Online to rent a streaming version of the movie.

4. Tap or click Download Movie to This Device to Watch Offline to rent a downloaded copy of the movie that can be played even when you're offline. (This option is not available for all movies.)

5. Tap or click Next.

6. Enter your PIN.

7. Tap or click Rent to confirm your rental purchase.

Payment Options

You can tap or click Change if you want to use a new credit card for your purchase.

Renting Movies

Movies that you rent and choose to download are added to Movies after you download them. You are given the opportunity to download the movie after your rental is complete.

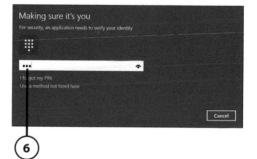

It's Not All Good

Streaming and Downloading

You will only be able to play a rented movie using the playback option (either streaming or downloading) you selected when you rented it. If you choose to stream the movie, you won't be able to download it, and vice versa. This is important to keep in mind because if you select the streaming option, you must be connected to the Internet the entire time you are watching the movie.

Buying Movies

If you want to add a movie to your music library without any time limits on watching it, you can purchase the movie. Most movies you purchase can be watched on your tablet or on your Xbox console.

1. After tapping or clicking a movie you want to purchase, tap or click to select between SD and HD.

2. Tap or click Buy.

Buying SD Movies
I don't recommend buying the SD version of movies. HD versions are usually only a few more dollars, and the increase in quality is definitely worth the few extra dollars.

3. Enter your PIN.

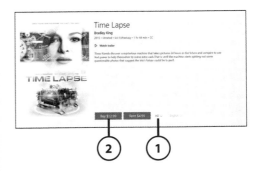

4. Tap or click Buy.

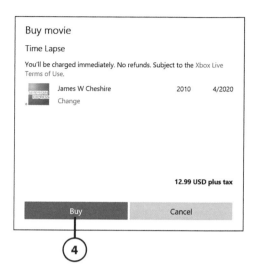

Buy movie

Time Lapse

You'll be charged immediately. No refunds. Subject to the Xbox Live
Terms of Use.

	James W Cheshire	2010	4/2020
	Change		

12.99 USD plus tax

Buy	Cancel

④

It's Not All Good

Copy Protection

When you buy a movie, you are actually just buying a license to play it whenever you want on your PC or Xbox. (You can play rented videos only on the
device on which you rented them.) You don't have the right to burn it to a
DVD or watch it on another device because copy protection will prevent
it. This might surprise you because most music you buy can be freely used
on any device. Unfortunately, the movie companies and television studios
haven't yet been persuaded to drop the copy protection from videos, so
some stiff restrictions are still in place even after you buy a video.

Buying TV Shows

In addition to movies, the Store provides access to a large number of television shows you can buy. You can buy single episodes, an entire season that
has already aired, or a season pass for a current season so you can keep up
with the show as it airs. (TV shows cannot be rented.)

1. Browse the Store to locate a TV series you want to purchase.

2. Tap or click a show's tile to see more about the show.

3. Tap or click Buy Season Pass to buy existing episodes and all upcoming episodes in the current season.

Buying in HD

Just as you did with movies earlier, you can select between HD and SD when buying TV shows. I always prefer HD, but the choice is yours.

4. Swipe up or scroll down to see additional seasons.

5. Tap or click a season to see episodes in that season.

6. Tap or click the price button for an individual episode to buy that episode.

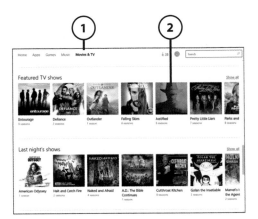

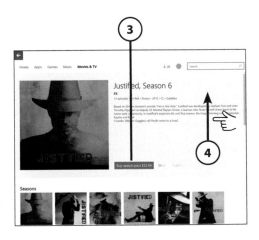

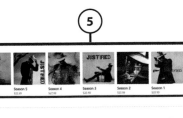

It's Not All Good

It's All or Nothing

When you buy a season pass, you must pay for the entire season up front. Many video stores enable you to pay for episodes as they are made available and cancel a season pass to stop being billed for episodes. The Windows Store doesn't offer this option.

I'll often buy season passes when I want to get caught up on a show that I've just started watching because it enables me to easily buy all episodes up to the current episode in one step. If you want to do this with Store purchases, you'll need to purchase each episode individually instead. The end result is the same, but it's a bit of a hassle.

Playing Videos

Your Windows 10 tablet likely has a high-resolution screen that is excellent for watching video.

Playing Videos on Your Tablet

Videos can be streamed or downloaded to your tablet. If you're going to stream videos, you'll need to be connected to the Internet throughout the playback of the video.

Your personal videos will have no restrictions on playback. However, if you're watching a movie or TV show you got from the Store, you might have to abide by playback restrictions imposed by the owner of the video rights.

Stream and Download

It's up to the rights owner of a video as to whether you can download a video. The Store lets you know what rights are available to you when you buy or rent a movie.

Notice that the images you see in this walkthrough show a video that allows for both streaming and downloading; therefore, I can tap Download to download a video for offline watching.

1. From the Movies & TV app, tap or click the video you would like to play.

2. Tap or click Play to play the video. (If you selected a television series in step 1, you'll need to tap an episode first.)

3. Tap or click Download to download the video to your tablet before playing it. (Downloaded videos can be played while you're not connected to the Internet.)

4. While a video is playing, tap or click the video to access playback controls.

5. Drag the scrubber handle to quickly move to a particular part of the video.

6. Tap or click Back to return to the Video app home screen.

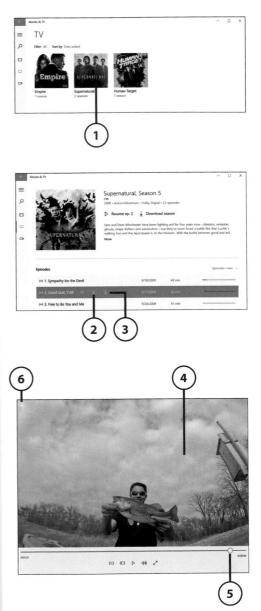

Edit your photos to make
them look their best.

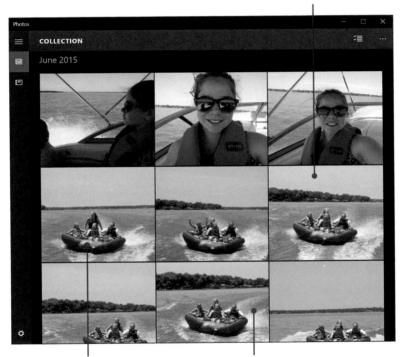

Browse photos in your
Pictures folder and on
your OneDrive.

Create a slide show of
your photos.

Windows 10 not only makes it easy to take pictures if you have a camera on your tablet, but it also provides a great app for organizing and editing your photos. In this chapter, you learn about the following:

→ Viewing Pictures and Video

→ Editing Pictures and Video

Using Photos

The Photos app makes it easy to browse photos in your Pictures folder on your tablet or on your OneDrive. You can also edit pictures to remove red eye, enhance them, and even apply cool effects.

Viewing Pictures and Video

Once you've added some pictures to your Pictures library or your OneDrive, you can view them in the Photos app. You also can watch a slide show of images and set a picture as your lock screen image.

Browsing Pictures

You can browse through all the pictures in your Pictures library and pictures from your OneDrive.

1. From the Start menu, tap or click Photos to launch the Photos app.

2. Tap or click the month and year to select a new time period.

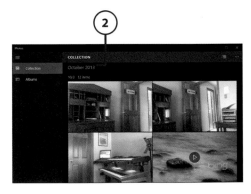

3. Swipe up or scroll down to see additional months.

4. Tap or click a month to see pictures taken in that month.

5. Tap or click a picture to select it and view a larger version.

6. Reverse pinch on the image or tap or click + to zoom in.

7. Tap or click and drag to scroll on a zoomed-in image.

8. Pinch on the image or tap or click – to zoom out.

9. Tap or click Back to return to all your photos.

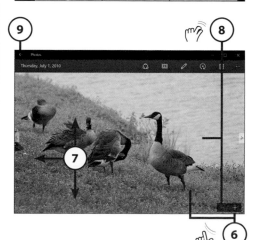

Watching a Slide Show

You can view a slide show of pictures. When you are viewing a slide show, the Photos app transitions through all your pictures. Each picture is displayed for 4 seconds.

1. In the Photos app, tap or click a picture that you want your slide show to start with.

2. Tap or click Slide Show.

3. Tap anywhere on the image during the slide show to return to your photos.

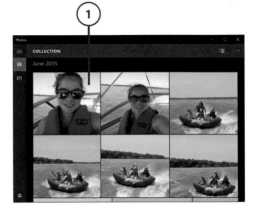

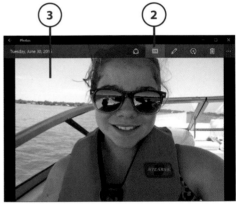

Watching Video

You can watch videos that you've added to your Pictures folder or your OneDrive.

1. Tap or click a video file. (Videos display a circle in the center with a Play icon.)

2. While the video is playing, tap it or hover your mouse pointer over it, and then tap or click Pause to pause playback.

3. Tap or click and drag the scrubber to change playback position.

4. Tap or click Back to return to your photos.

Deleting Pictures

You can delete pictures from the Photos app. Be careful when deleting photos from your OneDrive, however, because they are permanently deleted.

1. Tap or click Select.

2. Tap or click the check box in the upper-right corner of any pictures you want to delete.

3. Tap Delete.

4. Tap Delete to confirm the deletion.

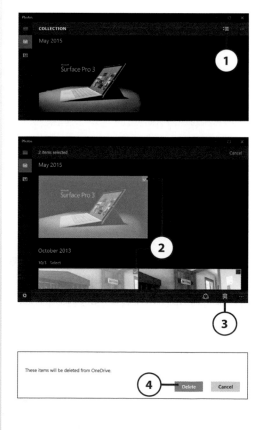

Using a Picture as Your Lock Screen

You can change the background image for your lock screen so that it displays one of your favorite pictures.

1. While viewing the picture you want to use as your lock screen background image, tap or click See More.

2. Tap or click Set as Lock Screen.

No Cropping

Windows 10 uses the full picture as your lock screen background. There is no option to crop the image or reposition it. If you want to use a cropped image for your background, you'll need to crop the image first and then set it as your lock screen picture. I show you how to crop images in the next section.

Editing Pictures and Video

The Photos app has basic photo editing features. You can crop pictures and rotate pictures, but you can also adjust color, contrast, and brightness as well as add effects, fix red eye, and much more.

Rotating Pictures

The most basic editing operation is rotating pictures.

1. While viewing the picture you want to rotate, tap or click Rotate.

2. If necessary, tap or click Rotate again. Each tap or click on Rotate rotates the picture 90 degrees clockwise.

Automatic Save

When you rotate a picture, the Photos app will automatically save the rotated version.

Automatically Enhancing Pictures

You can use the Photo app's Auto Enhance feature to automatically enhance a picture. This can help to fix problems with pictures that are too dark or are otherwise not to your liking.

1. Tap or click a picture you want to automatically enhance.

2. Tap or click Enhance to automatically enhance the picture.

3. If you don't like the changes, tap or click Enhance again to undo the enhancements.

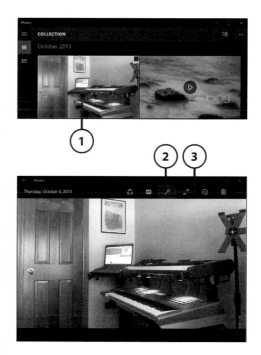

Cropping a Picture

If you want to keep only part of a picture, you can crop out the parts you don't want.

1. While viewing the picture you want to crop, tap or click Edit.

2. Tap or click Crop.

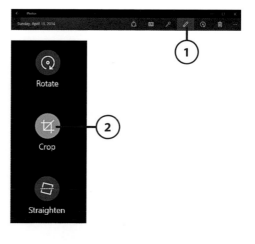

3. Tap or click Aspect Ratio and select an option if you want to restrict the aspect ratio while cropping.

4. Tap or click and drag to reposition the picture.

5. Tap or click and drag a corner to resize the cropping area.

6. Tap or click Apply to commit your changes.

7. Tap or click Save to overwrite the original picture with your changes.

8. Tap or click Save a Copy to save a new copy of the edited picture.

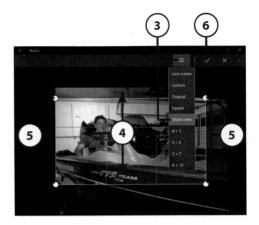

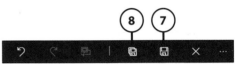

Removing Red Eye

You can easily remove red eye from a picture.

1. While viewing the picture you want to remove red eye from, tap or click Edit.

2. Reverse pinch on the photo or tap or click the + button to zoom in on the eyes. (You might also need to drag to reposition the photo on the eyes.)

3. Tap or click Red Eye.

4. Tap or click the eyes that are red.

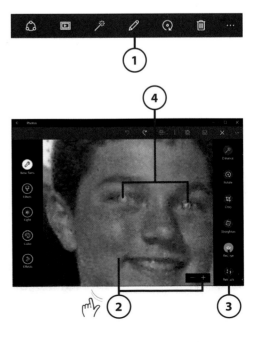

5. Tap or click Save As to save the edited photo as a copy.

6. Tap or click Save to overwrite the original photo.

Retouching a Photo

Retouching is a great way to remove blemishes, splotchy skin, and other qualities of a picture that you want to touch up. You can even use it to remove a specular highlight (bright area) caused by a flash reflecting off of a surface.

1. From the Editing screen, tap or click Basic Fixes.

2. Tap or click Retouch.

3. Tap or click an area that you want to retouch.

4. Tap or click the area multiple times if you need to retouch the photo some more.

5. Tap or click Save or Save As to save your change.

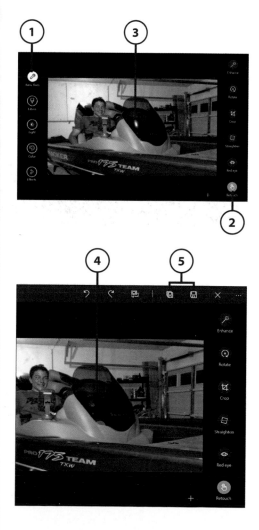

Using Filters

Filters provide a great way to fix up a photo quickly without complicated steps. The Photos app provides multiple filters you can use on your photos.

1. From the Editing screen, tap or click Filters.

2. Tap or click a filter to select it.

3. Tap or click Save or Save As to save your change.

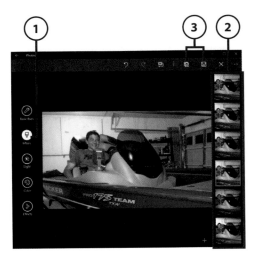

Adjusting Lighting

You can adjust the lighting of your picture. This includes brightness, contrast, highlights, and shadows.

1. From the Editing screen, tap or click Light.

2. Tap or click Brightness, Contrast, Highlights, or Shadows, depending on what you want to adjust.

3. Drag the white ball counterclockwise to decrease the value and clockwise to increase the value.

4. Tap or click Save or Save As to save your changes.

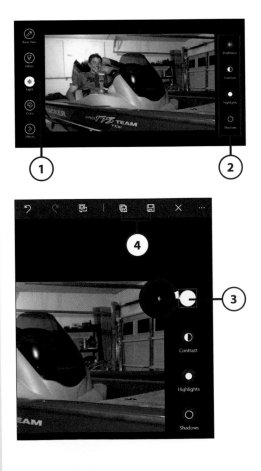

Adjusting Color

You can adjust the temperature, tint, and saturation of colors in a photo. You can also choose a particular color that you want to either boost or reduce.

1. From the Editing screen, tap Color.

2. Tap either Temperature, Tint, or Saturation.

3. Drag the white ball counterclockwise to decrease the value and clockwise to increase the value.

4. To boost or reduce a particular color, tap and hold or click and hold on Color Boost.

5. Drag the Color Boost pointer to the color you want to boost or reduce, and then release your finger or the mouse button.

6. Drag the white ball counterclockwise to reduce the color and clockwise to boost the color.

7. Tap or click Save or Save As to save your changes.

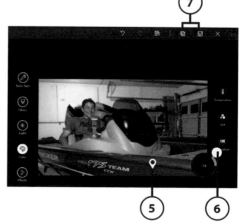

Applying a Vignette Effect

A vignette effect makes the edges of a photo either lighter or darker than the rest of the picture. It's a commonly used effect to draw attention to something in the center of an image.

1. From the Editing screen, tap or click Effects.

2. Tap or click Vignette.

3. Drag the white ball counterclockwise to apply a darkening to the edges of the picture.

4. Drag the white ball clockwise to apply a lightening to the edges of the picture.

5. Tap or click Save or Save As to save your changes.

Using Selective Focus

Another way you can emphasize the focal point of a picture is by using selective focus. This allows you to have one part of the picture in crystal-clear focus while the rest of the picture is blurred to a certain degree.

1. While in the Editing screen, tap or click Effects.

2. Tap or click Selective Focus.

3. Drag the ellipse to encompass the portion of the image you want to be in focus.

4. Use the sizing handles to resize and reshape the ellipse.

5. Tap or click Blur, and then tap or click a blurring strength to control how blurry the rest of the image is.

6. Tap Apply to apply the effect.

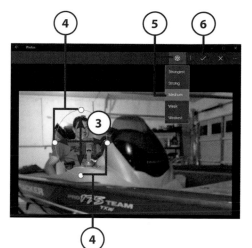

Trimming a Video

If you want to trim a video and save a portion of the video to a new file, you can easily do so right within the Photos app.

1. Tap or click the video you want to trim.

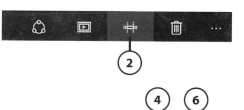

2. Tap or click Trim.

3. Tap or click Play to view the video or use the scrubber to locate the section you want to keep.

4. Tap or click and hold on the left handle to move it to the desired starting point for your video.

5. Tap or click and hold on the right handle to move it to the desired ending point for your video.

6. Tap or click Save a Copy to save a copy of your trimmed video.

Location of Saved Copy
The copy of your trimmed video is saved into the same folder as the original video.

Explore selected
places in 3D views.

Get turn-by-turn
directions and view
traffic incidents.

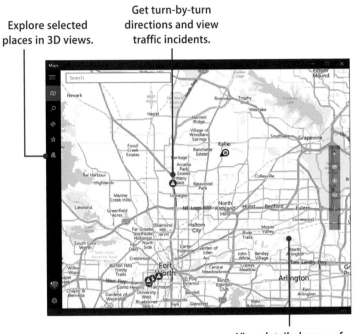

View detailed maps of
the entire world.

The Maps app makes it easy to explore new places and get directions to just about anywhere. In this chapter, you learn about

→ Exploring Maps

→ Searching Maps

→ Getting Directions

→ Updating Maps and Using Offline Maps

Using Maps

The Maps app enables you to use the Bing Maps service to explore maps, search for places and addresses, and find directions. You can view road maps with minimal clutter as well as aerial maps that provide a satellite view of an area. In many cases, you can also view an angled aerial view that provides a three-dimensional perspective of the map.

Exploring Maps

The Maps app provides maps of practically the entire world, and satellite imagery is available for most areas. Many of its tools enable you to easily explore any area you want.

Viewing and Zooming

While you are viewing the map, you can easily move around and zoom in and out using touch or using a mouse or trackpad.

1. From the Start menu, tap or click Maps to launch the Maps app.

2. If prompted, tap Yes to let the Maps app use your location or No to prevent the Maps app from using your location.

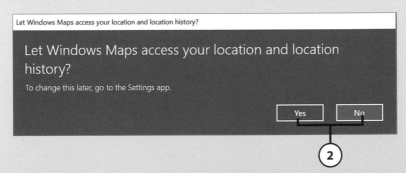

3. Tap or click, and then slide to move around on the map.

4. Reverse-pinch or tap Zoom In to zoom in on the map. (You can also press Ctrl+plus sign on your keyboard.)

5. Pinch or tap Zoom Out to zoom out on the map. (You can also press Ctrl+minus sign on your keyboard.)

6. Double-tap or double-click to zoom in and center the map on the point where you double-tapped or double-clicked.

7. Tap or click Show My Location to center the map on your current location.

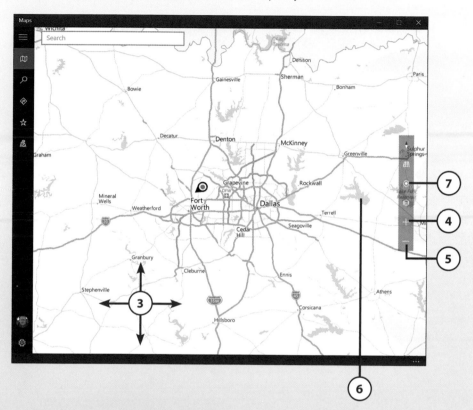

Location Services

Many apps you use might use location services to provide you with a better experience. The Maps app uses location services so that it can show you your current location on the map, and so it can provide a better experience when you are getting directions.

Every Wi-Fi access point transmits a unique identifier called a MAC address. There are companies that drive around the country collecting these MAC addresses and the approximate GPS coordinates of each one. Even if your tablet doesn't have a GPS built in, your tablet might use services provided by these companies to get your approximate location based on the MAC addresses your tablet picks up.

Changing the Units of Measurement

By default, the Maps app shows distances using miles as the unit. If you prefer, you can switch the Maps app to use a different unit of measurement.

1. While in the Maps app, tap or click Settings.

2. Tap or click the Units drop-down.

3. Tap Metric, Imperial, or US to change the unit of measurement.

Changing the Map Style

The Maps app shows maps using the Road style by default. This style of map is similar to paper maps and uses a solid-colored background and displays roads using different colors based on the size of the road. You can switch to Aerial style, which uses a satellite image for the map with colored roads drawn on top of the image. You can also switch to Traffic view so that you can see color-coded traffic conditions.

1. While viewing the map, tap or click Map Views.

2. Tap or click Aerial to switch to Aerial view.

3. Tap or click Traffic to overlay traffic conditions onto the map.

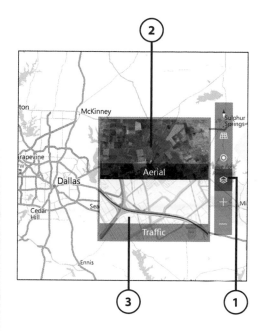

Traffic

I show you how to use Maps to analyze traffic conditions in the "Showing Traffic" section later in this chapter.

Exploring in 3D

Select cities in Maps are offered in 3D so that you can explore them just as though you were flying a helicopter over these cities.

1. Tap or click 3D Cities.

2. Swipe or scroll up and down to see additional cities.

3. Tap or click a city to explore that city in 3D.

4. Tap or click, and then drag to move around the map.

5. Use the Zoom control or pinch to zoom in and out.

6. Tap or click Tilt to switch to 3D mode.

7. Tap and hold or hover over Tilt, and then tap or click Tilt Down to tilt down.

8. Tap and hold or hover over Tilt, and then tap or click Tilt Up to tilt up.

9. Tap or click Go Back to 2D to return to 2D mode.

Showing Traffic

As you saw earlier, Maps can show you traffic congestion from Microsoft's Bing service. Maps uses colors overlaid on roads to indicate the speed of traffic. Areas where traffic is very slow are shown in red, slow traffic is orange, somewhat slow traffic is yellow, and fast traffic is green. If a road doesn't show any of these colors, traffic data for that road isn't available.

1. While viewing a map, tap or click Map Views.

2. Tap or click Traffic.

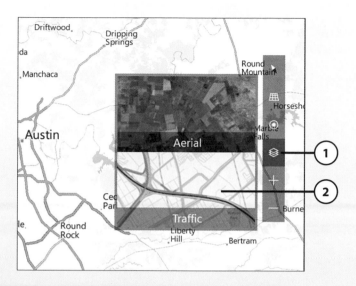

3. To see details on a traffic incident, tap or click the incident's icon.

4. Tap or click Back to remove the incident details from the screen.

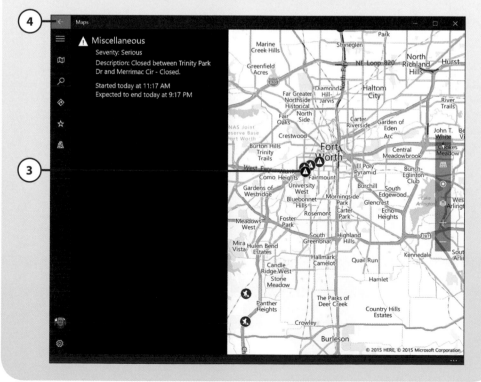

Searching Maps

In addition to browsing through a map, you can search the Maps app for an address or a place of interest.

Searching for a Place

You can search for a business or a place using the Maps app. For example, you can use the Maps app to find museums by entering **museum** in the Search box.

1. Tap or click inside the Search box.

2. Enter a search term.

Search Relative to Area on Map

When you search, you will see results that are closest to the location you were viewing on the map. If you want to see results close to your present location, tap or click Show My Location before searching.

---

3. To view a search result on the map, tap or click the result's icon.

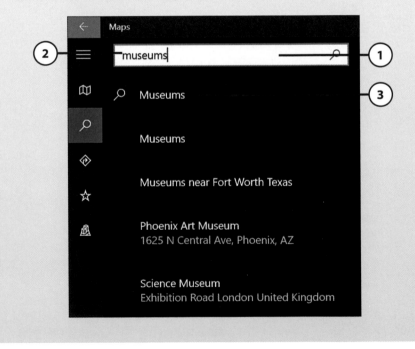

4. Tap or click Directions to get directions to a place.

5. Tap or click the phone number to call a place using Skype.

6. Tap or click on a place name for details on that place.

7. Tap or click Website to visit the location's website.

8. Tap or click Add to Favorites to add the location to your Favorites list in Maps.

9. Tap or click Nearby to see other interesting places nearby.

10. Tap or click Pin to Start to pin the location to the Start menu.

11. Drag up or scroll down for reviews and more information about the location.

12. Tap Back to return to the list of search results.

Finding an Address
You can use this same search technique to find an address on the map.

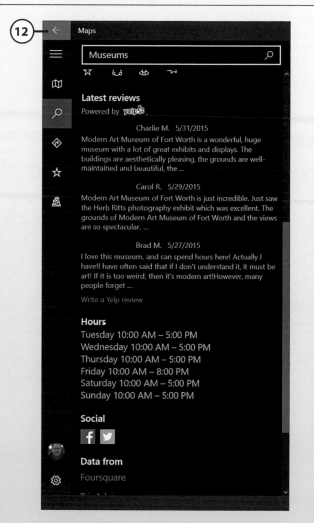

Adding Favorites

You can add a place on the map to your Favorites list. You use favorites to save a location on the map for future reference.

1. While exploring the map, tap or click and hold to select a location. (You can also search for a location.)

2. Tap or click Add to Favorites.

Editing or Deleting a Favorite

You can edit the details of one of your favorites. You can also delete a favorite if you no longer want it listed in your Favorites list.

1. Tap or click Favorites.

2. Tap or click the favorite you want to edit or delete.

3. Tap or click Edit or Delete Favorite.

4. Edit the favorite, and then tap or click Save to save changes.

5. Tap or click Delete This Favorite to delete the favorite.

Getting Directions

The Maps app can generate directions so that you can easily find an address or a place on the map.

Getting Directions

You've already seen how you can get directions to a place you've searched for. You can also get directions from your location to an address or from one place to another place using the Directions feature of Maps.

1. Tap or click Directions.

2. By default, the starting point is your current location. Tap or click inside the box and enter a new address to use a different starting location.

3. Enter a destination place name or address.

4. Tap or click the bus or the pedestrian symbol to get directions for public transit or walking directions.

5. Tap or click Options to choose between alternative routes.

6. Tap or click Reverse Directions to swap the starting and ending points for your directions.

7. Tap or click the arrow, or press Enter on the keyboard to generate the directions.

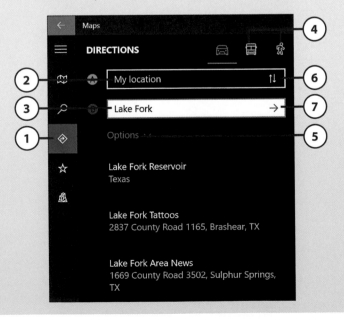

8. Tap or click one of the navigation steps to zoom in on that part of the route.

9. Slide up or scroll down to see additional turns on the route.

10. Tap or click Go to begin your turn-by-turn directions.

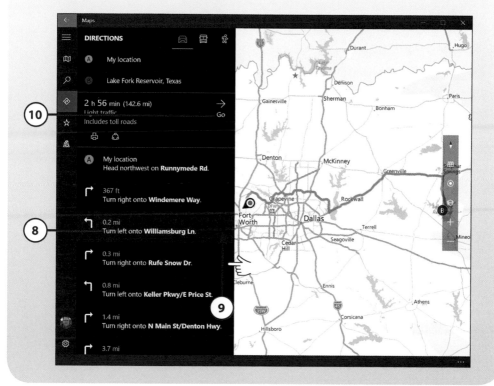

Updating Maps and Using Offline Maps

You can ensure that you always have the latest map data by updating your maps. After you've updated your maps, you can download maps to be used when you're offline.

Updating Maps

Keeping your maps updated will ensure that you always have the latest map and traffic data.

1. Tap or click Settings.

2. Tap or click Download or Update Maps.

3. Tap or click Check Now to check for downloads and to update your maps. (If Settings has already found available updates you'll instead have the option to tap or click Install Now.)

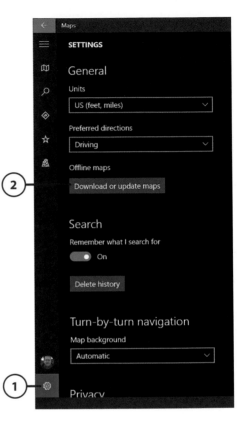

Downloading Maps

You can download maps so that you can use Maps when you're not online. This is useful if you are traveling and will be away from an Internet connection.

1. From the Offline Maps page in System Settings, tap or click Download Maps.

2. Tap or click a continent.

3. Tap or click a country.

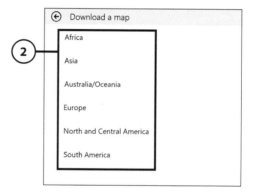

4. If your selected country requires it, tap or click a region, or tap or click All Regions to download the entire country.

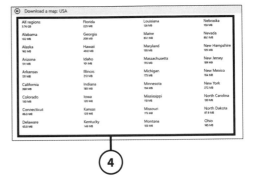

Close Maps When Downloading

Windows 10 will only download offline maps while the Maps app is closed. To ensure that your download completes, close the Maps application after you start your download.

Format text just the way you want it.

Share documents and collaborate with others.

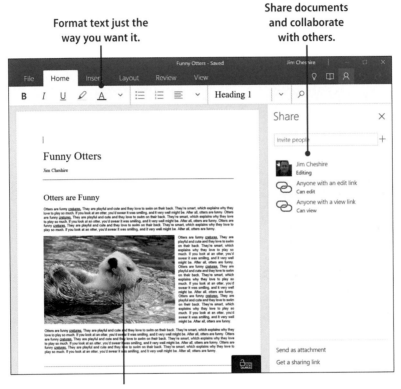

Add pictures and edit them right within Word.

If you need to create documents for any purpose, Microsoft Word is a great way to do it, and Microsoft Word Mobile is a great way to do it on your tablet. In this chapter, you learn about

→ Creating, Opening, and Saving Documents

→ Formatting Text

→ Adding and Formatting Pictures

→ Sharing Documents

→ Reading in Word Mobile

Creating Documents with Microsoft Word Mobile

Microsoft Word is a word processor with a long history. Along with Windows 10, Microsoft introduced a new mobile version of Word that offers cloud integration and a universal experience across devices. It's designed to work with documents that are stored in OneDrive (so that you can access those documents from any connected device). Even better, Word running on your Windows 10 tablet looks and works just like Word running on your Windows Phone or an iPhone, an Android phone, an iPad, and so forth.

In this chapter, my goal is to give you a taste of what you can do in Word Mobile. Obviously, I can't cover the entire application, but if you are interested in learning all about Word, I encourage you to read *My Office 2016*, Que Publishing, Fall 2015.

Creating, Opening, and Saving Documents

Word Mobile offers a wide array of templates you can use to create documents of all types. As you're creating your document, it gets saved to your OneDrive automatically so that it's available on any other devices you use. However, if you choose to, you can save a copy to another location.

Installing Word Mobile

Before you go further in this chapter, you should install Microsoft Word Mobile from the Windows Store. It's available as a free download.

Creating a New Blank Document

You can create a new blank document so that you can start from scratch without any included content.

1. Tap or click the Search field.

2. Enter **Word** and press Enter.

3. Tap or click Word Mobile to open Word Mobile.

4. Tap or click In OneDrive if you want to change the location for your new document.

5. Tap or click This PC > Documents to save the new document in the Documents library on your tablet.

6. Tap or click Select a Different Location if you want to choose a different folder for your document.

7. Tap or click Blank Document to create a new document.

8. Tap the document name to rename your document.

9. Enter a new name for your document and press Enter.

Using OneDrive

If you want to be able to access your document from other devices, you should create your document in OneDrive. Word Mobile will look for documents in OneDrive by default.

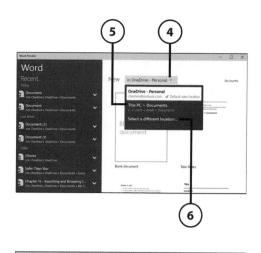

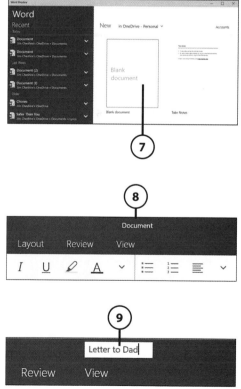

Creating a Document from a Template

Word Mobile comes with an assortment of templates to get you started on creating your document. Templates range from lists and journals to newsletters and resumes.

1. Launch Word Mobile from the Start menu.

2. Swipe up or scroll down to view additional templates.

3. Tap or click a template to create a new document based on that template.

Pinning Word Mobile

If you use Word Mobile a lot, you might want to consider pinning it to the Taskbar or the Start menu. For information on how to do that, see Chapter 3, "Using and Customizing the Start Menu and Taskbar."

Saving Documents

By default, Word Mobile automatically saves your document to OneDrive as you are working on it, assuming you chose to create your document on your OneDrive. If you want to, you can also save the document elsewhere.

1. Tap or click File.

2. Tap or click Save.

3. Tap or click Save a Copy of This File.

4. Navigate to the location where you want to save the file.

5. Enter a new name or accept the current document name.

6. Tap or click Save a Copy.

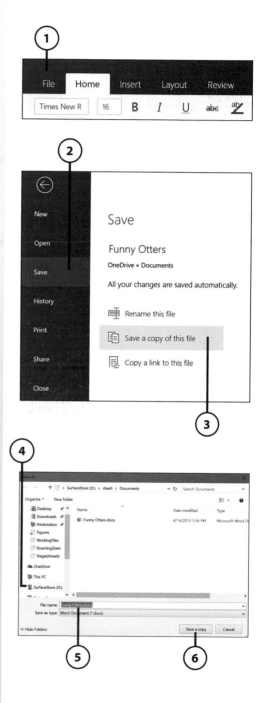

It's Not All Good

AutoSave Location Changes with New Copy

When you save a copy of your document to a new location, any changes you make to the document will be automatically saved to the new location from that point on. If you want your changes to be automatically saved to OneDrive again, make sure you open the document that's on your OneDrive before you start making edits again.

Opening Documents

When you open Word Mobile, you are provided with a list of documents you've recently worked on. You can also open documents that are not on the list.

Opening Documents

If you're currently working on a document and you want to open another document, you can tap or click File and then Open to open a document. After you do that, the steps to open the document are the same steps I've outlined here.

1. Tap or click a document in the Recent list to open that document.

2. Tap or click Browse to browse for a document that's not listed.

3. Browse to the folder that contains the document you want to open.

4. Tap or click the document.

5. Tap or click Open Document.

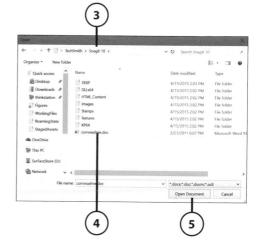

Managing Recent Documents

As you saw earlier, Word Mobile keeps a list of documents you've worked on recently so that you can access them quickly. You can remove documents from this list. You can also pin a document to the list so that it doesn't get moved off the list as you work on new documents.

Removing a document from the Recent list doesn't delete the document; it simply removes it from the list. If you want to open the document later, you'll need to browse to it.

1. Tap or click the down arrow to the right of the document you want to remove.

2. Tap or click Remove from List to remove the document from the Recent list.

3. Tap or click Pin to pin the document to the Recent list so that it will not be automatically removed as you work on new documents.

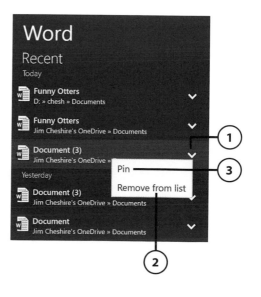

Formatting Text

Word Mobile offers features that make it easy to format text the way you want. In addition to directly formatting text by making it bold, italicized, and so forth, you can also apply a *style* to text so that the text takes on predefined formatting that is based on the style you apply.

Formatting Text

You can change the font, the font size, the style and color of the text, and so forth.

1. Select the text you want to format.

2. Tap or click Home.

3. Tap or click the Font drop-down, and then tap or click a font to change the font of the selected text.

4. Tap or click the Font Size drop-down, and tap or click a size to change the font size.

5. Tap or click Bold to make the selected text bold.

6. Tap or click Italic to make the selected text italic.

7. Tap or click Underline to underline the selected text.

8. Tap or click Strikethrough to strike through the selected text.

9. Tap or click Highlight to highlight the selected text in yellow.

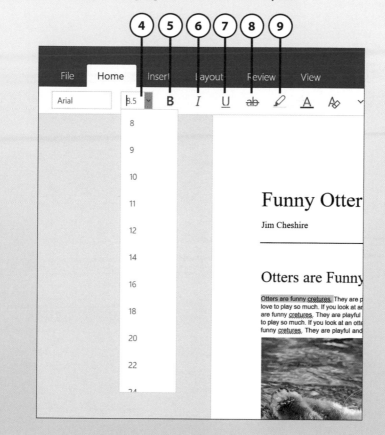

10. Tap or click Font Color, and then tap a new color for the selected text.

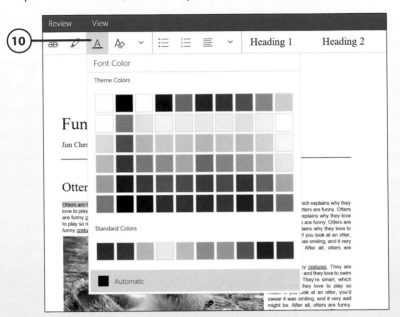

11. Open the Font menu.

12. Tap or click the down arrow, and then tap or click Subscript to make the selected text subscript.

13. Tap or click Superscript to make the selected text superscript.

Formatting New Text

If you want to format new text that you are about to add to a document, apply the formatting at the point where you are about to enter text and the new text you enter will have that formatting applied.

Formatting Text Using Styles

You can use a style to easily apply formatting to text. A *style* is a predefined set of formatting that you can apply to any text in one step. Styles are applied to an entire paragraph, so you don't have to select text before you apply a style.

1. Tap or click to place your insertion point inside the paragraph that you want to format with a style.

2. Tap or click Styles.

3. Tap or click the style you want to apply.

Adding and Formatting Pictures

Pictures can make a document more interesting. Word Mobile has plenty of tools to allow you to add and format pictures in a document.

Adding a Picture

You can add a picture from OneDrive or from your PC.

1. Place the insertion point where you want the picture to be.

2. Tap or click Insert.

3. Tap or click Pictures.

4. Navigate to the folder that contains the picture you want to add to the document.

5. Tap or click the picture to select it.

6. Tap or click Insert.

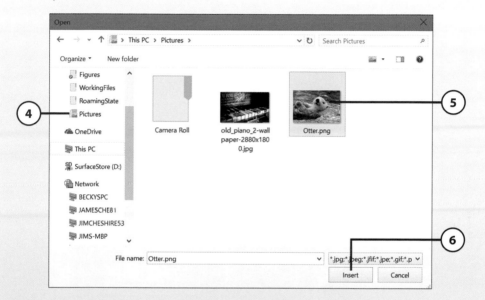

7. Tap or click and then drag one of the sizing handles to change the picture's size.

Applying a Picture Style

Much like the styles you can apply to text, picture styles enable you to apply formatting to a picture with a single tap or click.

1. Tap or click to select the picture to which you want to apply a style.

2. Tap or click Styles.

3. Swipe up or scroll down to see additional styles.

4. Tap or click the desired style.

Positioning a Picture

Word Mobile makes it easy to position a picture exactly where you want it. As you reposition a picture, the text in your document will automatically flow around it.

1. Tap or click your picture to select it.

2. Tap or click Wrap Text.

3. Tap or click a text-wrapping option for your picture using the icons as a guide.

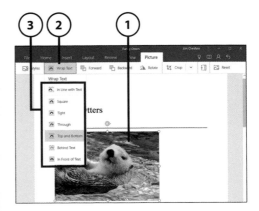

4. Tap or click and hold and then drag the picture to the desired location. Text will wrap around the picture automatically based on the setting you chose in step 3.

Wrapping Text

In the figure I've included, I am using the Square wrapping style. This style causes text to wrap around all sides of my picture.

Rotating a Picture

You might want to rotate a picture that you've inserted into your document. Word Mobile provides tools that make rotating pictures easy.

1. Tap or click the picture you want to rotate.

2. Tap or click Rotate.

3. Tap or click a rotation option to rotate the picture.

Fine Rotation Control

If you need to rotate a picture less than 90 degrees, you can tap or click the picture and drag the circular rotation control.

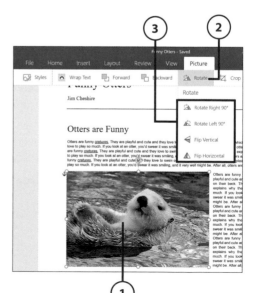

Cropping a Picture

You can crop a picture from within Word Mobile if you want to use only part of the picture in your document.

1. Tap or click the picture you want to crop.

2. Tap or click Crop.

3. Drag the handles to frame the portion of the picture that you want to keep.

4. Tap or click Crop again to complete the cropping.

Undoing

If you want to undo a crop to a picture, tap or click Reset and then tap or click Reset Size.

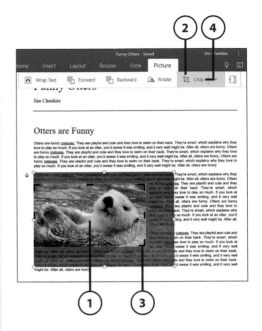

Sharing Documents

As long as your document is saved in OneDrive, you can share it easily with others and allow them to either view or edit the document. You can also get a link that allows either editing or viewing that you can share with anyone. Finally, you can send your document as an attachment in an email message.

Inviting Others to a Document

When you send an invitation to a document, you are giving the recipient permission to either view or edit the document directly on your OneDrive.

1. With the document that you want to share open in Word Mobile, tap or click Share.

2. Enter the email address of the person you want to share the document with.

3. Tap or click Can Edit, and tap or click Can View if you don't want to other person to be able to edit your document.

4. Enter a message.

5. Tap or click Share.

Microsoft Account Required

You can send an invitation to an email address that's not a Microsoft account, but in order for the recipient to access your document, they must sign in with a Microsoft account.

Getting Sharing Links to a Document

You might want to give someone a link that enables them to either edit or view your document using a method other than email. For example, you might be on a Skype call with someone and you want to send them a link that will allow them to edit your document. In that situation, you can get a sharing link that you can share with them.

1. From the Share pane, tap or click Get a Sharing Link. (If prompted, click Create an Edit link as well.)

2. Tap or click Copy to copy a link to the clipboard that enables the user to edit the document.

3. Tap or click Create a View-Only Link to get a link that enables the user to only view the document.

4. Tap or click Copy to copy the view-only link to your clipboard. You can then paste it wherever you need it.

Stop Sharing

The Share pane will show you with whom a document is shared. If you want to stop sharing with someone (including stopping sharing using a link), you can tap or click on the person in the Share pane and then tap or click Stop Sharing.

Sharing a Document Using Email

You can send a copy of your document to someone in email. When you use this method, the document is sent as an attachment. The user does not have access to the original document stored in OneDrive or elsewhere.

1. From the Share pane, tap or click Send as Attachment.

2. From the Windows 10 Share pane, tap or click Mail.

3. Enter an email address to which you want to send the document.

4. Enter a message.

5. Tap or click Send.

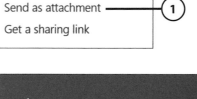

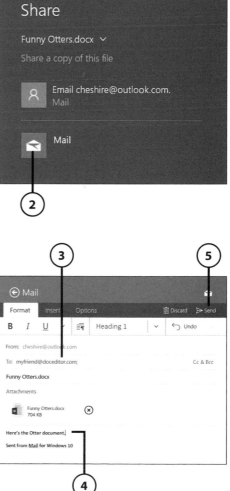

Reading in Word Mobile

Word Mobile offers a unique Read view that makes it easy to read Word documents on a tablet. You can easily swipe through a document to move from page to page. Read view also enables you to access the Insights feature in Word Mobile that makes it easy to get more information about topics in a document.

Using Read View

Once you switch to Read view, you'll have the ability to navigate a document much more easily using touch.

1. With your document open in Word Mobile, tap or click Read to switch to Read view.

2. Swipe left and right to move from page to page.

3. If you use a mouse or trackpad, click the left and right arrows to move from page to page.

4. To exit Read mode, tap or click the ellipsis.

5. Tap or click Edit to switch back to Edit mode.

Customizing Read View

After you click the ellipsis in step 4, you'll see options to change font size, background color, and more while in Read view. You can use these options to customize Read view to make it easier to read without modifying the original document.

Using Insights

The Insights feature enables you to use the Internet to get more information about topics in a document.

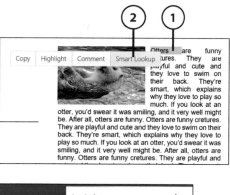

1. While in Read view, tap and hold or right-click on a word that you want more information on.

2. Tap or click Smart Lookup from the menu.

3. Swipe up and down to read more in the Insights pane.

4. Tap More to get additional information.

5. Tap outside the Insights pane to close it.

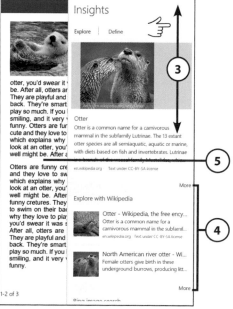

Format data
exactly the way
you want it.

Compute values
using formulas.

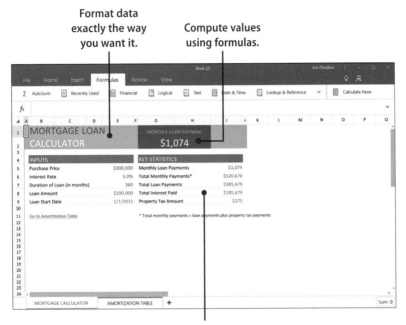

Insert and edit
tables of data.

Microsoft Excel Mobile makes it easy to create and edit Excel workbooks anywhere you go right on your tablet. In this chapter, you learn about

→ Creating, Opening, and Saving Workbooks

→ Entering Data

→ Working with Sheets

→ Creating Formulas

→ Sharing Workbooks

Crunching Numbers with Microsoft Excel Mobile

Microsoft Excel Mobile is designed to make working with numerical data quick and easy. Over the years, Excel has made complex numerical data analysis easier and easier, and the latest version makes that even easier by focusing on a touch interface. As you'll see in this chapter, you can use Excel Mobile for everything—from planning your household budget to keeping track of gifts you're buying for that special occasion.

Creating, Opening, and Saving Workbooks

Before we get started, it's important for you to understand some Excel vernacular. A *workbook* is a file that opens in Excel. Each workbook contains one or more *sheets* that are represented by tabs within the workbook. You can use sheets to organize data within your workbook. Each sheet is made up of rows and columns of *cells*.

Now that you know these basics, let's see how you can work with workbooks in Excel Mobile.

Creating a Workbook

Excel Mobile includes a large number of templates you can use to create workbooks. These templates vary from simple lists to complex sales trackers. You can also create a blank workbook so that you can start from scratch.

1. From the Start menu, tap or click Excel Mobile to launch the app.

2. Tap or click the location drop-down and choose a new location for your workbook if you want to. (By default, Excel Mobile stores files in OneDrive.)

3. Swipe up or scroll down to see additional workbook templates.

4. Tap or click a template to create a new workbook based on that template.

OneDrive and Excel Mobile

It's recommended that you store your Excel Mobile workbooks in OneDrive because you can then access them from any device. You'll also be able to share workbooks with others if they are stored in OneDrive.

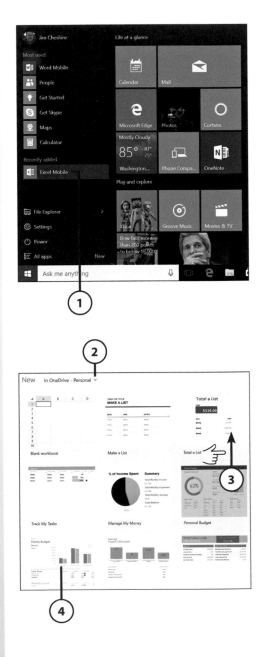

Opening Workbooks

If you want to work on a workbook that you've saved, you'll need to open it first.

1. From within Excel Mobile, tap or click File.

2. If your workbook is listed in the list of recent workbooks, tap or click it to open it.

3. If your workbook isn't listed, tap or click Browse.

4. Browse to the location where your workbook is saved.

5. Tap or click your workbook to select it.

6. Tap or click Open Workbook.

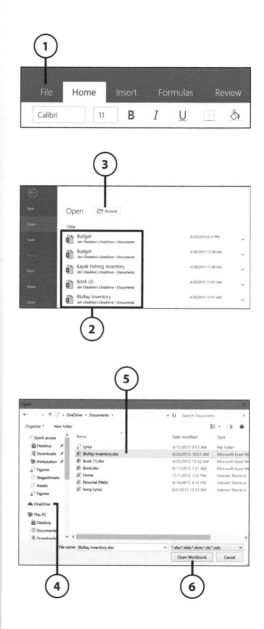

Saving Workbooks

Excel Mobile saves your workbooks automatically as you work on them. However, if you want to, you can choose to save a copy of your workbook in a different location.

1. From within Excel Mobile, tap or click File.

2. Tap or click Save.

3. Tap or click Save a Copy of This File.

4. Browse to the location where you want to save the workbook.

5. Enter a new filename or accept the existing filename.

6. Tap or click Save a Copy.

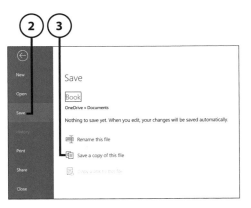

Entering Data

You can add both text and numbers to your Excel Mobile workbook. You can adjust the width of columns to account for your data, and you can format your data using fonts, font sizes, styles, and colors. You can also have Excel Mobile format your data for you in a table with one easy step. You can organize your data by creating new sheets within your workbook.

Adding Data

You add data to your Excel Mobile workbook by clicking in a cell and typing to enter your data.

1. Tap or click within the cell where you want your data to be added.

2. Enter the text or numbers you want to add.

3. To modify data in a cell, tap and hold or double-click on the cell.

4. Modify the data in the cell and press Enter.

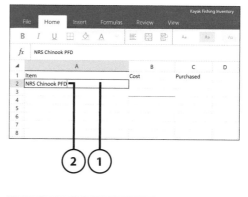

Excel Mobile Is Smart

Excel Mobile is pretty smart when it comes to understanding your data. For example, if you enter "$100" in a cell, Excel Mobile knows that you are entering data formatted as currency, and it will automatically recognize that cell as having a monetary value. The benefit of this will become obvious to you when you read the "Creating Formulas" section later in this chapter.

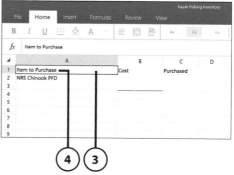

Resizing a Column

You might find that the data you enter in a cell is wider than the column that the cell is in. When that happens, you can adjust the width of the column. (You can also, naturally, make a column narrower if you want to.)

Resizing Using a Mouse

These steps walk you through resizing a column using touch. If you want to resize a column using a mouse, move your mouse pointer to the column header's right edge until you see a mouse pointer with an arrow pointing left and right. You can then click and drag to resize the column.

1. Tap the header of the column you want to resize.

2. Tap and hold the sizing handle.

3. Drag the handle left to make the column more narrow.

4. Drag the handle to the right to make the column wider.

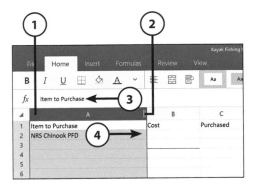

Changing Data Formatting

Just because you're typically dealing with numbers in Excel Mobile doesn't mean you can't make your data look pretty. Excel Mobile has plenty of features to make formatting your data easy.

Formatting Is Applied to Cells

Formatting in Excel Mobile is applied to cells; therefore, you cannot format some parts of a cell differently than other parts. If, for example, you want to make text in a cell bold, all the text in the cell must be bolded. You cannot bold only some of the characters within the cell.

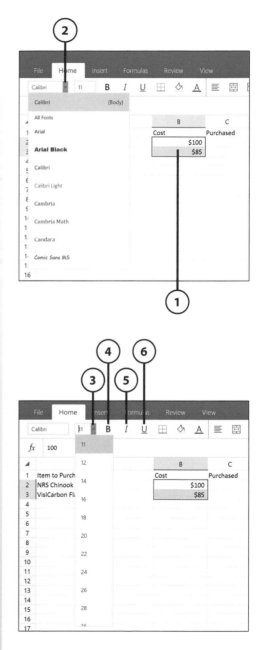

1. Tap or click the cell or cells you want to format. (Tap or click and drag to select multiple contiguous cells.)

2. Tap or click the Font drop-down, and then tap or click a font to change the font.

3. Tap or click the Font Size drop-down, and then select a new font size to change the size of text.

4. Tap or click Bold to make the text bold.

5. Tap or click Italic to make the text italic.

6. Tap or click Underline to underline the text.

7. Tap or click the Borders drop-down to add a border to the cells and to change the line style and line color of the border.

8. Tap or click the Fill Color drop-down, and then tap or click a color to add a fill color to the cells. (Tap or click No Fill to remove a fill color.)

9. Tap or click the Font Color drop-down, and then tap or click a color to change the font color.

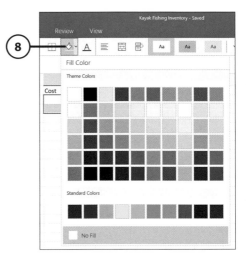

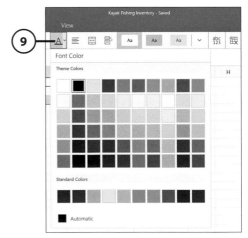

10. Tap or click Choose Text Alignment, and then tap or click an alignment option to align the text in the cell horizontally and vertically.

11. Tap or click the Cell Styles drop-down, and then tap or click a style to format cells using a preformatted style.

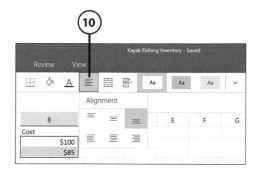

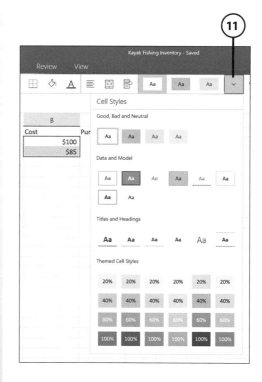

12. Tap or click Number Format to select a number format for the data in the selected cells.

Formatting Entire Rows or Columns

If you want to format an entire row or column, you can tap or click the row number or the column header to select the entire row or column in step 1. Any formatting that you apply will then format the entire row or column.

Why Choose a Number Format?

Step 12 shows you how to choose a number format for one or more cells. If you choose a number format for your cells, Excel Mobile will automatically format data you enter to match the chosen format.

Adding a Table

A lot of the data you will use in Excel Mobile is likely well-suited to a table. When you format tabular data as a table, Excel Mobile will format your table with a color scheme that makes it easier to visualize the data. You will also have the ability to filter and sort information based on columns.

1. Tap or click any cell containing data.

2. Tap or click Insert.

3. Tap or click Table.

4. Excel Mobile will automatically detect whether your table uses headers. If Excel Mobile fails to recognize that your table does have headers in the first row, tap or click Table Has Headers to check the box.

5. Tap any cell to deselect the table.

	File	Home	Insert	Formulas	Review	View	Table

Insert Above   Insert Below   Insert Left   Insert Right   De

fx   Category

	A	B	C
1	Category ▼	Budget ▼	Actual ▼
2	Housing	1500	1500
3	Groceries ✓ Table has headers	250	280
4	Telephone	38	38
5	Electric	65	78
6	Water/Sewer/Trash	25	21
7	Cable TV	75	85
8	Internet	60	65
9	Insurance	255	255
10			
11			

5   4

6. To sort or filter based on a column, tap or click the arrow at the right edge of the header cell.

7. Tap or click A to Z to sort the table in ascending order by the values in the column.

8. Tap or click Z to A to sort the table in descending order by the values in the column.

9. Tap or click one or more values to see only data for the values you select.

10. Tap Select All to see data for all values.

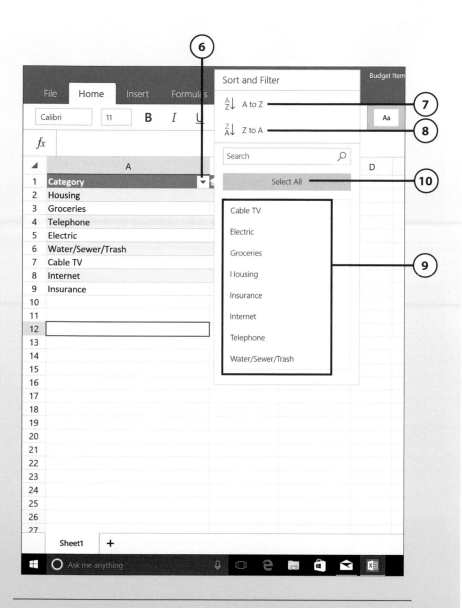

Alternating Colors

Notice that Excel Mobile added alternating colors to the rows in your table. If you add new data to your table, Excel Mobile will automatically add highlight colors to the rows of the table.

Working with Sheets

You might find it convenient to organize data in your workbook using sheets. Excel Mobile creates one sheet by default (called Sheet1), but you can create additional sheets as needed. You can also color-code your sheets, rename sheets, and organize sheet tabs.

Creating Sheets

You can create new sheets to better organize data that you're entering into your Excel workbook. For example, if you're creating a yearly budget, you might want to have one sheet for each month of expenses.

1. Tap or click the + sign at the bottom of the Excel window.

2. Tap or click a sheet's tab to change to that sheet.

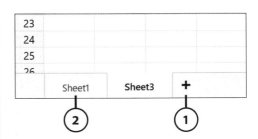

Renaming Sheets

Excel uses a generic name for new sheets, so you'll likely want to rename your sheets to a more descriptive name.

1. Tap and hold or right-click on a sheet name.

2. Tap or click Rename.

3. Enter a new name for the sheet and press Enter.

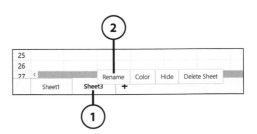

Faster Renaming

You can also double-tap or double-click a sheet to rename it.

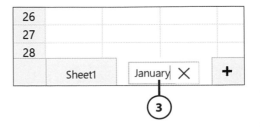

Coloring Sheets

You can further categorize sheets by applying a color to the sheet's tab. When a tab is not selected, the color you choose will appear in a border at the top of the tab. When you select the tab, the sheet's name will appear in the color you selected and a colored border at the bottom of the sheet.

1. **Tap and hold or right-click on a sheet's tab.**

2. **Tap or click Color.**

3. **Tap a color for the sheet's tab.**

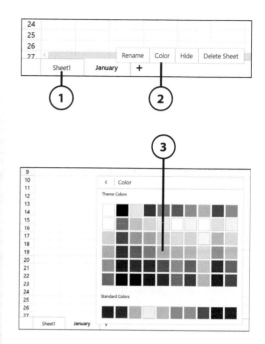

Organizing Sheets

You can change the order of sheet tabs so that your sheets are in the order you choose.

1. **Tap and hold or click and hold on the sheet you want to move.**

2. **Drag the sheet to the desired position and release your finger or mouse button.**

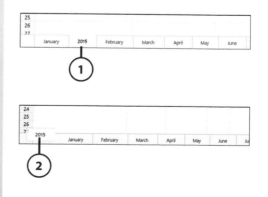

Deleting Sheets

If you no longer need a sheet, you can delete it. Deleting a sheet also deletes all the data on that sheet.

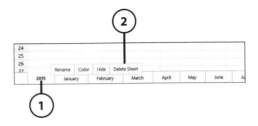

1. Tap and hold or right-click on the sheet you want to delete.

2. Tap or click Delete Sheet.

3. Tap or click Delete to confirm that you want to delete the sheet.

Canceling a Delete

If you change your mind and don't want to delete the sheet, simply tap or click anywhere outside the confirmation dialog to cancel the delete.

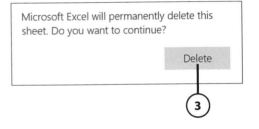

Creating Formulas

The true power of Excel Mobile is realized when you start using formulas. Excel Mobile is kind of like a super calculator in that it has the capability to calculate and analyze numerical data just about any way you can imagine. It does that with formulas, and Excel Mobile makes it easy to use formulas, even when you're not a math whiz.

You can enter formulas directly, or you can use the Formulas bar or Formulas ribbon for easier entry.

Directly Entering a Formula

You might want to enter a formula directly if you're using a very simple formula to do something such as add some numbers together. In this step-by-step, you'll see how to enter a formula that sums a group of cells.

1. Tap or click the cell where you want the result of your formula to be entered.

2. Type **=sum(** in the cell.

3. Tap or click in the first cell containing the numbers you want to add.

4. Tap or click the blue handle and drag it to enclose all the cells you want added.

5. Press Enter to add your formula and see the total of the numbers.

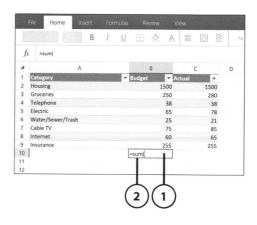

Formulas in Action

If you change one of the numbers used in your formula, Excel Mobile will automatically change the total that it computed. This is the power of Excel Mobile in action.

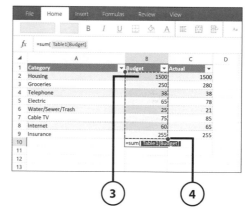

More Formulas

You might have noticed that Excel Mobile displayed a list of formulas after you entered the SUM formula in step 2. You can select any of these formulas to see information on how the formula works and how you can use it in your workbooks. This example was only a small example of the true power of Excel Mobile.

Using the Formulas Toolbar

In the example you just completed, you knew to use the SUM formula because I told you to do that. There might be times when you don't know the name of a formula, and in those situations, the Formulas toolbar is a great solution.

The Formulas toolbar has buttons that represent categories of formulas so that you can find exactly the formula you need.

1. Tap or click the cell where you want the formula's result to be entered.

2. Tap or click Formulas to activate the Formulas toolbar.

3. Tap or click a formula category, or tap or click the down arrow for more categories.

4. Tap or click the formula you want to use.

Lookup & Reference	∨	Calculate Now

< | Statistical

AVEDEV	>
AVERAGE	>
AVERAGEA	>
AVERAGEIF	>
AVERAGEIFS	>
BETA.DIST	>
BETA.INV	>
BINOM.DIST	>
BINOM.DIST.RANGE	>
BINOM.INV	>
CHISQ.DIST	>
CHISQ.DIST.RT	>
CHISQ.INV	>

4

5. Tap or click the cell that contains the first number to be used in your formula.

6. If additional numbers are needed, tap or click the cell containing the additional number or select multiple cells using the handle.

File	Home	Insert	Formulas	Review	View

∑ AutoSum ☆ Recently Used 📇 Financial ? Logical

fx =AVERAGE(B2:B4 , number2 , …)

◢	A	B	C
1	Angler ▼	Pounds of Bass ▼	
2	Kevin VanDam	32	⑤
3	Timmy Horton	28	
4	Jason Christie	28	⑥
5	Shaw Grigsby	27	
6	Gerald Swindle	25	
7	Skeet Reese	23	
8	Brent Ehrler	23	
9	Tommy Biffle	23	
10	AVERAGE POUNDS	ERAGE(B2:B4 , nu	
11			

7. Press Enter to accept the formula and display the result.

File	Home	Insert	Formulas	Review	View

Σ AutoSum   ☆ Recently Used   🗐 Financial   [?] Logical

fx

◢	A	B	C
1	**Angler** ▼	**Pounds of Bass** ▼	
2	Kevin VanDam	32	
3	Timmy Horton	28	
4	Jason Christie	28	
5	Shaw Grigsby	27	
6	Gerald Swindle	25	
7	Skeet Reese	23	
8	Brent Ehrler	23	
9	Tommy Biffle	23	
10	AVERAGE POUNDS	26	
11			
12			

⑦

Sharing Workbooks

Excel Mobile enables you to easily share workbooks with others. You can share a workbook with other people you are collaborating with on the workbook. You also can use sharing to send an email with the workbook attached to it in case you need to send the workbook to someone.

Sharing features in Excel Mobile are identical to the sharing features in the other Office apps. You can find out how to use these features by reading the section called "Sharing Documents" in Chapter 18, "Creating Documents with Microsoft Word Mobile."

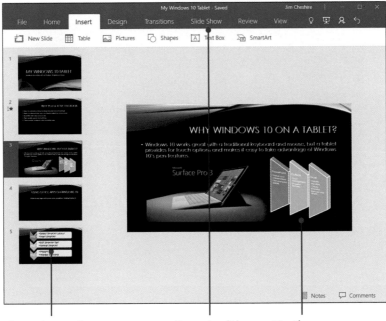

Create interesting content using text, pictures, and SmartArt.

Present a slide show complete with slide transitions.

Use themes to give your presentation a polished look.

Presenting your ideas using PowerPoint can open up new possibilities for getting your point across. In this chapter, you learn about using PowerPoint Mobile. You learn about

→ Creating, Opening, and Saving Presentations

→ Creating Slides and Content

→ Using SmartArt

→ Presenting with PowerPoint Mobile

Presenting with Microsoft PowerPoint Mobile

Microsoft PowerPoint Mobile makes it easy to create compelling presentations on any topic. By combining interesting content with attractive themes and transitions, you can keep your audience's attention while getting your point across.

Office 365 Required

PowerPoint Mobile requires an Office 365 subscription. You can find out about purchasing an Office 365 subscription at http://products.office.com.

In this chapter, you learn how you can use PowerPoint Mobile to create a presentation and how you can use the unique capabilities of your tablet to present your presentation in a way that will impress your audience.

Creating, Opening, and Saving Presentations

PowerPoint files are called *presentations*. As you work on your presentation, PowerPoint Mobile automatically saves it to your OneDrive; however, you can save a copy somewhere else if you'd like to.

Creating a Presentation

When you create a presentation, you can choose between multiple templates that will apply graphics and colors to your presentation. You can also create a blank presentation and set the colors and add graphics yourself.

1. From the Start menu, tap or click PowerPoint Mobile to launch the app.

2. Tap or click In OneDrive - Personal to create your presentation somewhere other than on your OneDrive.

3. Swipe up or scroll down to see additional templates.

4. Tap or click a template that you like.

5. Tap or click the presentation name so that you can give it a unique name.

6. Enter a name for your presentation and press Enter.

OneDrive

It's recommended that you create your new presentation in OneDrive so that you can access it easily from other PCs and so that you can easily share it with others if you need to.

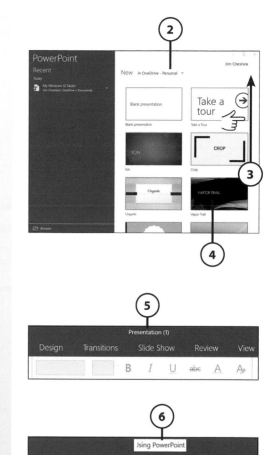

Opening a Presentation

You might not finish working on your presentation in one session, and that's okay. PowerPoint Mobile will save your presentation for you so that you won't lose any of your work when you close it. When you open PowerPoint Mobile again, you can open the presentation you were working on earlier.

1. Launch PowerPoint Mobile from the Start menu.

2. If your presentation is in the Recent list, tap or click it to open it.

3. If your presentation is not in the Recent list, tap or click Browse.

4. Browse to the location of your presentation.

5. Tap or click your presentation.

6. Tap or click Open Presentation.

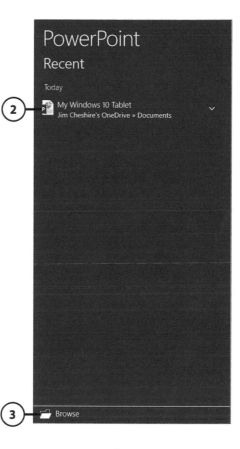

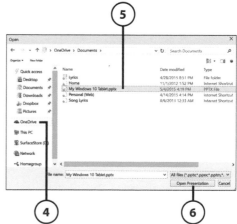

Saving a Presentation

PowerPoint Mobile automatically saves your presentation as you work on it, but there might be times when you want to save a copy manually. For example, if you want to change where PowerPoint Mobile saves your file when it performs an auto-save, you'll need to manually save your presentation to the new location.

1. Tap or click File.

2. Tap or click Save.

3. Tap or click Save a Copy of This File.

4. Browse to the location where you want to save the presentation.

5. Enter a new filename if you want to.

6. Tap or click Save a Copy.

Saving to a New Location

After you save your presentation to a new location, PowerPoint Mobile will begin auto-saving to the new location.

Sharing Presentations

After you save your presentation, you can easily share it with others using the sharing features built in to Office applications. For more information on how to do that, see "Sharing Documents" in Chapter 18, "Creating Documents with Microsoft Word Mobile."

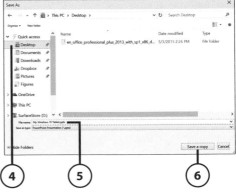

Creating Slides and Content

A PowerPoint presentation consists of one or more slides, and each slide can contain text, pictures, shapes, and so forth. PowerPoint Mobile offers pre-defined layouts for slides so that you can easily create content without having to build everything from scratch.

Adding a New Slide

A new slide can be easily added to your presentation. After you add a new slide, you can change its layout. I'll show you how to do that in the next step-by-step.

1. Tap or click the slide after which you want to insert a new slide.

2. Tap or click Home.

3. Tap or click New Slide to insert a new slide.

Changing a Slide's Layout

PowerPoint Mobile offers many pre-defined slide layouts so that you can quickly add new content without having to manually configure text areas and so forth. These predefined layouts also make it easy to maintain a consistent appearance in your presentation. You can easily change a slide's layout after you add it to your presentation.

Default Layout

By default, any new slide you add to your presentation will use a layout that provides a place for a title and an area for text.

1. Tap or click the slide for which you'd like to change the layout.

2. Tap or click Layout.

3. Swipe up or scroll down to see additional layouts.

4. Tap or click the desired layout to apply it to your slide. Any existing content on the slide will be moved to fit into the new layout.

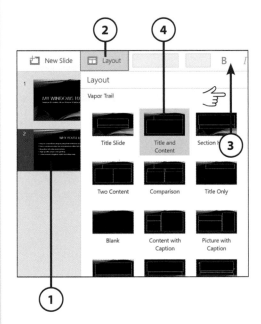

Trying a Layout

If you don't know which layout you'd like to use, feel free to try out a few. The current layout for the slide will be highlighted when you tap or click Layout, so you can always return to the original layout easily.

You're Not Locked In

You're not locked in to the configuration of a particular layout. After you apply a layout, you can remove or resize elements, add new elements, and so forth. You'll learn how to do that next.

Adding and Formatting Text

Even if you prefer a presentation that uses graphics and pictures, you'll still want to add some text to make your point. PowerPoint Mobile has powerful text features that are similar to Word Mobile's, so they should feel familiar to you.

You can add text to any slide using a Text Box. After you've added your text, you can configure that text to look just the way you want it to.

1. Tap or click the slide on which you would like to add text.

2. If the slide has a Text Box added automatically by the slide's layout, double-tap inside the box to replace the layout's text with your own text.

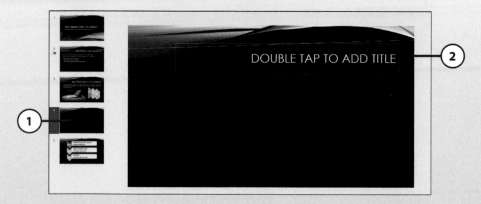

3. To add your own text, tap or click Insert.

4. Tap or click Text Box.

5. Tap and drag inside the Text Box to move it to a new position on the slide.

6. If you're using a mouse, hover over a border of the Text Box until you see a four-way arrow, and click and hold while dragging the Text Box to a new location.

7. Tap or click inside a Text Box and enter some text.

8. Tap or click and drag a sizing handle to resize a Text Box.

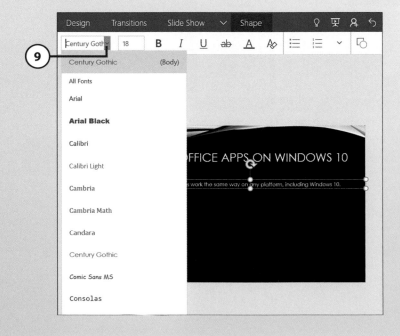

9. Tap or click the Font drop-down to select a new font for selected text or new text.

10. Tap or click the Font Size drop-down to select a new font size for selected text or new text.

11. Tap or click Bold to make selected text or new text bold.

12. Tap or click Italic to make selected text or new text italic.

13. Tap or click Underline to make selected text or new text underlined.

14. Tap or click Strikethrough to make selected text or new text strikethrough text.

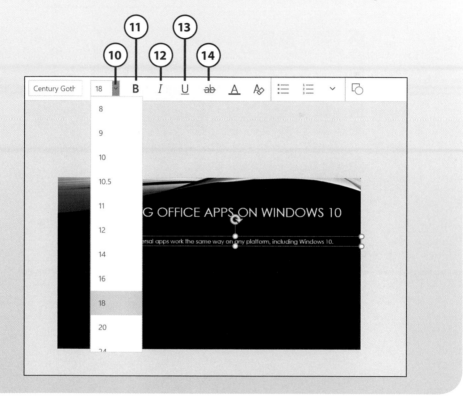

15. Tap or click the Font Color drop-down to select a new color for selected or new text.

16. Tap or click Clear All Formatting to clear any formatting you've applied to the selected text.

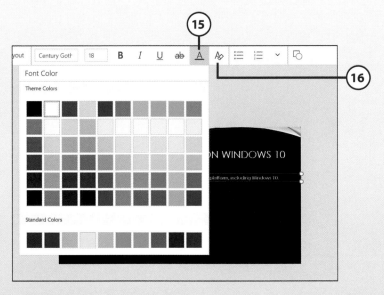

17. Tap or click Bullets to add a new bulleted list.

18. Tap or click Numbering to add a new numbered list.

19. Tap or click Paragraph Formatting to access additional formatting options for paragraphs.

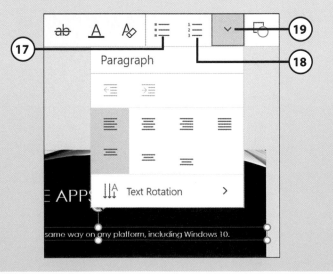

Inserting and Formatting Pictures

Pictures are an important part of any presentation. Pictures can be added from your tablet or from OneDrive. After you add a picture to a slide, you can format the picture using the tools provided by PowerPoint Mobile.

1. Tap or click the slide to which you want to add a picture.

2. Tap or click Insert.

3. Tap or click Pictures.

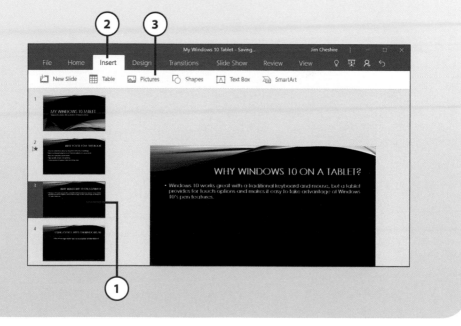

4. Browse to the picture you want to insert, and then tap or click it.

5. Tap or click Insert.

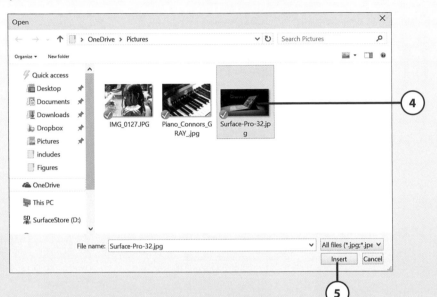

6. Tap or click and drag a sizing handle to resize the picture.

7. Tap or click and drag the picture to move it to a new location on the slide.

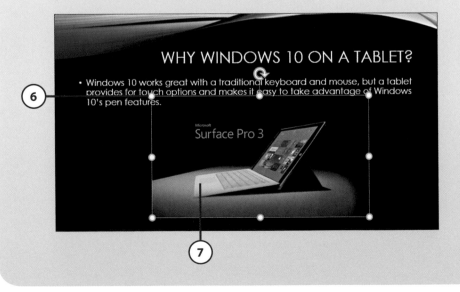

8. Tap or click Styles, and then tap or click a style to apply it to your picture.

9. Tap or click Forward to move the picture in front of other elements on the slide.

10. Tap or click Backward to move the picture behind other elements on the slide.

11. Tap or click Rotate to rotate the picture.

12. Tap or click Crop, and then drag the cropping handles to crop the picture.

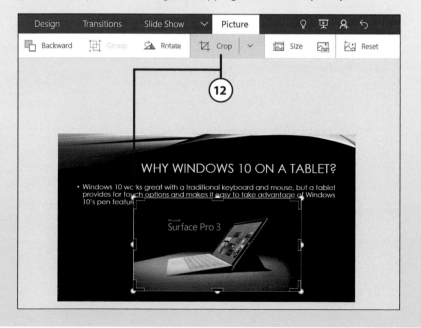

Using SmartArt

SmartArt makes it easy for anyone to add professional-looking diagrams to a presentation. You can choose from a large assortment of SmartArt diagrams, all of which can be customized for your particular needs.

Inserting SmartArt

PowerPoint Mobile's SmartArt assists in diagraming lists, processes, relationships, and more.

1. Tap or click the slide on which you want to insert SmartArt.

2. Tap or click Insert.

3. Tap or click SmartArt.

4. Tap or click a SmartArt category to see a list of diagrams you can add.

5. Tap or click a SmartArt diagram to insert it.

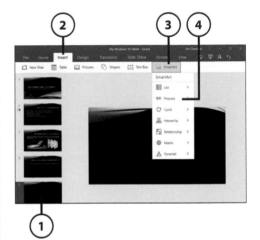

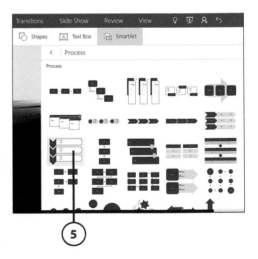

Editing SmartArt Text

SmartArt is made up of graphical and textual elements. You can edit SmartArt text directly on the SmartArt. You can also use the Text Pane to edit SmartArt text.

1. Tap or click the SmartArt whose text you want to edit.

2. Tap or click a text element and enter new text directly on the SmartArt.

3. To use the Text Pane, tap or click Show or Hide Text Pane.

4. Enter your text in the Text Pane.

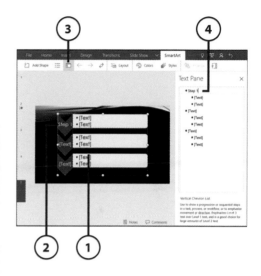

Formatting SmartArt

You're not stuck with the boring default look of your SmartArt. You can change the colors and the style to give your SmartArt an impressive look.

1. Tap or click the SmartArt you want to format.

2. Tap or click SmartArt (if it's not already selected).

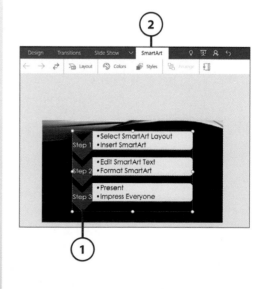

3. Tap or click Colors to apply a color scheme.

4. Swipe up or scroll down for additional color schemes.

5. Tap or click a color scheme to apply it.

6. Tap or click Styles.

7. Tap or click a style to apply it.

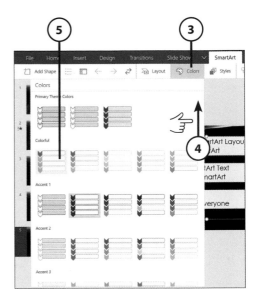

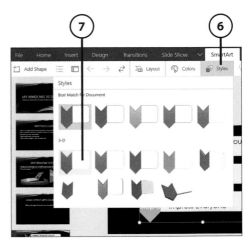

Presenting with PowerPoint Mobile

Once you've finished creating your presentation, you can present it in full-screen mode. You can also apply slide transitions to give your presentation a bit of flair.

Adding Transitions

Transitions are effects that happen when you move from slide to slide. Adding transitions can give your presentation a more polished look.

1. Tap or click the slide before which you want to add a transition.

2. Tap or click Transitions.

3. Tap or click a transition to apply it.

4. Tap or click the Transition drop-down to see more transitions that you can apply.

5. Swipe up or scroll down to see more transitions.

6. Tap or click a transition to apply it.

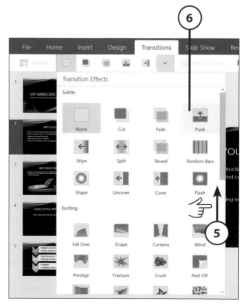

7. Tap or click Effect Options to see options for the selected transition.

8. Tap or click an effect to apply it.

Previewing Transitions

Transitions are visible only when you are presenting in Slide Show mode. However, you can preview a transition by tapping or clicking the Preview button on the Transition menu bar after inserting the transition.

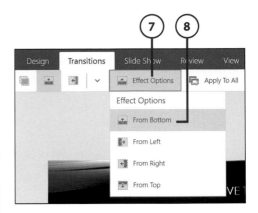

Using Slide Show

Slide Show enables you to present your presentation so that your slides fill the entire screen. Any transitions you applied will also be visible in Slide Show mode.

1. Tap or click Slide Show.

2. Tap or click From Beginning to start a slide show from the first slide.

3. Tap or click From Current Slide to start the slide show from the currently selected slide.

4. Swipe left or click to move forward one slide.

5. Swipe right to move back one slide.

6. Tap or click and hold to activate a virtual laser pointer that you can use to highlight things of interest on a slide.

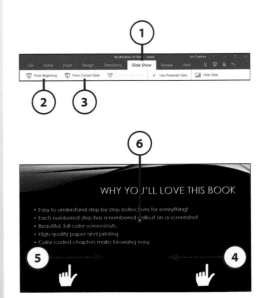

7. Right-click or tap above the current slide to display the inking controls.

8. Tap or click Ink Tools.

9. Tap or click a pen color to draw in that color on a slide.

10. Tap or click a highlighter color to highlight using that color on a slide.

11. Tap or click Eraser to erase previously added inking.

12. Tap or click Erase All to erase all previously added inking.

13. Tap or click End Show to end the slide show.

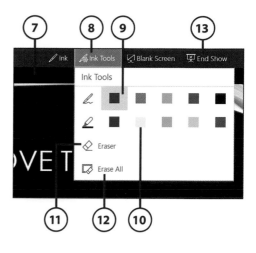

Use pictures to
make your notes
more effective.

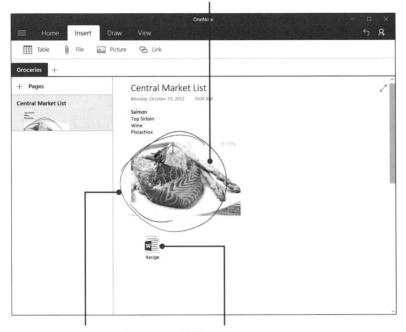

Create text notes and use
your finger or a stylus
to draw inside of your
notes.

Add files to your notes
and access them from
anywhere.

Microsoft OneNote is a powerful and easy-to-use application for keeping notes on just about everything. In this chapter, you learn about

→ Working with Notebooks

→ Creating and Organizing Sections

→ Creating and Editing Pages

Organizing Notes with Microsoft OneNote

Chances are you use your computer for taking notes. Maybe it's a shopping list or a list of things you need to take on your vacation. Whatever your purpose for taking notes, OneNote offers the tools you need to manage and organize your notes and to easily access them from any device.

OneNote and Office 365

Unlike the other Microsoft Office apps I've covered, OneNote does not require an Office 365 subscription. OneNote comes with Windows 10 and is available to use at no extra charge.

In this chapter, I show you the basics of OneNote as part of the universal Office apps. If you want to read a full guide on using OneNote 2016, read *Microsoft OneNote 2016 Step By Step* from Microsoft Press.

Working with Notebooks

OneNote stores notes in notebooks. You can have any number of notebooks in OneNote. Each notebook is organized into sections and pages. You'll learn how to use sections and pages later in this chapter.

You don't have to save a notebook when you are adding notes. OneNote takes care of that for you, and changes are synchronized to all your devices automatically.

Creating a Notebook

You'll need to create a new notebook before you can start taking notes.

1. Tap or click OneNote on the Start menu to launch OneNote.

2. Tap or click Show Navigation.

3. Tap or click the plus sign next to Notebooks.

4. Enter a name for your notebook and press Enter.

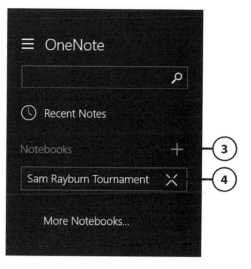

Switching, Opening, and Closing Notebooks

When I'm working in OneNote, I usually leave all my notebooks open so that I can switch to them and immediately see any changes I made on another device. In this section, you learn how you can switch between notebooks, how to open notebooks, and how to close a notebook.

1. Tap or click Show Navigation.

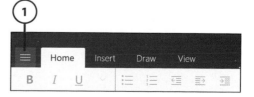

2. To switch to another open note-book, tap or click the notebook name.

3. To close a notebook, tap and hold or right-click the notebook name, and then tap or click Close This Notebook.

4. To open a notebook, tap or click More Notebooks.

5. Tap or click a notebook to open it.

Other Accounts

If your notebook is saved in another Microsoft account, you can tap or click Add Account to add that account and access your notebook.

Deleting Notebooks

You might have noticed that I didn't show you how to delete a notebook. If you want to delete a notebook, you'll have to browse to your OneDrive in a web browser and delete it from there. You cannot delete it from the OneNote app.

More Notebooks...

cheshire@outlook.com

Home   Song Lyrics

Add Account...

Cancel

⑤

Creating and Organizing Sections

Notebooks are organized using sections. Each section is represented as a tab in your notebook. You can organize these tabs, change the color of a tab, and more.

Creating a Section

When you create a new notebook, a section is created for you automatically. You can create additional sections as needed.

1. Tap or click the plus sign.

≡   Home   **Insert**   Draw   View

⊞ Table   📎 File   🖼 Picture   🔗 Link

+

Pages

①

2. Enter a name for the new section and press Enter.

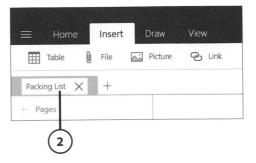

Changing a Section's Color

You can change the color of a section's tab. You might want to do this just because you like some colors more than others, but you also might want to color-code sections based on importance and so forth.

1. Tap and hold or right-click a section's tab.

2. Tap or click Section Color.

3. Tap or click the color you'd like to use for the section.

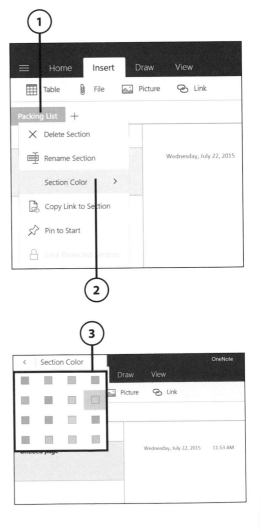

Renaming a Section

You might want to rename a section so that it's more descriptive of the content you're adding to the section.

1. Tap and hold or right-click the section's tab.

2. Tap or click Rename Section.

3. Enter a new name for the section and press Enter.

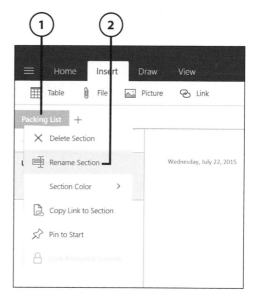

Changing the Order of Sections

You can change the order of sections to better organize your notebooks.

1. Tap or click and hold on the section you want to move.

2. Drag the section's tab to a new location and release it.

Deleting a Section

You can delete a section if you no longer need it. When you delete a section, it is permanently deleted. There isn't a way to recover a deleted section.

1. Tap and hold or right-click the section you want to delete.

2. Tap or click Delete Section.

3. Tap or click Delete Section to delete the section. (If you change your mind, just tap or click outside the box.)

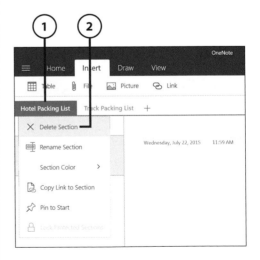

Creating and Editing Pages

Each section contains one or more pages. A page is represented as a tab along the left edge of the section. Notes that you add to a notebook are added to a page.

Creating a Page

You can create pages to better organize your notes. For example, if you're creating a notebook to keep track of notes for a trip, you might want to create a section for packing lists and then create a page for packing lists for each segment of your trip.

1. Tap or click the plus sign next to Pages.

2. Tap or click in the header section for the new page.

3. Enter a page title and press Enter.

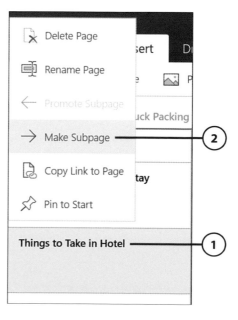

Creating a Subpage

A subpage is a page whose tab appears indented under another page. Using subpages is a great way to better organize larger pages.

No Connection Between Pages and Subpages

There isn't technically any connection between a page and a subpage. Subpages just provide a visual way to better organize your notes because the subpage's tab is indented.

1. Tap and hold or right-click the tab for the page that you want to make a subpage.

2. Tap or click Make Subpage.

Promoting a Subpage

If you want a subpage's tab to not be indented anymore, you can promote the page.

1. Tap and hold or right-click the tab for the subpage.

2. Tap or click Promote Subpage.

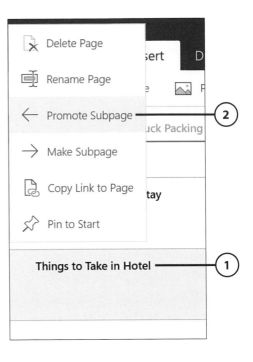

Renaming a Page

A page's name appears as a header for that page. It also appears in the page's tab. When you rename a page, the new name appears in both places.

1. Tap or click the heading on the page you want to rename.

2. Edit the name at the top of the page and press Enter.

Changing the Order of Pages

You might want to change the order of pages. For example, if there's a page that has especially important information in it, you might want that page's tab to appear at the top of the list of pages.

1. Tap or click and hold on the tab for the page you want to reorder.

2. Drag the tab to the desired location and release it.

Hotel Packing List	Truck Packing List
+ Pages	
Shopping List for Ho...	
Things to Take in Ho... ———— ①	

Hotel Packing List	Truck Packing List
+ Pages	
Things to Take in Ho...	
———— ②	
Shopping List for Ho...	

Deleting a Page

You can delete a page at any time. Be careful when deciding to delete a page because there isn't a way to undo it.

1. Tap and hold or right-click the tab for the page you want to delete.

2. Tap or click Delete Page.

3. Tap or click Delete Page to confirm that you want to delete the page.

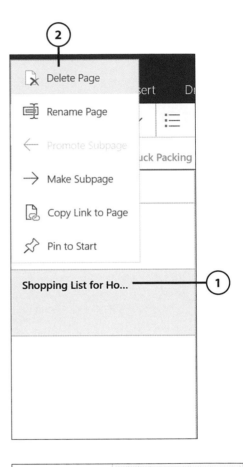

Adding Text to a Page

OneNote is very much like Word or any other word processor. You can easily format text the way you want it.

1. Tap or click inside the page.

2. Enter text on your keyboard.

3. Tap or click Bold, Italic, or Underline to stylize the text.

4. Tap or click Bulleted List to make a bulleted list.

5. Tap or click Numbered List to make a numbered list.

6. Tap or click Decrease Indent or Increase Indent to format the indentation for text.

7. Tap or click Tag as To Do to tag the selected line as a To Do item.

To Do Items

A To Do item has a check box next to it that you can click to check. It's a convenient way to make a list that you can check items off of. In the shopping list I'm making, I've made each item a To Do item so that I can check them off when I've purchased them.

---

8. Tap or click Paragraph Formatting, and then tap or click Left, Center, or Right to align a paragraph.

9. Tap or click a tag to tag a paragraph with an icon.

Adding Pictures to a Page

Pictures are a great way to add a visual element to your notes. For example, if you're making a grocery list for a special dish, you might want to add a picture of the finished dish. If you're making a list of places you want to fish on a lake, you might want to add a picture showing the place instead of trying to describe it with text.

1. Tap or click the place in your page where you want to insert your picture.

2. Tap or click Insert.

3. Tap or click Picture.

4. Browse to your picture, and then tap or click it to select it.

5. Tap or click Open to insert the picture.

6. Drag the picture to move it on the page.

7. Tap or click and drag a sizing handle to resize the picture.

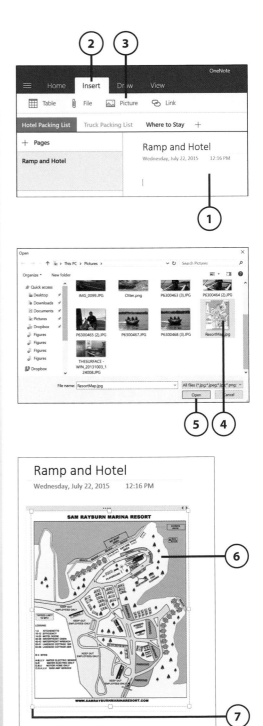

Adding Files to a Page

One of the great advantages to keeping notes in OneNote is that you can add virtually anything to a page. You can add a file to a page so that anyone viewing the page can access the file. You can also use this method to ensure you can access the file from any of your devices.

1. Tap or click the page where you want to insert a file.

2. Tap or click Insert.

3. Tap or click File.

4. Tap or click Insert as Attachment to attach the file to your notebook.

5. Tap or click Insert PDF Printout if your file is a PDF file and you want the contents of it added to your page.

6. Browse to the location of your file, and then tap or click it to select it.

7. Tap or click Open to insert your file.

Attached Files

Attached files show up as an icon on the page. Double-tapping or double-clicking the icon opens the file.

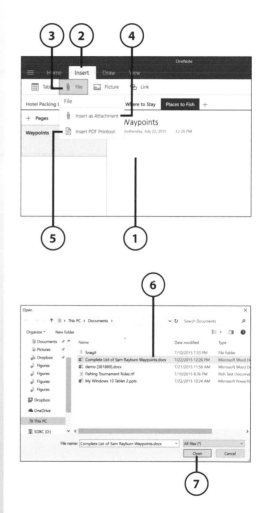

Drawing on a Page

One of the most natural ways to take notes is with pen and paper, and the drawing features of Windows 10 bring that experience to apps such as OneNote. You can draw on a page with a stylus or with your finger.

1. Tap or click Draw.

2. Tap or click Thin to draw with a thin pen.

3. Tap or click Medium to draw with a highlighter.

4. Tap or click Ink Color, and then tap or click a color to change ink color.

5. Tap or click Draw to draw with your finger instead of a stylus.

6. Tap or click the Eraser drop-down to erase.

7. Tap or click Medium Eraser to erase instead of draw.

8. Tap or click Stroke Eraser to erase entire strokes easily.

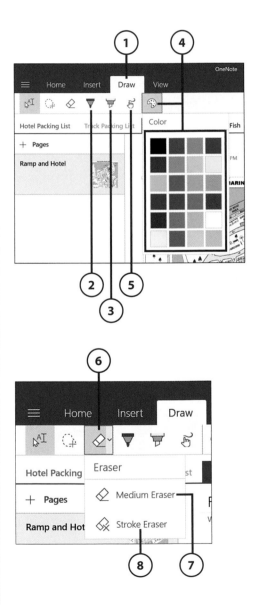

Filter to find just the
apps you want.

Update your apps.

Try and buy thousands
of apps in the Store.

The Windows Store offers hundreds of thousands of apps that you can install on your tablet. There are games, reference apps, weather and news apps, and much more. In this chapter, you learn about

→ Browsing the Store

→ Installing and Uninstalling Apps

→ Updating Apps

Enhancing Windows with Apps

Your Windows 10 tablet has enormous capabilities straight out of the box, but by adding additional apps from the Store, you can make it even more powerful. The Store makes it easy to browse for just the app you want, and once you find it, you can install it and update it right from within the Store.

Browsing the Store

The Store is the source of apps for your tablet. Apps are categorized for easier browsing, but you can also search for apps.

Browsing Categories

Browsing apps by category is one of the easiest ways to discover new apps for your tablet.

1. From the Start menu, tap or click Store.

2. In the Store, tap or click App Categories.

3. Tap or click a category to see apps in that category.

4. Slide up or scroll down to see additional categories.

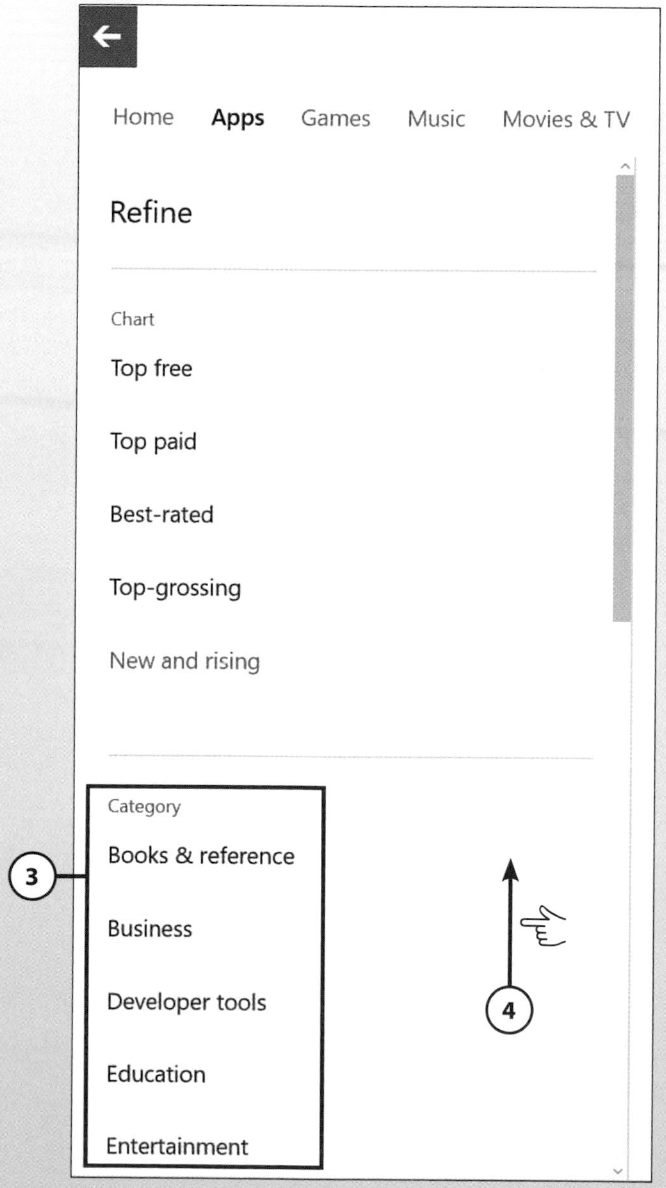

Home   **Apps**   Games   Music   Movies & TV

Refine

Chart

Top free

Top paid

Best-rated

Top-grossing

New and rising

Category

Books & reference

Business

Developer tools

Education

Entertainment

5. Slide up or scroll down to see additional apps in the selected category.

6. Tap or click a Chart option to refine the app list.

7. Tap or click the X to show all apps and return to the list of categories.

Exploring Apps

Plenty of information is available to help you decide whether you want to purchase an app. You can view screenshots, reviews of the app from other users, and more.

1. Tap or click an app in the Store that you're interested in.

2. Tap or click More to see more information on the app.

3. Swipe left or hover on the right edge of screenshots and click the right arrow to see additional screenshots.

4. Swipe up or scroll down to see reviews on the app.

5. Tap or click Yes or No to vote on whether a review is helpful.

6. Tap or click a flag, and then tap an option to report a review as being inappropriate due to spam or content issues.

7. Tap or click View All to drill further into the app's reviews.

8. Tap or click a rating to see only reviews with that rating.

9. Tap or click the Sort By drop-down to change sort order.

10. Tap or click Back to return to the app's details.

11. Swipe up or scroll down to see additional details on the app and related apps.

Searching for Apps

When you need to find a specific app or a specific type of app, searching for apps is often your best choice.

1. In the Store, tap or click in the Search box, enter a search term, and press Enter on your keyboard.

2. Tap or click a type to refine your search.

3. Tap or click Show All to see all apps that match your search.

4. Tap an app to view more details on the app or to install it.

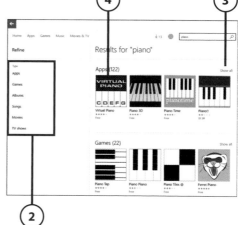

Installing and Uninstalling Apps

When you have found an app that you want to use, you'll need to install it on your tablet. If you later decide you don't want the app, you can remove it from your tablet by uninstalling it. Finally, you can easily locate apps that you've purchased and uninstalled and then reinstall them on your tablet.

Installing Apps

Many apps are free, whereas other apps require you to pay for them. However, many (but not all) of these paid apps offer trial versions so that you can try the app and decide whether it's worth purchasing. You can install any of these apps onto your tablet immediately via the Store.

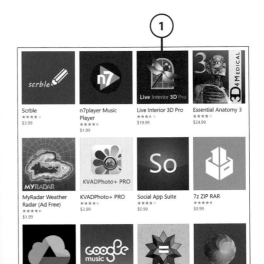

1. Locate an app that you want to install, and tap or click it to view the details on the app.

2. Tap or click the price button to purchase the app. You'll be able to confirm your choice before the purchase is finalized.

3. Tap or click Free Trial to install a trial version of the app.

4. Tap or click Pause to pause the download of the app.

5. Tap or click Cancel to cancel the app's installation.

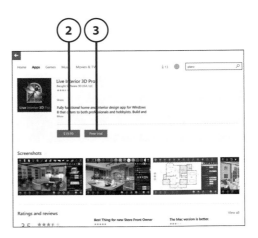

Canceling the Installation of a Purchased App

If you cancel the installation of an app that you purchased, you can install the app later without paying for it again. I show you how in the "Reinstalling Purchased Apps" section of this chapter.

Uninstalling Apps

If you want to free up space on your tablet, you can uninstall apps that you no longer want. You can always reinstall the app later without having to pay for it again, and I show you how in the next section.

1. Locate the app's tile on the Start menu, and tap and hold or right-click it to display the context menu.

2. Tap or click Uninstall to uninstall the app.

3. Tap Uninstall to confirm the uninstall of the app.

Reinstalling Purchased Apps

Microsoft keeps track of the apps you purchase, and you can reinstall any apps you've purchased under your Microsoft account.

1. From the Store, tap or click the Account button, and tap or click My Library.

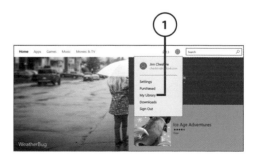

2. Your most recent apps are shown. Tap or click Show All to see all apps in your library.

3. Tap or click Download to reinstall an app.

Details While Reinstalling Apps

You can tap or click an app's tile to see details of the app before you decide to reinstall it.

It's Not All Good

Removed Apps

Just because you purchased an app doesn't mean you can always reinstall it. I've encountered a few situations where I tried to reinstall an app and was notified that the app was removed and is no longer available.

Updating Apps

Updates for apps are free, and you should install them when they're available because they often fix bugs and provide added stability.

Installing Updates

App updates can be installed at any time. You don't have to update all apps at once. You can select which apps you want to update.

1. From the Store, tap or click the Download Updates button. (If you don't see the Download Updates button, there are no updates available for your apps.)

2. Tap or click Check for Updates to ensure that all available updates are displayed.

3. Tap or click Download to update a specific app.

4. Tap or click Update All to update all apps.

5. Tap or click Pause to pause an app update.

6. Tap or click Cancel to cancel an app update.

7. Tap or click Retry to retry a failed update.

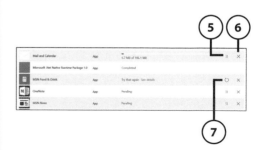

Wipe everything off of your PC and reinstall Windows.

Keep Windows up to date with Windows Update.

← Settings   — □ ✕

⚙ **UPDATE & SECURITY** | Find a setting   🔍 |

Windows Update	**Windows Update**
Windows Defender	Updates are available.
Backup	• Security Update for Windows 10 for x64-based Systems (KB3074674).
Recovery	Details
Activation	**A restart has been scheduled**
For developers	If you want, you can restart now. Or, you can reschedule the restart to a more convenient time. Be sure your device is plugged in at the scheduled time. The install may take 10-20 minutes.

◉ We'll schedule a restart during a time you usually don't use your device (right now 3:30 AM tomorrow looks good).

○ Select a restart time

Time:

| 3 | 30 | AM |

Day:

| Tomorrow ∨ |

Restart now

Advanced options

Refresh your PC and keep all of your files and settings.

It's important to keep Windows updated to avoid any problems. However, if you do encounter problems with your tablet, Windows 10 provides options to help you fix them. In this chapter, you learn about

→ Updating with Windows Update

→ Troubleshooting Windows 10

Updating and Troubleshooting Windows 10

Updating with Windows Update

Windows Update automatically keeps your tablet up to date. By default, updates are downloaded automatically, and many updates install automatically behind the scenes without your even knowing about it. However, if a restart is required to install an update, you'll be notified.

What's In a Name?

Windows Update's name isn't a fluke. Windows Update downloads and installs updates only for Windows (and Office) and drivers that let it communicate with your device hardware. Updates for Windows apps, including those that came with your tablet, are installed through the Store app and not Windows Update. I cover this in Chapter 22, "Enhancing Windows with Apps."

Checking for and Installing Updates Manually

Your tablet checks for updates to Windows every day. However, you can force a manual check for updates if you want to and then choose to manually install any updates that are available.

1. From the Settings app, tap or click Update & Security.

2. Tap or click Windows Update.

3. Tap or click Check for Updates. Any available updates will be downloaded and installed automatically.

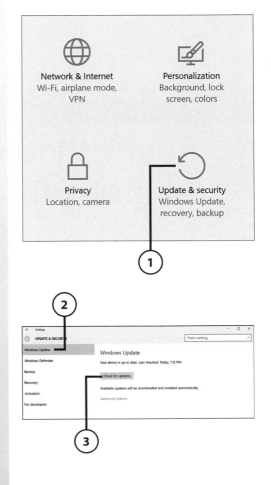

Turning Off Forced Restarts After Updates

When Windows installs updates that require your computer to be restarted, Windows will ask you to restart when the updates are installed. You'll be provided with the option to delay that restart for a set number of hours, but after that time period elapses, you'll be forced to restart.

If you want, you can configure Windows to allow you to schedule a specific time for a restart to install updates. If an update requiring a restart is installed after you configure this setting, you'll see a dialog allowing you to tell Windows what time to restart to complete the update.

1. From the Windows Update screen, tap or click Advanced Options.

2. Tap or click Choose How Updates Are Installed.

3. Tap or click Notify to Schedule Restart.

Windows Update

Your device is up to date. Last checked: Today, 1:12 PM

Check for updates

Available updates will be downloaded and installed automatically.

Advanced options

(1)

⚙ ADVANCED OPTIONS

Choose how updates are installed

Automatic (recommended) ⌄

Keep everything running smoothly. We'll restart your device automatically when you're not using it. Updates won't download over a metered connection (where charges may apply).

☑ Give me updates for other Microsoft products when I update Windows.

(2)

⚙ ADVANCED OPTIONS

Choose how updates are installed

Automatic (recommended)

Notify to schedule restart

thly. We'll restart your device automatically when you're not using it. Updates won't download over a metered connection (where charges may apply).

☑ Give me updates for other Microsoft products when I update Windows.

(3)

Troubleshooting Windows 10

If you are having trouble with Windows 10 on your tablet, you have a couple options for troubleshooting. You can reset your PC and keep your files, a process that restores all Windows settings while keeping all your personal files. You can also reset your PC and remove all your files, a process whereby Windows 10 is reinstalled and all your personal files are removed.

Resetting and Keeping Your Files

If you find that your tablet is having problems and not operating correctly, you often can fix it by refreshing and repairing your PC. When you do so, your personal files are not impacted and will remain on the device.

What About Apps?

When you refresh or repair your tablet, any Windows apps you've installed remain on the device. However, you will have to reinstall Windows Desktop apps. Windows will notify you of any apps that you must reinstall.

Before you start this process, plug in your tablet so that it's running on AC power and not the battery.

1. From the Settings app, tap or click Update & Security.

2. Tap or click Recovery.

3. Tap or click Get Started under Reset this PC.

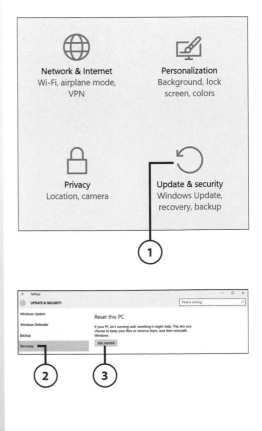

4. Tap or click Keep My Files.

5. Take note of the apps you will need to reinstall after the refresh. Tap or click Next.

6. Tap or click Reset to reset your PC. Your PC will restart and reset to its original settings without affecting your pictures, music, and other personal files.

Refreshing to Defaults

After you run a reset on your PC, your PC reverts to the settings that existed when you powered it on for the first time. After you reset, checking for updates and installing any available from Windows Update and the Store app is a good idea.

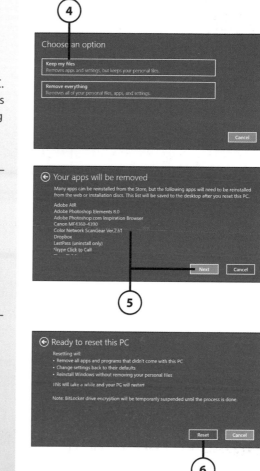

It's Not All Good

When to Reset

There's a good chance that you will never have to reset your PC. However, when it comes to technology, there's always the possibility that things can go wrong. How will you know when you need to reset? There aren't any specific rules for when to reset, but if you notice that you are seeing numerous errors, if your tablet restarts on its own, or if you are experiencing slowness when using your tablet, resetting your PC is a good first step. There's a good chance that resetting will fix any problems you're having.

Resetting and Deleting Your Files

You can reset Windows 10 completely, restoring your tablet to the state it was in when it was new and deleting all of your personal files. This is a good idea if you are giving or selling your tablet to someone else.

Before you go through this process, make sure you plug in your tablet.

1. From the Update & Security screen, tap or click Get Started under Reset This PC.

2. Tap or click Remove Everything.

3. To remove your personal files and reset settings while leaving the current Windows 10 installation intact, tap or click Just Remove My Files. This is a good choice if you are giving or selling your tablet to someone else.

4. To fully clean the drive and reinstall Windows 10, tap or click Remove Files and Clean the Drive.

Use File History

If you use File History to back up your files, you can safely reinstall Windows and then restore your files. For information on using File History, see Chapter 6, "Backing Up Your Data with File History."

5. Tap or click Reset to reset your PC.

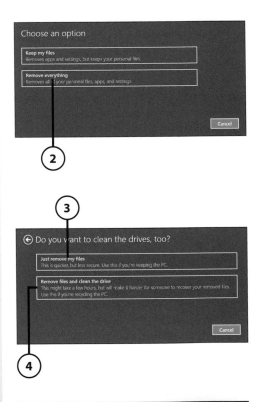

Reset this PC

If your PC isn't running well, resetting it might help. This lets you choose to keep your files or remove them, and then reinstalls Windows.

Get started

Choose an option

Keep my files
Removes apps and settings, but keeps your personal files.

Remove everything
Removes all your personal files, apps, and settings.

Cancel

← Do you want to clean the drives, too?

Just remove my files
This is quicker, but less secure. Use this if you're keeping the PC.

Remove files and clean the drive
This might take a few hours, but will make it harder for someone to recover your removed files. Use this if you're recycling the PC.

Cancel

← Ready to reset this PC

Resetting will remove:
 • All the personal files and user accounts on this PC
 • Any apps and programs that didn't come with this PC
 • Any changes made to settings

This will take a while and your PC will restart.
Note: BitLocker drive encryption will be turned off.

Reset   Cancel

Index

Symbols

3D maps, viewing, 348

A

accessing
  files on OneDrive (remotely), 280-282
  HomeGroups, sharing files, 275
  local news, 263. *See also* News app
  Microsoft Family, 99
    adding accounts, 100-101
    configuring accounts, 103-107
    deleting accounts, 102-103
    managing, 108-114
    reviewing, 118-120, 123
    scheduling, 115, 118
  networks
    Airplane Mode, 31
    connecting, 27
    disconnecting, 29
    forgetting, 30
    remoting, 35-39
    resources, 34-35
    sharing, 31-32
    Wi-Fi, 28-29

Start menus, 8
user accounts, formatting, 90-92
videos, 332
websites, allowing explicitly, 105

accounts
  blocking, 115
  Exchange, 207-208
  Google, 209
  iCloud, 211
  IMAP, 212-215
  MAIL app, 218-219
  Microsoft Family
    adding, 100-101, 204
    applying, 39
    configuring, 103-114
    deleting, 102-103
    reviewing, 118-120, 123
    scheduling, 115, 118
  Office 365, 207-208
  passwords, 64-68
  POP, 212-215
  unblocking, 116
  users
    assigning access, 90-92
    deleting, 88
    managing, 84-87
    modifying, 89
    switching, 93-96

C

D

E

N

O

Q

R

W

Z

More Best-Selling **My** Books!

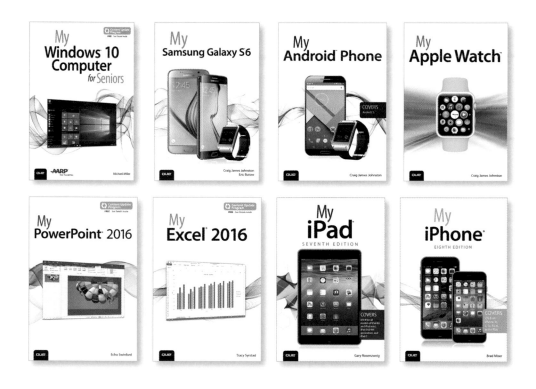

REGISTER THIS PRODUCT
SAVE 35%*
ON YOUR NEXT PURCHASE!

How to Register Your Product

- Go to quepublishing.com/register
- Sign in or create an account
- Enter ISBN: 10- or 13-digit ISBN that appears on the back cover of your product

Benefits of Registering

- Ability to download product updates
- Access to bonus chapters and workshop files
- A 35% coupon to be used on your next purchase – valid for 30 days
  - To obtain your coupon, click on "Manage Codes" in the right column of your Account page
- Receive special offers on new editions and related Que products

Please note that the benefits for registering may vary by product. Benefits will be listed on your Account page under Registered Products.

We value and respect your privacy. Your email address will not be sold to any third party company.

quepublishing.com